ROAD AHEAD CLOSED

My life's journey along a winding pathway

Geoffrey Smales

STAN

Life is a long lesson in humility.
James Matthew Barrie

Preface - To Be Read

My story could have been written as follows: "I did this, I did that; I went here, and I went there." That would have been easy, and no eyebrows would be raised. But the most important part of my story is found when I add these words: "I think this, I think that; I believe this, and I believe that." And now most certainly eyebrows will be raised here and there!

Some readers might think I've been ridiculously sympathetic towards folk who have 'deviated' from the norm. Others will wonder how I can possibly be so naïve as to believe that God has helped me, sometimes miraculously. There will also be some who will be checking my every word, in case a weakness in my faith, or an error in my doctrine comes to light.

Meanwhile, I simply seek to be honest with my readers, whatever the outcome, hoping that most of you will find a measure of encouragement from my story.

Thanks

Thank you to my wife, Mary, who has been so patient with me when I've hidden myself in my study, writing and re-writing.

Thank you to our children, Andrew and Margaret, for allowing me to write some embarrassing things about them.

Thank you to Ruth Howlett for her careful reading of the script and for her helpful comments and suggestions.

Names of People

In most cases I have used the actual names of people, but here and there you'll find a name in *italics*, and that's when I've used a pseudonym.

CONTENTS

Chapter 1

A Little Peep

Bullied,

Attacked by voodoo,

Threatened with a knife at my throat,

    … these are some of the ASSAULTS made upon me.

"You're a sissy,"

"You're not to be trusted,"

"You've got a warped mind,"

    … these are some of the ACCUSATIONS made about me.

Sacked from a pastorate,

Thrown out of several houses,

Barred from entering a church,

    … these are some of the ACTIONS taken against me.

That's a list of some of the bad experiences that life has thrown at me, but my 'good' list is far, far longer, as we shall see in due course. My life has been diverse and exciting - things which are seemingly impossible have happened to me. Was all this by chance? Or was it by miracle? Because of ill health, I wasn't expected to reach the age of twenty, but I did, and here I am in my eighties! Was I just lucky? Or is there another explanation? Does God come into the equation?

My life has been full of contrasts, rise-and-fall experiences, joy and pain, success and failure. It's also been a life of searching, finding, and then searching again, and discovering that after all, I don't know very much anyway. But thankfully, not knowing much isn't quite the same as not knowing anything, or not believing anything.

Even from early boyhood, one aspect of my life has remained constant - my longing to know the purpose of life. Why are we here? Is there a supreme being? Who is God? Where is God? Can we experience God in our lives? These are big questions, but are they too hard for me to answer? My search for the answers has consumed years of my life, even causing me to fail an important mathematics exam.

T S Elliot wrote 'We shall never cease from exploration, and the end of all our exploring will be to arrive where we started and know the place for the first time'. Well, those words seem to fit my own explorations to a T.

My life can be likened to a long journey, sometimes along winding and unwelcoming tracks, with poor visibility. I have encountered several roadblocks, and had to make detours; unfortunately I've also experienced a few crashes. Nevertheless, I have for the most part enjoyed my journey, despite all my bruises and scars, and I look back on my life with immeasurable thankfulness.

On the other hand, I've quite a list of regrets for my various misdeeds and 'miswords', and also for my incessant teasing that has sometimes gone badly wrong. And I admit that there have also been occasions when I have been somewhat economical with the truth in order to make things easier for me, and then I have felt ashamed - but all too late. I have more than once pretended to be ill in order to avoid a difficult situation. Oh what a sinner I am!

The moving finger writes, and having writ
Moves on. Nor all thy piety nor wit
Shall lure it back to cancel half a line,
Nor all thy tears wash out a word of it.
(Omar Khayyám)

Biggie Bow-wow with Geoffrey

Grandpa White, alias Humble Grandpa, with Geoffrey

Grandma White, alias Humble Grandma

Grandpa (be-a-man) Smales, alias Posh Grandpa

Mam and Geoffrey in the garden at Torquay

Dad plus cigarette and cricket bat

Chapter 2

The Fifth Green Bottle

My parents' troubles all began in Sheffield, in September 1929. That's when I was born, in the suburb of Ecclesall. And yes, that's right, I'm a Yorkshireman, and proud of it!

I didn't want to be an only child, or to be so poorly and frail, but what could I do? Well, what I did was to cuddle up to my lovely friend Biggie Bow-wow, and then I felt safe. But Biggie Bow-wow once got me into biggie trouble - all I did, at his request, was to wash his head in a fatty frying pan, thus incurring the wrath of my mother, who I called Mam.

Oh, I nearly forgot to mention my other cuddly bow-wow, Dimmon Demmon. He was a spotty Dalmatian who looked really sad. His name was supposed to be Dismal Desmond, but I couldn't get my tongue round the words! However, he was a good friend in times of trouble and always forgave me for my poor diction. Good old Dimmon Demmon!

I have very few memories of my first few years, but the bald patch on the side of my head is a permanent reminder of one particular day - that's the day when I leaned on the baby gate at the top of the stairs, but it wasn't properly secured, and down the stairs I came - CRASH! I had quite a long cut in my head, and Mam has always regretted not taking me to hospital to have it stitched.

In 1934, we moved to Torquay, all because Dad had been promoted - I think he must have been very important! But I was a bit of a misery-guts, because my gums were still bleeding after all my teeth had been extracted in hospital, just before moving. True, I was sans teeth, but I wasn't sans everything, because I still had my two friends Biggie Bow-wow and Dimmon Demmon, so I just snuggled up to them, and held them tightly.

Mam and Dad were loving and caring parents, despite the baby-gate problem! Mam in particular was very patient with me, especially in helping me to correct my diction. Pronunciation was a big problem for me; in fact, the 'th' sound completely eluded me - perhaps having no teef wasn't making things any easier for me. It's a good excuse, anyway.

At my new school, I had the honour of being dressed as a hot water bottle for the end-of-term concert. Maybe 'Miss' had got the wrong sort of bottle in mind, but whether she was right or wrong didn't really matter. What mattered to me was the fact that as the fifth green bottle in the song, I became confused and fell down on the stage two bottles too soon, amidst the laughter of the audience!

Looking back, there have been many minor incidents in my life which have made a major impact on me, and typified all my other muddles and fears. Green Bottle No. 5 was my first of these. But let's move from the stage to the school playground, where it was the custom for the children to bring some cake each day for playtime treats. Sad to say, the villains around me often snatched mine from me, and I just let it happen! It soon became known that I was a soft touch, and the thefts just increased. I felt intimidated by others, sometimes I felt panic-stricken. I was just a frightened green bottle.

I had enough trouble with thieves in the playground, but I didn't expect to meet one with Mam at my side! She'd bought me a bag of my favourite chocolate biscuits from *Woolworths*, and then taken me to nearby Paignton Zoo. I was really generous, and offered one of my precious biscuits to an elephant, who enjoyed it so much that in a split second he'd snatched the bag out of my hand, and sucked the whole lot into his trunk. He waved his trunk in triumph! I didn't like Jumbo any more.

It was one thing after another! One Christmas Dad's father, Grandpa Smales, gave me an expensive pedal car with padded seat, loud horn, and other extras. Maybe driving this was even better than eating chocolate biscuits! So there I was one day, proudly driving along the pavement, when a little girl walked past with her mum. The girl said 'I like your car, I wish I had one like that!' But worse was to come, as she actually asked me to give it to her! I felt trapped, and daren't refuse. I climbed out of my car and Megan the Thief climbed in - and unbelievably, her mum let it all happen! I watched my lovely car disappearing into the distance and felt dismayed. What HAD I done? That was bad enough, but when I got back into the house, Mam was furious with me. The following day Mummy and Megan came down the road once again, minus pedal car, and invited me for tea; I went, but no, I didn't enjoy my visit, especially when I saw my car in the back garden - in pieces!

My bedroom sometimes became a sort of camping ground, with me in my little tent! This needs explaining: because of bronchial troubles, I often had to sleep in a steam tent, which Mam erected for me over my bed, She made it from a couple of sheets held up by some bamboo canes. A kettle was kept boiling throughout the night, and the steam was directed inside the tent. Sleeping in my steam-filled tent is a vivid memory, but I have no recollection of how the kettle was heated. Maybe poor Mam had to get up several times through the night to refill the kettle. What troubles I caused!

By now, I was beginning to form the opinion that anything that CAN go wrong WILL go wrong. At the time I hadn't heard of Murphy's Law, but perhaps I was thinking on the same lines.

Time went by, and I think that my 'vast' experience of life and my version of Murphy's Law made me start thinking and questioning in a new way. This needed real concentration! So I waited until I was in bed, with no household distractions, to engage in this new level of thinking! I readily admit that it's rather odd for a young child to ponder over abstract matters as I did, but I merely describe myself.

Let's peep into my little bedroom where my 'journey' began at the age of seven. It was at the back of the house, overlooking a densely wooded area just behind our tiny garden. The room was small, dark and dingy, but the hooting of the owls kept me company at night. The creaking door, the drab lino on the floor, the little blue mat, the brown wallpaper - all this is vividly clear. Other than the bed, there was the chair where Biggie Bow-wow used to sit, and the dressing table where Mam used to put glasses of water - that's when I'd failed to swallow my tablets, and was sent up to my little bedroom in disgrace, and not allowed to come downstairs until successful. I drank all the water, but the tablets just remained in my mouth, and so I had to stay upstairs until my parents admitted defeat. I wonder why I didn't cheat.

Much worse than the tablet-problem was the problem of understanding the meaning of existence. Why do things go wrong? Why are we here anyway? Is there anybody else out there? What does 'always' mean? Is space infinite? Is time infinite? I wouldn't have known the word 'infinite' at my young age, but who cares about a word anyway? I knew what I meant by my question, with or without the word. Debussy once asked 'Can't you listen to chords without knowing their names?'

My childish thoughts led me to believe, not in God as such, but in space. I firmly believed that space and matter go on for ever. Night after night I set off on an imagined journey into the unknown universe - on and on I went, far past the sun, far past the stars. But what happens if eventually I bump into something solid? Is that the end of my journey? No, no! I'll simply get a gigantic drill and bore through it. And if I don't bump? Well, I'll just carry on travelling. I decided that cessation of space and matter was inconceivable.

But what about time? Tucked away in my little bedroom, I tried to unfold the mystery of time - quite a task for a child! I decided that there must be three types of time. Imagine something which has been alive for ever in the past, but suddenly dies. As it had been there for ever, it must be infinity-past. Or imagine something which suddenly appears but never dies. That must be infinity-future. Or imagine something which has no beginning and no end. Could this be called complete infinity? Is this in fact a picture of God, from everlasting to everlasting? Many years later I was to learn how mathematicians deal with different types and sizes of infinity.

My bedtime imagination used to work overtime. In my mind I held a piece of string which stretched for ever in both directions, but what happens if I use my scissors? SNIP! I've now got a piece of string with no beginning, but here's the end, and another with a beginning (in my other hand) but no end. Half infinity to the left, half to the right, but when I join the pieces together again, I've got complete infinity. I was in good company, as the poet William Blake also held infinity in the palm of his hand:

> To see the world in a grain of sand
> And heaven in a wild flower,
> Hold infinity in the palm of your hand
> And eternity in an hour ...

Blake then wanders through thirty-five verses, considering the robin, the bat, the lamb, even the caterpillar - he shows us that God is found in all these creatures. Lastly he considers the faith of a little child. Perhaps he was writing about me! He continues:

> He who mocks an infant's faith
> Shall be mocked in age and death.
> God appears, and God is light,
> To those poor souls who dwell in night.

I was frequently off school through illness, so my little bedroom became my den, and I loved it there. It was my private place where I could think just as I wanted, and how I wanted. I certainly didn't tell Mam and Dad my thoughts, much less my so-called conclusions. In my private little bedroom I was entitled to my private little ponderings. That's happiness!

Come to think of it, there was no wonder that I kept my thoughts to myself, as I wouldn't have had the ability to describe them. I merely thought my thoughts and there is no way I could have clothed them in words. Perhaps I still can't! Mind you, I did discuss infinity with Biggie Bow-wow, and he seemed to understand what I meant.

Inside my little room I felt safe, especially with Biggie Bow-wow on guard, but outside my room I was frail and frightened. I had a friend called Derek, and I remember the two of us going to sail our boats on a nearby pond, but soon Derek got fed up. 'Let's go,' he said, so off we went! Derek clutched his boat under his arm, but at the time mine hadn't reached port, so I had to leave without it. I was too scared to remind him that I had a boat too. Today I'd probably be called a wimp, but again, I merely describe myself. Would I ever learn to assert myself?

After we parted company I went back to the pond, but my lovely little boat had gone!

What with missing my turn as a green hot water bottle with everyone laughing at me, the theft of my cake and my pedal car, and then Mam of all people letting an elephant steal all my chocolate biscuits, I thought that life was so unfair! And now, thanks to Derek, someone's stolen my lovely boat. "Whatever next?" I asked myself.

I wonder why our non-churchgoing parents decided we should both go to Sunday School. We went once, but didn't like it, so the following Sunday we set off, but never reached our destination. We simply returned and explained (Derek's idea!) that Sunday School had been cancelled! Surely they didn't believe us, but we never went again.

I won't easily forget the Great Storm of 1937 and the impression it made on my thinking. The thunder and lightning and the torrential rain continued throughout the day and the ensuing night. There was flooding and extensive damage, and consequently not many people went to work the following morning. Teachers and pupils were in short supply in the schools. In addition, the sea 'turned to blood' - well, so read the headline in the local paper. Devon is well known for its red sandstone rock, and therefore for its red soil and sand. The tumult of the sea during that storm stirred up the seabed so much that the sea became red - hence the newspaper headline.

We actually lived in Preston, a few miles from Torquay, and we had our very own Preston beach. A couple of days after the storm I ran down the concrete slope to the beach, and fell off the end. The beach had disappeared in the storm! For months lorries plied to and fro, importing more and more sand - it was a mammoth task. I learned a lot from this experience about the power and the seeming unpredictability of nature, and also of the uncertainty of life. It gave a new dimension to my childish questioning, and made me feel very, very small.

In contrast with my new awareness of nature's uncertainties, I felt convinced that I would only live to the age of twenty. It was an inevitability which I frequently dwelt upon, and eventually discovered to be almost prophetic. It wasn't age nineteen or age twenty-one I had in mind. This 'twenty' cut-off point was clearly written on my time-map, but it never worried me as age twenty seemed a hundred years away.

Maybe I was some strange sort of child philosopher in my little bedroom, and a frightened little boy outside my room, but there was still ample scope for naughtiness in my young life. Once, having taken the lid off a tin of yummy chocolate biscuits, I asked Mam if I could have one. 'Only if there are some broken ones!' she replied. Oh dear, there weren't any! I distinctly recall my defiance as I took the tin, crouched under the dining table with my back to Mam, and set to work breaking biscuits in two.

Then there was my canary-pester. Despite all my weaknesses, I seemed reasonably adept at the art of pestering, so let's have a go! Yes, I longed to have a canary - not an X-box, or a PlayStation, mind you, or whatever children long for these days. All I wanted was an ordinary little yellow canary! So Operation Pester began in earnest! Eventually I was told I could have my canary, but only if I cleaned out the cage each week. 'I will, I will, I will!' was my eager response - but apparently I didn't, I didn't, I didn't. And that was a crime I was going to regret in a few years' time, as I was yet to discover.

But I had a pal in Grandpa White (that's Mam's father, a maths teacher), because he was the one who understood my feelings, and was happy to have a muddled green bottle as a grandson. When we lived in Torquay, he visited us from Barnsley two or three times a year. I looked forward to his visits, because he used to buy me a Crunchie Bar on the way to the beach, plus one for himself. Then we'd sit on a bench, eating our Crunchies, and chatting like two old men. More to the point, he used to teach me things that mattered, and showed me tricks and short cuts in arithmetic. Grandpa encouraged me to experiment with numbers and patterns, and gave me a leather-covered box containing dividers and two posh pairs of compasses. With these instruments, plus a ruler and a setsquare, I was a happy little fellow.

Furthermore, he encouraged me to be creative in writing, and to play about with words. He told me to aim high, and work hard to reach perfection; he was for ever urging me to heed St Jerome's well-known words:

Good, better, best,
Never let it rest,
Till your good is better,
And your better, best.

So after breakfast one morning (*Kellogg's* Rice Krispies) I felt 'inspired' to write my first ever poem:

Snap, crackle, pop,
Never let it drop,
Till your snap is crackle,
And your crackle, pop.

I was just having fun with words as Grandpa told me to do. Maybe what I wrote was a load of nonsense, but I used to like nonsense, and to this day I still write nonsense poems, usually to tease people!

Grandma White was a little lady, and also a lovely lady. I liked her very much - far better than Grandma Smales, as this Grandma had no airs and graces, and just lived a simple life. She was my Humble Grandma! She wasn't possessed with an abundance of skills; she was just ordinary, and I really like 'ordinary'! But she could play a few hymns on her incredibly out-of-tune piano, and that really impressed me. I remember too how she always brushed her teeth using Vim instead of toothpaste - but it seemed to do her no harm!

Grandpa had his own quirks, including looking up to the ceiling, cracking an egg over his wide-open mouth and swallowing the whole lot in one big gulp! He was without doubt my special Grandpa, my Humble Grandpa.

I remember playing a game of 'I spy' at Grandma's house one evening, when we were all staying there for a few days. It was my turn. "I spy with my little eye something beginning with B." So far so good, but after they'd tried a few words, they gave up.

"Well, what DID you spy?" asked Dad.

"A bosom," I replied.

They all looked stunned. Everyone went quiet. All I knew is that a bosom was a mysterious bulge near the top of a woman. I felt confused and just couldn't understand their response. I couldn't bear the tension any longer, so I broke the silence.

"What's wrong with bosom?" I enquired.

"Nothing's wrong with it," Dad replied.

But if there's nothing wrong with my word, why did they all look aghast? Adults have strange reactions!

It was one of those weeks when I was staying at Grandma and Grandpa's home in Barnsley, without my parents. By now I was used to being wakened early each morning by the coal miners walking down the street in their clogs, on their way to the pit. The lace curtains never looked clean - somehow coal dust seemed to permeate the house. Maybe that's why Grandma used to say to me a hundred times a day, "Go and wash your hands and face, Geoffrey!"

When I returned home, Mam checked my appearance and immediately became rather cross. "Geoffrey, have you washed your neck lately?"

"No," I replied, "Grandma only mentioned my hands and face!"

Then there's Grandpa (be-a-man) Smales, who lived in Sheffield. I called him Posh Grandpa. He was a very strict man. Sometimes he would take me out for a meal, just the two of us, man-to-man and all that! But when I chose chicken, I got the reply "Chicken for women, beef for men," so beef it was! He was ridiculously concerned about my lips. "You have the lips of a girl," he used to say, and he would put his fingers in my mouth, trying to stretch my lips outwards. Oh dear, I didn't like Posh Grandpa's beef-rule and lip-stretching exercises. I much preferred Humble Grandpa's help with learning and experimenting.

Grandma (must-be-tidy) Smales was Dad's stepmother. She was a bit odd, with her many Rules of Residence! For example, she wouldn't let me go into her front room except on Tuesdays in case I got the place untidy. If I wrecked her holiest of holies on Tuesday, it didn't matter all that much as the cleaning lady was allowed into this sacred place on Wednesday. But the Britannica Encyclopaedias were kept there, and as I wanted to look at them I used to feel a bit annoyed about her petty restrictions. I thought it was a silly rule anyway.

I've always had an aversion to peas, but with Posh Grandma, aversions and fads were forbidden. Come dinnertime, I would force myself to eat my peas first, so that I could then enjoy the good things on my plate. But it never worked. She would say, "Oh Geoffrey, you've finished your peas already," and even as she spoke she'd give me another dollop of those wretched things!

Posh Grandma and Grandpa lived in a semi-detached house, not the sort of home where you'd expect to find a maid. But there she was, in residence - Maid Ann. She was really nice, and I liked her typical maid's apparel. She didn't do any cleaning, but simply looked the part, and served meals with a 'thank you, Ma'am' thrown in here and there. I was most impressed, but I preferred the down-to-earthness of Humble Grandma's simple home. Grandma Smales was a bit too 'up there' for my liking. Grandpa would tell me in her hearing, "You might like THIS Grandma, but you'd have liked the first one much better!" Maybe that's so, but I never met the first version.

Mam and Dad didn't really have much idea how to help me to know things, and I learnt very little from them educationally. Mam had no hobbies and no particular interests or abilities, apart from knitting. She was just lovely and 'ordinary', like her own mother, and that made her special! I think 'extra ordinary' would be a better description. She was a loving mother, who taught me my manners and helped me with my speech. But it took her a long time and a lot of patience to promote me from TEEF to TEETH, and from MIRROW to MIRROR.

Mam must have carried many worries about my health on her shoulders, and at the time Dad was far too busy with his work to deal with what he thought were a mother's responsibilities. He would work into the early hours of the morning preparing for the next day, smoking cigarette after cigarette. Dad was a workaholic - sometimes when on holiday he would sit on a deckchair on the beach, working away, complete with his old-fashioned swimming costume, plus bowler hat, briefcase and the inevitable cigarette!

Dad's shopping methods were a bit strange - he would frequently say to the shopkeeper, "But haven't you got anything more expensive?" He must have been a shopkeeper's delight. Dad bought Posh Grandpa an expensive umbrella one Christmas when he was visiting us, but Grandpa said, "You keep it Son, I've got a good one at home." Poor old Dad hadn't reached high enough that time!

And then there was his driving logic - we went down narrow winding country lanes at frightening speeds. He reasoned that if there is danger ahead, 'just drive as quickly as possible in order to get it over and done with!'

Dad had an office staff of about two hundred men and thirty women. Once a year he booked a room in a conference centre for those of 'higher rank', and a grandiose meal was followed by a grandiose speech from the Boss - a sort of pep talk, and Dad spoke for about two hours! But I'm not convinced that the Boss was a good speaker. Two hours? Wow! Maybe it was a pretty boring occasion. Sorry, Dad!

You should have heard Dad sneeze - it was an experience to be remembered. Just turn the word 'rickshaw' into an elongated fortissimo sneeze, and you'll know what Mam and I had to endure. Try it. My own sneeze is a highly dignified 'tissue', probably man-sized! What's your word?

Well, that's the family. It's also a peep at my life from age nought to eight, confessing that I reached this age still believing in Father Christmas, still believing that evil would befall me if I walked on the cracks in the pavement, as well as believing in infinite space, infinite matter and infinite time! I also remember being worried every year from Good Friday till Easter Sunday, wondering how the world would survive without God for three days! What a muddled green bottle I was!

I've mentioned the serious bits of my life, a few naughty bits, and a little nonsense rhyme thrown in for good measure. But all this proved to be a mere genesis. A big exodus into the unknown wilderness of life awaited me, with all its adventure and exploration, as well as all its dangers.

Chapter 3

Thank You Mr Sparrow

It's September 1939 and we've just moved near to Manchester, because of Dad's further promotion.

Two weeks after moving I went to the Junior Department of Manchester Grammar School. We're at war with Germany and soon my new school is evacuated to the 'safety' of Ormskirk, but Mam and Dad decide that I will not go to this 'safe' town. So my time in this new classroom turns out to be quite brief.

We actually lived a few miles away from Manchester, in the village of Gatley in Cheshire. At the time of evacuation to Ormskirk, we ourselves received two evacuees from the city centre to the 'safety' of Gatley. So it did seem rather ridiculous to receive Frank and Eddie into our home for safety's sake, and to send me away for the same reason. Hence a change of school was necessary.

So off I went, complete with gas mask, to Gatley High School, a private school in the village. Not a good idea as it turned out! It was quite usual for teachers to miss lessons, though there was one conscientious teacher, Miss Nairn, who used all her free periods in search of classrooms where no other teacher had turned up, and that class would then have some extra tuition in French! As for my maths teacher, he once called me to the front of the class to illustrate an inverted fraction. He grabbed hold of me quite forcibly: 'Well, just for a start,' he said, 'here's an inverted Smales!' I didn't enjoy the experience. I think he must have chosen me because I was skinny, and he would need minimum strength to perform his trick.

My time at this chaotic place of 'learning' came to an unexpected end. I kept complaining to Mam and Dad that I had chest pains, and I don't blame them for saying "Don't make such a fuss!" as I'd frequently told them I didn't feel well in years gone by, so why should this be anything worse? Time passed by, but my chest pains didn't, and eventually a doctor came to see me, and that was the end of my schooling for two years. The road ahead was suddenly closed. Today, some tuition would have been organised, but alas, I was living in 'yesterday'.

On my last day at school before my two-year absence, my algebra was causing me problems and Mr Spoonley, the teacher who had inverted me, was far from pleased with me. I explained to him that I felt ill, but my excuse was met with a rebuke. "Feeling ill is to do with the body, but you are supposed to be using your brain!" I wonder how he felt when he knew I was suffering from rheumatic fever and that my heart was badly affected. But I never knew, as he died of lung cancer during my absence.

Initially I was told, "You'll have to stay in bed for a month to six weeks!" I felt quite proud as other boys only seemed to be poorly for a couple of weeks at most, but I had a winning score. I felt proud enough to write to my relations to tell them! But my heart problem worsened, and in next to no time a consultant and two doctors came to visit me, all three in one visit! Now I felt really important! Mr Langley, the consultant, asked me, "Do you hope to become as strong as Samson?"

"Who's he?" I enquired. Maybe Derek's plan to 'abolish' Sunday Schools wasn't such a good idea after all!

Mr Langley 'planted' me in the back garden and 'fed' me on aspirins! Part of the downstairs of our house was set back under one of the bedrooms, and there was just enough room for my camp bed in that space. This complied with the consultant's orders for me to live outside, day and night, summer and winter.

I had a sweaty waterproof sheet over my bed, and during cold winter nights I wore a lilac and purple pixie-hood which had Mam knitted for me - it tied with a bow under my chin, and it was lovely and warm. That's where I lived, come frost, come snow, though I still don't really understand how facing these adverse elements was good for my heart. After my return to school I continued sleeping outside on my unyielding camp bed for a further eight years (doctor's orders), but at that point I allowed myself to sleep indoors during the coldest winter nights.

Back to the present time, sometimes it rained, of course. However, the vertical sort caused me no problems, though I did get wet when the wind was in my direction. My pride in having a long illness had gone by now, but

I never thought I was having a bad time. In fact, in a way it was a wonderful time for continuing to think. And now, thanks to the absence of light pollution, I had a starlit night sky to aid my 'infinity' explorations. My books on astronomy just amazed me. The vastness of the universe simply confirmed my earlier 'conclusion' that space really does go on for ever. Of course, during my outside-illness there was a wartime blackout - so I couldn't read during winter evenings.

Within the first few weeks of my illness, I made a request: "Dad, can I have a dictionary and a Bible please!" Why on earth did I ask for these books? They were certainly unusual wants for a young lad. Maybe some hard-to-understand words in my books on astronomy prompted my dictionary-request, but whatever the reason, I started to read and learn the dictionary. It's a wonder that even to the present day all my big words don't begin with the letter A, because I never reached letter B in those two years. It all seemed to take so much time, and I really needed a second dictionary to explain the first, as some of the definitions seemed rather obscure to me.

I wonder why I wanted a Bible. Was it God who prompted me to ask? Anyway, Dad brought one to me straight away - it was leather-bound and unused. I started reading Genesis but hadn't got very far when Dad suggested that I should skip the Old Testament, and so I remained ignorant about the story of Samson! Jumping to the New Testament, I read the four Gospels, feeling that my exploration might have taken a new turn. Maybe I was beginning to believe in an everlasting God, not merely in endless space. Might this prove to be a book which could show me something about the purpose of life?

At first, a few friends, Lionel and Co, came to visit me on Sunday afternoons. It was good to see them, and somehow or other we managed to play Monopoly, despite my semi-horizontal position and the rakish angle of the board.

Maybe the Bible was to blame for a decision which I was about to make, because having read the four Gospels and a little bit more, I was suddenly made aware of the need to 'please God' (quoting the apostle Paul) rather than Lionel and Co, and so on the next Sunday I declared that I couldn't play Monopoly on this holy day! "Well, you needn't actually play," they replied, "you could become the banker instead." But I turned down their thoughtful suggestion, and their Sunday visits ceased. I didn't like Monopoly anyway!

This was the first time in my life I'd dared to say 'no' to anybody (except Mam and Dad of course!) and it didn't happen again for another seven years, when I stubbornly refused to take some exams. So, was it God who gave me strength of will on Monopoly Termination Day?

My Sunday decision threw my parents into total confusion - Dad didn't know what to do or what to say. In a state of embarrassment, he searched through the records and played 'Bless this House', sung by the tenor Webster Booth. I still remember hearing this song through the open French window:

Bless this house, O Lord we pray,
Make it safe by night and day.
Bless these walls, so firm and stout,
Keeping want and trouble out.

Maybe the words of the song were not a perfect match for the situation in hand, but they did express something of Dad's feelings. There was an air of seriousness in the family, and I was very much aware of the baffling effect my decision had made on my parents, and I felt that this was an emotional and very important day.

Round about this time I read a biography of Albert Schweitzer, and discovered his belief in what he called 'reverence for life' and how he stressed that the same respect should be shown to all living things, 'from elephants to blades of grass'. This made me ask whether anyone knows the size of creatures below which cruelty doesn't matter? A centimetre in length, perhaps? Or is squashing a midge with your thumb just as bad as driving a steamroller over a cat? How would we like to be flattened by a gargantuan fly swat? Let the politicians deal with their war plans if they liked, but I wanted to know how to help a midge!

I thought that if the Lord God really has made all creatures great and small, who are we to trample SOME of them under foot? Perhaps we are allowed to trample on God's small creatures, but not on His great creatures, but that didn't seem logical. Albert Schweitzer might have gone to extremes, but with doctorates in medicine, in theology and in music, he was no ignoramus. In fact, he must have been extremely clever - but was he clever, but crazy? Or maybe clever and caring? He always tried to avoid walking on grass, if there was a path nearby. Was he silly? But whatever we think, and whatever definition we give to 'reverence for life', it seems to be in short supply in today's world.

Books and events seemed destined to make me question and wonder - they just crowded into my life. The war itself made an impact upon my thinking. When the air-raid sirens shrieked their warning note, I came inside the house for a while, and we went into our indoor air-raid shelter in the dining room. We heard bombs whistling down, and wondered where they would fall. Some nearby houses were destroyed, but we remained safe. Was the Lord in fact blessing our house and making it safe by night and day?

On one occasion Dad came back from work and described a horrific scene after a blitz in the centre of Manchester, with corpses being picked up in the streets and dumped into lorries! These experiences of war heightened my realization of the seriousness of life, and made me more aware of the comparison between infinity and that which is finite, between beauty and ugliness, harmony and discord.

In contrast with the horrors of war I began to enjoy the beauties of poetry, and found *Palgrave's Golden Treasury* to be a lovely oasis. I began to memorise Wordsworth, Burns and others. Mam and Dad asked me to recite poetry to their friends when they visited us, but I felt embarrassed and always pulled the bedclothes over my face before I started my performance! I also began to write poetry, quite serious stuff for a lad, expressions of my own feelings! One poem was about 'a piece of tangled string' - it explained that even amidst troubles there is hope! Maybe someone came along and disentangled the string, but I can't remember how the poem continued.

Anyway, my poetic efforts were now far removed from the 'snap, crackle, pop' nonsense of earlier days, and fame came my way when one of my attempts was actually printed in a newspaper, together with a short article about me!

Scott was a neighbour's son who was a young entrepreneur. He decided to publish a monthly magazine called *The Companion*. He was the editor, and he appointed me as the sub-editor. Scott's art teacher designed a spectacular cover, and month by month we filled about twenty quarto pages with stories, poems, and whatever. So thank you Scott for encouraging me to experiment with writing fiction. It was an enjoyable addition to my busy life!

During part of my illness I corresponded with Neville, the son of one of Dad's colleagues. He was also ill in bed, though he was indoors in a normal bed. We exchanged some of our 'creations'. He sent me pictures he'd drawn, and I sent him poems I'd written. But our helpful correspondence came to an abrupt end, and I found his sudden death rather hard to accept, especially knowing he had the same heart problem as myself. Neville was 'fed' on a much bigger dose of aspirin than I was, and at first it appeared that he was the one who was improving .

After my Sunday decision, Dad tried to find a religious book for me, and came up with the 'John Bunyan' idea. *Pilgrim's Progress* made exciting reading, but I had two concerns. The first was my feeling of sadness that Christian should walk away from his wife Christiana (as she was eventually called) while he went on his travels, leaving her to work hard at home and fend for herself. All right, maybe the story is an allegory, but I'm still left thinking to this day that a Christian can give his Christiana quite a hard time because of his 'higher' beliefs.

Also, I hesitated at the wicket gate. Pilgrim went through the gate and lost his burden of sin, but I stumbled there, because I didn't understand what had happened to him - it all seemed so sudden. Am I also expected to go through some sort of wicket gate? And if I don't, what will happen to me? Have I also got a burden of sin?

Leaving the spiritual for a moment, I did have some practical uses in my outside bedroom. One night, while Mandy (my rival girl-poet from next door) and her parents were away on holiday, I was awakened by a scraping sound, just over the fence, about a couple of yards away from me. Was there someone in their garden? So, in a childish squeak I merely said an innocent 'hello', upon which two frightened men fled. They were trying to force open a window, but a 'ghost' interrupted their thieving plans!

Mind you, maybe Mr Next-door deserved to be robbed, as he regularly stole building materials from nearby building sites. He even stole from me, a child philatelist - and he pinched my most valuable stamps. He robbed a poorly boy!

Thinking of thieves reminds me of our two teenage evacuees Frank and Eddie, who gave Mam and Dad extra problems. One day these lads heard my parents say they'd like a rockery in the front garden, so within one week a lovely rockery appeared, fully planted. It was Frank and Eddie's attempt to placate my parents after being caught stealing money from Mam's purse to buy cigarettes. The rockery was stolen from gardens around the estate, though we never discovered which gardens, and so the rockery remained in our possession! Neither did we discover how they worked out the complicated logistics. Anyway, I suppose the boys were quite helpful, in an inverted sort of way.

The behaviour of Frank and Eddie, our helpful thieves, together with the fact that they had to be taught how to use a knife and fork, and that their grammar was up a gum tree, made quite an impression on me. It once again emphasized contrasts - the different backgrounds from which folk came, the different opportunities they have, the different talents. It was all so baffling. Why was I ill but Frank and Eddie were well? Is there anyone who understands? What about this God I'm supposed to be pleasing? Does He have any answers? Does God make any decisions? Does God decide on our backgrounds, our talents? Is there such a thing as chance? Good luck and bad luck? Can God and chance coexist?

I was never bored during my illness. In any case my doctor had given me hundreds of old postage stamps and that was when my interest in philately began. And there were also my night sky, my books on astronomy, my dictionary, my Bible, my books of poetry, my desire to memorise and to write poetry, not to mention all my thoughts and wonderings. What more could a young lad want?

Tuition during long illnesses wasn't the norm in those days, but it's a wonder that Dad didn't arrange some for me privately. Perhaps he thought I'd never return to school, especially after the consultant had called him aside for some reason or other. It was years later that I unearthed the reason, and only then did I understand why Dad had been so secretive! But come to think of it, would I have had time to squeeze private lessons into my already busy life?

Well, my in-bed schedule continued happily, day by day, and month by month, but my friends Lionel and Co had by now vanished into thin air. As for my friendly owls, I'd left them all behind in Torquay, and not surprisingly my old pals Biggie Bow-wow and Dimmon Demmon had long since met their demise. But suddenly two new friends appeared on the scene - a boy and a bird!

The paperboy somehow discovered I was in bed at the back of the house, and he came to see me every morning round about 8 a.m. I enjoyed his brief visits, but they came to a sudden end when the thief-man next door popped his head out of his bedroom window and shouted to my Paper Friend, "Just leave that boy alone, he's very ill!" Ah well, all good things come to an end!

Mr Sparrow couldn't fly, but he hopped to my bedside every morning, week after week. Why did this poor flightless bird come to see me? And why didn't the neighbour's cat gobble him up? I felt that this was something which God had planned especially for me! What, a lame sparrow coming to give a poorly boy some comfort? Wow, that's just amazing. Apart from the '3 a.m. event' which I have yet to describe, this was the biggest event of my illness, and one that often comes to my mind. Thank you Mr Sparrow.

I had one other visitor, but that was a one-off visit from a black cat! One cold winter's night I awoke with a start, and there he was, lying across my face, purring! Without thinking, I threw this black bundle of fur to the ground, and I can still visualize this terrified cat looking back at me with staring eyes, with legs and body making a backwards parallelogram. Poor thing, he'd just found a warm spot for the night!

Time went on, but I didn't seem to be solving any of life's problems, and the explanation of infinity was still beyond my grasp. Health-wise, I was quite accustomed to my continuing illness, but after almost two years of being in bed, something happened which changed the situation. It was the 3 a.m. event.

I'm fast asleep. It's the middle of the night and I dream that Jesus is at my bedside. He stretches out His hand and gently touches me. In my sleep I shout out, "I'm better now!" Mam hears me from the bedroom above my outside den and comes running out to see what's wrong, but I keep repeating the good news. Mam notes the time as 3 a.m. and says, "All right, all right, just settle down Geoffrey!"

That was my dream, but there was a happy sequel when my lady doctor came a few days later and found a vast improvement. 'However can this have happened so suddenly?' she asked. Soon we discovered that at 3 o'clock during the same night as my dream, Scott's dying mother suddenly awoke, and prayed for me. So was my dramatic improvement by chance or by miracle? Things began to happen - I hadn't been dressed for two years, but now I was allowed to get dressed each day and walk around for five minutes. Soon my doctor allowed ten minutes, and little by little she extended the time. It was exciting. I already believed in God, but was this dream-come-true yet another indication that God is not merely 'there', but that He cares, and acts?

A physiotherapist came each week, to help me to walk again. Quite needless, I thought, as I'd been walking to the toilet quite easily for the last two years. Anyway, let's have all the help I can get, eh?

Walking down our road for the first time is still a vivid memory. I felt like a king, and wanted to greet everybody as kings do, but I saw no one. What an experience, what freedom! And how things had changed - many houses were now painted a different colour, gardens had grown, trees were big, gnomes had appeared. It was all so wonderful, and I often relive the huge emotion of that solitary walk.

Soon I'd be walking a little further - back to school. What a relief for Mam and Dad, who had been so worried about me. And of course they'd had no holidays for two years, and never gone out together - but now their restrictions had been lifted!

It was exciting to think that my education would soon be back on track, even though I had to return to Gatley High School, which we now knew was not the best of schools. This is because my doctor insisted I went to a school close to home, with minimum walking involved. But it was still an exciting prospect, though somewhat daunting.

My two-year gap was filled with many unanswered questions. Some of these questions arose from my books - what really happened to Pilgrim when his burden dropped off? How should we interpret 'reverence for life'? Other questions arose from events - why had I been so ill? The lady next door knew the answer - it's because I lived at No. 13, and that's what brought me bad luck! If so, could she explain why I was suddenly so much better? What about my dream? Was God somehow involved in all this? Perhaps I should say that God had been good to me, but if so, had God been bad to Neville? My questions just won't go away.

Geoffrey, aged nearly 15. This is the first time he'd been dressed for two years

Chapter 4

Rock Bottom

So far in my life I've had no exams to pass, but that's all going to change.

Going back to school had a feeling of unreality about it. However, the fact that I was now two years behind the others was a reality, though a stark one. Unfortunately it didn't seem that my attempts to understand the purpose of life, which had been claiming my attention for the last two years or more, were on the curriculum! Maybe ignorance is bliss at times, but not when it comes to taking exams.

Two years without tuition isn't good, but it was also two years of forgetting all the things I'd previously been taught. No wonder I was dreading these wretched exams. But there was no escape, and the day came when I had to sit at my desk and take them, and that's when I suddenly fell to rock bottom - bang! I came bottom of the class in every subject, gaining a mere 5% in French and in maths - it hurt. How strange to think that sometime in the future I would be Head of Mathematics in a well-known school!

But nobody bothered about my poor performance. Nobody came to help me. I was on my own, and seemingly in a desperate situation. I believe so much in the need to help others, and have at least tried to do so in my adult life. But the fact that I had no help whatsoever turned out to be the best thing that could have happened to me.

I visited bookshops, and bought books on various school subjects.

Buying the books was the easy-peasy bit, but then I had to study them all! And I must say it was a big struggle to catch up, but these books became my ladder, and I just had to make myself think 'rung by rung' and 'day by day'. When Sir Ranulph Fiennes climbed to the summit of Mount Everest in 2009 at the age of sixty-five, he said that his mantra 'plod on, plod on,' got him to the summit. It was 'plod by plod', it was 'plod for ever'. Thankfully I wasn't climbing a literal Mount Everest, but I was certainly climbing an educational Mount Everest. At long weary last, I got there. What a view!

At first, I was hopeless at French. One of my difficulties was the division of words into masculine and feminine - what a nuisance! Why is a knife a boy, but a fork a girl? A road a boy, but a street a girl? The sun a boy, but the moon a girl? Day a boy, but night a girl? I had enough trouble with my sex education anyway, without meeting this barrier as well.

However, despite all my problems with learning French, I devised a plan to help me. Surely, I thought, the words 'what a pity' could be fitted into almost any essay, so *'quel dommage'* became my starting point. I asked Miss Nairn to teach me the French for more and more phrases, and then set to work learning them all. They were then ready to be used at a moment's notice:

Against all odds
Believe it or not
As a matter of fact
In the very middle of
It almost took my breath away
You'll never guess what happened next

This proved to be a huge help to me. After all, you can learn a hundred nouns with the hope that one of them might come in handy now and then, but learn twenty phases such as the above, and you'll be able to use lots of them in every story or essay. Simple!

But how did I cope with mathematics? Well, although catching up with other subjects was a struggle, it was less so with maths. Here was a subject which required minimum remembering, and maximum thinking, and it suited me to a T. Maths became addictive. Apparently I used the toilet roll as maths notepaper when I spent time in the 'little room'. And I was once caught having fun with maths during the French lesson, upon which Miss Nairn made me write out 500 lines: 'You cannot whistle and eat porridge at the same time!' I wonder why I was told to write these lines in English. I think Miss Nairn missed a big teaching opportunity there. Hence I never learnt the verb *'siffler'*, and so I was never able to whistle in French. *Quel dommage!*

The maths teacher who had inverted me years earlier had died, and now we had a new teacher who couldn't have had much knowledge of maths. His main qualification was that of being the Head's son. Maybe that was his only qualification! One day, after I'd caught up, this so-called maths teacher came and sat next to me before he 'taught' the lesson, and with a look of embarrassment, he hesitantly asked me for help! I remember drawing a diagram for him - with circles, tangents, chords, and so on. The scenario was repeated with some algebra a few weeks later. What must the others have thought about the teacher who was taught by a pupil? And this is the education for which my parents paid!

What a school! Half way through the final year of preparing for School Certificates (the GCSEs of yesteryear), it was discovered that we'd been studying the wrong books for English Literature, and so an urgent change of course was needed. Neither did we as pupils have any idea that the geography examination included a paper on world geography. So here's a big 'thank you' to my doctor for giving me all those stamps, thus enabling me to have some knowledge of other countries. It was my doctor who got me through that exam, not the teacher.

I was good at thinking abstract thoughts, but pretty bad at remembering solid facts, and it is the latter which I needed most if I were to pass my exams. I devised mnemonics galore (as I still do to this day) to aid my appalling memory. I got into the habit of doing this, and kept on producing mnemonics for French words, formulae in maths, the Great Lakes in America, names of roads, telephone numbers, just about anything. Here, for example, is one which I still use - my time-zone mnemonic:

Try your best
To get the knack
That 15 west
Is one hour back.

Then at least
You can't go wrong
With 15 east
Is one hour on.

‒ Throughout my time of preparing for all these exams, I was not too well. Sometimes I was taken ill at school and had to be sent home. So, hadn't God done a very good job of repairing my body? But I wasn't confined to bed any more, and that was mind-blowing.

I was still a frail and frightened boy, who was bullied by his so-called friends. I was also naïve in so many ways. I hadn't had much interrelation with other boys, and so I knew nothing of boys' talk and desires.

These lads wrote down a list of strange words, and one day in the High Street, they told me to read them out at the top of my voice. I daren't disobey, or they would have hit me. It seemed a strange demand, but I thought that there's no harm in shouting out some mumbo jumbo. But I wondered why all the shoppers gazed at me, looking aghast. Little did I know at the time that I'd shouted out a string of expletives, words completely unknown to me. Meanwhile these bullies just laughed. I felt much safer in my little outside den than in the big outside world.

These same lads made me steal from *Woolworths*, while they just watched and laughed. There seemed to be nothing within me to withstand these things, and I was far too scared to refuse! They used to hit me with a stick which they always carried with them, and I daren't risk the consequences of refusing to steal. I did the dirty work, but they received the booty! I never told Mam and Dad about this bullying, though Mam sometimes saw me in the bath and asked me what I'd done to get my bruises. I lied, and told her I didn't know.

Being hit with a stick would have been bad enough if there'd been a reason for it, but these lads just hit me for fun. It was their entertainment!

Lionel was back in the picture now, but he was different from all the others. I'd first met him at school several years earlier and remember that the maths teacher who had been so displeased with me, caned him for not understanding some formula or other. We seemed to have different outlooks on life, but we got on well. He never bullied me, though he did take the lead in deciding what we should do, including playing truant one day - and I hated every minute of it.

He also devised an outdoor game - we were to take turns in lying down on the lawn, face-up, arms and legs outstretched and eyes closed, while the other one threw a dart high into the air. We tried to look brave. After many uneventful throws, the game came to an abrupt end when a dart pierced my cheek. There was blood and panic!

Soon after this event, the two of us dismantled the Anderson air-raid shelter in Lionel's parents' garden. Work completed, Lionel threw his spanner high into the air, with an ear-splitting shout of triumph - it was one of those heavy adjustable spanners. I thought I'd better do likewise, so using every bit of energy I could muster, I threw my spanner high into the air, but it landed on Lionel's head! There was blood and panic! He ran round the garden, holding his head and screaming with pain - it could easily have killed him.

Far from bullying me, Lionel was helpful to me, and for our mutual good he pushed out a knot in the wooden garage at his home. That was to enable us to gaze through the peephole at the neighbour's teenage daughter as she sunbathed in the garden, scantily dressed. Lionel said, "We'll take it turns to peep." I didn't want to look silly, so I took my turn and simply thought, 'Yes, she's a girl, I know that!' But he appeared to be thinking different thoughts, and that was very puzzling for me!

Watch out, hold tight, something strange is about to happen! I've already recounted experiences which I believe to be God-events, but what sort of eerie events are these which I'm now going to describe?

It was one of those cold winter spells when I allowed myself to sleep indoors: I was awakened night after night by the sound of someone sweeping the road, as though with a stiff broom. Each time I heard this sweeping sound I got up, looked out of the window, but saw nothing. The blackout had ceased, and so the streetlights were now lit, and that should have given me every opportunity of seeing my nocturnal road sweeper.

After several weeks of hearing the sweeping and seeing nothing, the night came when I was rewarded. On this particular night I heard, I looked, and then I actually saw! I had a perfect view of a woman dressed in a full-length luminous robe. She was on the road outside our house, holding a broom, but the sweeping had stopped. She moved around as though gliding, with no hint of leg movement. This was not ordinary walking, and neither was this an ordinary woman. This was something extraordinary!

I woke my parents and asked them to come quickly. Dad wouldn't come (don't be silly, Geoffrey!) but Mam did, and we watched our gliding lady for several minutes, until she disintegrated into a mist, which gradually dispersed. She'd gone, broom 'n' all! I never heard the sound of sweeping again.

My own mind was spinning - from God to ghosts. Wherever was I in the midst of all this?

The next evening, whilst walking down the road, with no one in sight and not a sound to be heard, a glass bottle hurtled past my eyes; it came down from the sky and smashed at my feet. I felt that the road sweeping and the smashed bottle were connected in some strange way, but what a pity my luminous road sweeper hadn't hung around a little longer, and then she could have swept up the broken glass! Or was she the one who actually threw the bottle at me?

But whatever the explanation of these strange events, at least they made me think that there must be other aspects of life to explore, mysterious things, things about which I felt rather uneasy. Brushing all this under the carpet and ignoring it seemed wrong.

So I decided I must face up to these things, and I paid my one and only visit to a Spiritualist Church. The children's song warns us that 'if you go down to the woods today, you're sure of a big surprise'. Well, this church made me feel to be in thick woodland spiritually, with no light getting through. And yes, I DID get a big surprise, and I think home would have been a far safer place. And the surprise? There was actually a message for me from 'the other side'. The medium seemed to point to me, so I tried to shrink, and hide behind the lady in front of me, but it was in vain. "Yes," the medium said, "that's you, behind the lady in the yellow hat!" Anyway, the message didn't seem relevant, and I have by now forgotten the contents. Was it a case of mistaken identity or was the whole thing a complete fake?

Soon I discovered that the poet William Blake experienced visions from a very early age, and claimed supernatural aid in his writings. About his book, *Milton*, Blake said, "I have written this poem from immediate dictation, sometimes against my will." This, he claimed, was automatic writing. He lived his life on the edge of poverty, because he wouldn't adjust his poetic output to the fashions of the day. How could he? After all, he had claimed direct guidance, and that's that.

I thought I'd have a go at this automatic writing myself. So I sat holding my pencil, endeavouring to get into an abstract state of mind, and then I waited… and waited. But nothing ever happened, despite several attempts! Perhaps I was far too willing to put these paranormal things to the test.

But having read about ESP cards, I found a pack of ordinary playing cards and repeatedly cut the pack, making sure I did not part the cards until I felt quite certain in my mind that I would obtain a red card. To my amazement, I obtained thirty-five red cards in succession. So did I have some extrasensory perception (ESP)? But I didn't test the next cut, as I was beginning to think the whole thing was a bit scary.

Now for some maths! The chance of obtaining thirty-five red cards in succession is 1 in 2 to the power 35, which is 1 in 3,435,973,836 which means that if I tried this card-cutting experiment about three and a half thousand million times, maybe I would succeed once. But it worked on my first attempt! Subsequent attempts were met with zero success, I'm glad to say!

Well, my period of experiencing strange happenings came to an abrupt end. Phew! However they were soon replaced by strange dreams and those dreaded doodlebugs (Hitler's flying bombs). One of these bombs dropped from the sky near enough to our house to destroy it, but it failed to explode - was the Lord once again keeping us safe by night and by day? As for my dreams, two of them recurred night after night, and continued for several years. These dreams were so convincing, that the world of dreams and the world of reality seemed to merge.

One dream was of my having the ability to walk with no contact with the ground! No, I didn't float around in space, I simply walked along normal pathways, but always a few inches above ground level. Whilst asleep, I walked long distances in this way. I just couldn't disregard such a persistent dream, a dream which was so real that I began to wonder whether I actually had the power to do this. I felt a bit disappointed when my attempts failed!

My other persistent dream concerned what today would be called flying saucers. The first official sighting of these strange objects was reported in 1947, but my dreams preceded all this by several years. I experienced my own 'sightings' hundreds of times. A massive disc-like object with windows around the circumference, moved overhead very slowly and in total silence, barely above roof height - it was so large that it took ages to pass over. The location was on Gatley Road, just by my school. I kept absolutely still while it passed over, looking up towards it with awe. Once again I felt that this was no empty dream, and that I'd peeped into an unknown world.

But my life was not entirely made up of strange dreams and spiritual enquiry, God-wards or other-wards. My parents had some friends who had a daughter Brenda, just a little younger than I was. They were frequent visitors, the grown-ups playing cards while Brenda and I entertained ourselves.

So one day, trying to find something different to do, we moved all the furniture in the dining room to one side, rolled up the carpet square, and took it into the loft, finally returning the furniture to the original position. Not a very good idea for someone with heart problems! But please note that it was Brenda's idea to do this, and earlier in my life it was Derek's idea to cancel Sunday School, and it was my bullies' idea to make me steal from *Woolworths*. On my own I would never have dared to do any of these things, but I was also too weak to refuse. So on carpet-day I climbed up the shelves of the airing cupboard, underneath the loft opening, and Brenda fed the carpet to me whilst I obediently heaved it upwards. Mam, now aged 107, recently asked me "Do you remember when you and Brenda took up the carpet?" So although her memory has all but gone, the carpet saga still remains fresh in her mind.

My ignorance and naivety were highlighted as Brenda began to investigate sexual matters. Every time she visited us, it seemed that she'd made yet another discovery. "And what have YOU discovered?" she would ask. But I wasn't looking for anything, not in that line anyway. To me, her quest for sexual information was boring, unnecessary, and irrelevant to life.

During my exam preparation I met the word 'adultery' in one of Shakespeare's plays and asked Dad what the word meant. So much for my

34

having studied the 'A' section of the dictionary! Poor Dad was confused yet again, and totally ignored my question. All he said was "I'll buy you a book." Sure enough, the next day I received this strange book, complete with rude pictures and diagrams. And that was my sex education out of the way! But Dad was no help to me at all, as I was still left in the dark about the meaning of adultery - not even a mention of the word in the whole book. A few days later, Dad decided that he'd better check up on my progress on the facts of life:

Have you read that book, Geoffrey? Yes.
All of it? Yes.
Did you understand it? Most of it, I suppose.
Oh good!

And that was it. *Quel dommage*, perhaps I should have listened to Brenda a little more! But how could it be that I should reach the age of nearly seventeen and not know these things? Most youngsters just know somehow, but I certainly didn't. Quite apart from Brenda, maybe I should have asked Lionel a few questions as we peeped through that knothole at the girl next door. Maybe I was still too busy with my brand of philosophy to consider things so mundane!

Mind you, I thought that Mary (the girl who sat in front of me at school) was very nice, and I admired her incredible ability at art and her witty personality. Her name was Mary Frederica St James Smith, which I thought was most impressive - well, apart from the 'Smith' bit! By now I'd read 'the book', but that had no bearing on my simply liking Mary. To my surprise she invited me to her seventeenth birthday party, and I was the only boy there! Soon afterwards our exams were taken and the school year ended - so I never saw her again at school, and never dared to ask to see her subsequently.

However, we did contact each other by letter. Mary was the first to write. She said 'There is something of SINGULAR importance I want to tell you'. I admired her English, and replied 'There is something I want to ASCERTAIN.' What a silly pair! A few more letters passed between us, but her last letter to me remained unanswered. For some reason I daren't write again. So that was that!

Despite ghosts, smashed bottles, carpet removals, parties with girls, and other interruptions to my education, somehow I had to find time to sit the School Certificate examinations. Now Gatley High School was too small to be accepted as an examination centre, so the Head had to find a centre where the exams of the Oxford Board were taken, and that just happened to be in the solemnity of a convent school. Have you ever knocked a nun over? Probably not. But I had the privilege of racing along a corridor of this holy establishment, whizzing round a corner and bumping into a nun, who fell flat on the floor!

There were several puzzling happenings during this exam period. For example, just before the French exam, and with an English-French dictionary to hand, I looked up a word at random - it was the word 'skater', which I found to be *'patineur'*. Maybe I should have known the word already, but I didn't. In any case I didn't bother much with learning nouns; as a matter of fact (or as some would say, *comme une question de fait*), I just specialized in phrases.

And guess what? The exam paper included a comic strip of a boy skating on an ice rink. I had to describe the various scenes in French, and oh how I enjoyed telling that story! I used my brand new word, plus some of the phrases which I'd prepared earlier:

John was a good skater. As *a matter of fact* he was much better than all the others. There he was *in the very middle* of the rink, enjoying himself, but *you'll never guess what happened next…*

Not all my puzzling events were good. Why did I walk out of an exam when I hadn't finished and wasn't even in difficulty? It was a crazy thing to do. Our maths exams were under separate subjects, and I was enjoying my trigonometry exam, but when Lionel gave up and walked out, I followed him! I didn't deserve my maths distinction after that.

And why was there one subject for which I did no studying? That was history. However, two weeks before the exam I panicked and crammed, racing through the Tudor and Stuart periods and enjoying history so much that I began to feel addicted.

I had worked hard to catch up, but not at history. In fact, I did no work whatsoever towards the exam, as I found the teacher so boring. And it was easy to get away with it, as the only homework we'd ever been given was to 'read the next chapter'. It's hard to understand how someone who tried his best had such a big exception, and did nothing. But that's not the only time in my life I've known this contradiction.

Nevertheless, despite my lack of work, I was suddenly in the position of knowing quite a lot about the Tudors and Stuarts, temporarily! Come the exam, I wrote and wrote at an immensely fast rate, completely immersed in my answers and living in the period of which I was writing, so much so that when the nun shouted out 'Five minutes remaining', I didn't know where I was. It seemed as though I'd come out of a trance - an experience which I'll never forget, though I have to confess I've forgotten most of the history of the Tudors and Stuarts, except for my mnemonic for remembering the names of Henry's wives, and the order in which he had them!

When I received my School Certificate results, I was taken aback that I'd done well, as I had no belief in myself. I was even granted matriculation by Oxford University - whatever that means!

This has been a chapter of failure and success, of storm and sunshine. An old Arabian motto explains that 'all sun makes a desert,' but I became more and more thankful when the sun shone, and successes came my way - they put the bad things in perspective.

Quite out of the blue, Dad made a dramatic announcement, "We're going to start going to church!" Whatever next? I think it was supposed to be as a thanksgiving to God for my exam success. My parents and my parents' parents were Methodists by name, though not by attendance, so off we went, week by week to Eden Place Methodist Church in Cheadle, fairly near our home in Gatley.

Now, believing in God is one thing, and that is done in the heart. But going to church? That's another thing. Why do we need to enter a building? Isn't belief enough on its own?

And for that matter, what would Derek think if he knew I was now attending a church? Hadn't Derek and I already implied that church was a non-starter when we fled from Sunday School? But he needn't worry, I'm not committed - but I am a bit curious.

Chapter 5

Presto

After the slowness of a long illness, the slowness of catching up educationally, and the slowness of growing up, the tempo suddenly changed from adagio to presto. The change seemed to be so rapid that it almost took my breath away! In other words, *cela m'a presque coupé le souffle!*

I managed to get a place at Altrincham Grammar School for Boys. Going to a new school was necessary, as the previous apology of a school didn't take pupils beyond School Certificate.

I really believed that in going to the Sixth Form I would be meeting young men who were dedicated to their studies. As I was intending to study mathematics, it seemed obvious that I'd better show some dedication myself, and do some work in preparation for this great new adventure. So I spent much of my holidays enjoying maths. I worked through a few books, including one on higher algebra and another on calculus. It was such fun, and I managed to do all the exercises, but I had the bad habit of defacing all my books with heavy underlining, and in this case, by drawing great big lines through every question I'd answered. The big lines were my expressions of triumph, always drawn with a quick flourish! When I'd finished, the books looked a real mess, but the mess meant 'done it!' Little did I know at the time how much I'd learned at what turned out to be a presto rate.

The holidays now over, I went off to this new academy of learning and had a couple of shocks. Firstly, I discovered that if I took maths then I had to take physics too, but at the previous school no sciences were taught. So I had to take the Sixth Form course with no prior knowledge of the subject. Not surprisingly, I struggled in the physics class.

Secondly, generally speaking, the dedicated young men I was expecting to meet didn't seem to be there! With some of the boys there wasn't the seriousness of approach which I'd imagined. I was completely taken aback by this.

My doctor didn't allow me to play games or to do gym, so this new boy, still frightened and frail, was taunted by the others. They viewed me as a weak freak. "You're a sissy, you're a sissy," they kept jeering. I just had to put up with it, feeling lonely and miserable. I sometimes wondered whether the boys might have been a little gentler with me if I'd been on crutches or in a wheelchair. Maybe not, but I'll never know. All I knew at the time is that I felt incredibly unhappy.

I'm close to despair,
Do you know how it feels?
They shout and they swear,
They're close on my heels.

Is there no one who likes me?
Is there no one who cares?
I hope Jesus likes me,
But He lives 'upstairs'!

As for 'downstairs', the division between the boys and myself widened when, after a month, I was placed in the Second-year Sixth maths class. It was dawning on me that I had already covered almost the entire maths syllabus in the holiday period. That did not go down at all well with the others.

To make matters even worse, soon after that, I was promoted to the Scholarship Sixth (the third-year Sixth), where I began to struggle - my second promotion was too big a leap. Physics was a non-starter, maths had gone wrong, and my other two subjects didn't work out either. I wasn't happy. My life was in a mess!

One day we were all sent home early, as one of those dreaded pea-soup fogs had descended on us - the kind of fog rarely experienced these days. I caught the bus, which was driven for about half a mile at far less than walking pace, but soon the driver abandoned all hope and left the passengers to their own devices. Walking home when I could hardly see my own hand was very difficult. It was also a silent, eerie and thought-provoking six-mile walk, or creep. This smog experience was a picture of my life, and I became more and more sombre. Dad was also returning home early - he'd abandoned his car and eventually found the road where we lived, only to walk into the kitchen of a neighbour's house! As for myself, I was in the fog of bewilderment about my life's direction. What confusion I felt!

My maths was doubly confusing. It just seemed uncanny that I could have learnt so much, so quickly, and on my own. But was I on my own? Was I helped in some way by a power outside myself? Maybe in some inexplicable way God had come downstairs to help me: 'I will restore to you the years that the locusts have eaten.' (Joel, chapter 2). I felt sure that the Lord must have opened my head and popped mathematics into it. God must have come into the equation somehow, and yet, confusion upon confusion, suddenly I'm out of my depth in the third-year Sixth! And so this became my first rise-and-fall experience. I'd risen rapidly through my maths classes, and then BANG - down I came!

Not surprisingly, after three months at my new school, I left. It seemed that once again the road ahead was closed. I was becoming experienced at staying at schools briefly! Mind you, I think that my teachers must have been glad when I left, as they didn't seem to know what to do with me. However, something happened while I was still there which turned out to be a turning point in my life.

And this 'something'? We had a lesson each week taken by a be-collared clergyman, whose subject was Logic. This was a misnomer, for in practice the lessons were on anything this reverend gentleman could think up, and the subject of Logic became Bassett's Educational Allsorts!

The day came when Revvy (as we called him) thought up the idea of assessing our personalities. He handed out multiple-choice questionnaires and we were to circle the numbers 1, 2 or 3 of the choices in each of ten questions. Our answers concerned our opinions, likes and dislikes, and not our academia. Afterwards, he went round the class to ask us for the ten-digit number each of us had produced, such as 1,323,112,321. He then looked up this number in his massive book of nearly 60,000 different combinations, and read out a short description of each personality. My number was 3,333,333,333, the last number in his big book. He seemed completely taken aback by this and refused to describe my personality, explaining that he would only do so if I went to see him privately. Of course I wanted to know but I never dared to ask. Was it something really bad? If it had been something good, wouldn't he have told me there and then?

Soon after this, Revvy thought up the idea of debates, and chose me as one of the contenders, with the motion 'Gambling is harmless'. "Yes," he said, glaring at me, "you've got to speak, Smales!" I was extremely scared, and felt I'd been given a massive kick - it really hurt and made me fear worse to come! Was it my 3,333,333,333 which prompted him to choose me? And guess what? The boys tittered at his choice of speaker.

I did my 'homework', first of all writing to the 'sinners' (Vernon's Pools), asking for info. I received a very helpful reply together with various pamphlets. Then I plucked up courage to see the 'saints' (the Christian Bookshop in Manchester) and asked if they had any books on gambling. The girl looked quite shocked. "Will you just wait a minute please?" Maybe she'd gone to fetch me a suitable book, but no, she'd gone to fetch me a suitable preacher, the manageress, who without asking me a single question, simply 'went for me'. I daren't tell her that what I really wanted was a book discussing the evils of gambling, just to get the full picture. Oh dear, that was a bad start - no book, just a telling-off! I left the shop feeling quite dejected and asking myself why the sinners had been more helpful than the saints. But I believed in God, and hoped that HE might help me, even if His saints hadn't.

Eventually the dreaded time came, and the debate began. I was shaking uncontrollably, and was 'doing a Belshazzar', with my knees 'smiting one against the other' (Daniel, chapter 5). But after a few moments of speaking, the tittering stopped. The boys listened in stunned silence. I'd never known anything like this before. It was unbelievable.

A few weeks later I spoke at another debate - I was shaking again, but it was another positive step forward for me. It was worth bearing all the pain I'd felt in this school, simply to receive so much eventual help by being told, "You've got to speak, Smales!" And that is all I got from the school, nothing more - but to me it was gold bullion. It was such a presto change from DAREN'T and CAN'T, to DARE and CAN - and DID!

Anything I had achieved previously had been done in private, but when others were around I was weak and scared. But I'd now done something while others were watching. It was only a small beginning, but it turned out to be a life-changing turning point. So thank you, Mr Reverend!

When life goes all pear-shaped and I feel I can't cope,
Bewildered, perplexed, and it seems there's no hope,
When all seems against me, and I've nowhere to go,
And my life is a list of woe upon woe…

Sometimes I think 'Shall I pack it all in?
Shall I dump all my hopes and dreams in a bin?'

But perhaps all I need is a push and a shove:
Someone to kick me? Someone above?

They say that you shouldn't kick a man when he's down, but I think it depends who it is, and when it is - kicks won't help everybody, but maybe there are times when kicks are just what we need. I certainly needed one. Well, Revvy is the one who kicked me by making me speak, but I think it must have been God who actually set things in motion, and then enabled this frightened boy to speak. So thank You, Lord!

'Sometimes life will push you, beat you down and stomp your face to the floor. Never give up, because you are alive and here for a reason. Stand up after all the scars have tried to tear you down. Nothing should stop you, and God will enable you.' (Anon)

Chapter 6

The Three M's

So here I am, with no A-levels, as we call them nowadays, so what next? Will my passion for mathematics lead me anywhere? Will my desire to understand spiritual matters come to anything? Or will a new roadway appear on the map? The answers to those questions cover my life from age seventeen to twenty-one. I reached conscription age, but my 'medical' yielded a Grade 4 result, which I have since discovered was the 'permanently and totally unfit' category. And so I never went into the armed forces.

When I was a 'big' boy aged seventeen, Dad decided that I should go for a holiday for young people, minus Mummy and Daddy. I was still fearful of others and dreaded it. Why was there a middle-aged man in the group? He shared a bedroom with me, and took a very strange interest in me! A few days later I went to reception to explain what was happening to me each night, and thankfully the fellow was never seen again. Because of my fear of others I pretended to be ill twice, to avoid going on an outing. Worse still, on the last night we had to sit on the floor, huddled together, for a sing-song. At midnight the lights were turned off. Suddenly, in darkness, I felt someone's lips against mine. Oh dear, whatever's happening? It must have been that girl sitting next to me, the one who nobody liked. Maybe this frightened boy was her last hope! How naïve I was. Yes, it was a rotten holiday.

M for MUSIC

Just before I left the Grammar School, as a major misfit, Mandy (the girl next door) started having piano lessons. Now, during my illness Mandy was my rival at writing poetry, with the aim, I think, of proving that girls make better poets than boys, and in particular that her skills were greater than mine.

"What, Mandy learning to play the piano?" Suddenly my feelings of rivalry were stirred. "I'll show her!" But I needed a piano teacher in order to 'show her', so I began to exercise my tried-and-trusted pestering techniques, pleading with Mam and Dad to let me have lessons. "Of course I'll practise," I kept repeating, "I promise."

The trouble is that neither Mam nor Dad had forgotten a previous promise I'd made - to clean out the birdcage each week. "No Geoffrey, just remember the canary," they said repeatedly. They seemed convinced that I would never persist in practising and that I'd soon lose interest. I was definitely getting nowhere.

Admittedly, my reason for wanting to play the piano was not altogether a holy one. But there was already a piano in the house, which had belonged to Grandma Smales No. 1, the one who had been a piano teacher. So why not use it? But for a long time my pestering didn't seem to be paying off. However I was a persistent pesterer, and...

Mrs Goulden's fees were half a crown an hour, or 12½ pence. That turned out to be gross overcharging, as she was such a rotten teacher. She called her semi-detached house, complete with her hideous piano, 'The Gatley School of Music', with a brass plate by the front door to prove it! But at least I was having lessons and I soon found that my initial poor motive of rivalling Mandy was eclipsed by a new and more noble motive - love! Yes, I loved playing, and couldn't get enough of it. Unfortunately my teacher gave me unsuitable music - arrangements of orchestral music. I soon became adept at playing *Les Patineurs* by Waldteufel, which I enjoyed despite its unsuitableness, and I especially enjoyed the title. After all, I knew a lot about skating, in French!

A business colleague of Dad's, who was a pianist, heard me play and told Dad he must find a good teacher for me post-haste! And so, only one week later I was under Teacher No. 2, Mr Whitehead, much to the annoyance of *Mrs Goulden*. What a difference! Sadly, I'd only been under him for a couple of months when he died suddenly. What HAD I done?

Teacher No. 3, *Miss Thoms*, was a well-known musician, but she seemed to have no musical interest except in her own performances. Sometimes I would go for my lesson and she wasn't there - she'd forgotten to tell me she was broadcasting. Fortunately it wasn't long before she got married and left the area. Quite timely, I thought! I remember the day she'd said to me,

"Look Geoffrey," holding out her left hand and showing me her new ring.

"Yes, it's very nice," I replied curtly, never cottoning on as to what sort of a ring it was. And that was the end of the conversation! After all, I'd come for a piano lesson, hadn't I? So why did I need to look at my teacher's new ring? Perhaps I didn't live in the real world. Maybe I still don't!

So now I'm with Teacher No. 4 - what will she be like? My previous three teachers only taught me, in total, for about a year. Will No. 4 last any longer? Well, Beryl Dallen turned out to be a teacher-par-excellence. Sometimes she seemed over-severe; nonetheless she soon sorted me out, and after about a year with her, she was rewarded by my Grade 8 distinction. Mind you, I nearly didn't take the exam, because I had a high temperature on exam day. So Mam rang Beryl to explain that I was ill in bed, but our Beryl was having none of that, and so I had to get up and take the exam - ill or not. Saying 'no' to Beryl wasn't an option!

Beryl had three pupils who were neck and neck, namely Hazel, Margaret and myself. We were a mutual encouragement to each other, as well as being friendly rivals, especially when we entered music competitions, usually coming back with several trophies between us. We enjoyed playing trios - and I was the lucky boy who sat in the middle!

My progress from nothing to Grade 8 was another presto experience. It was on a different level from my speedy learning of maths, in that I actually know others who have reached this same stage in piano playing in just as short a time. Beginning piano lessons in my late teens was not ideal, but there was a plus side, as surely an older person can learn easier than a child, and if addicted to playing as I was, there is every hope of speedy learning.

The time came when Beryl decided that I was good enough to become the accompanist of her choir, the well-known Maia Girls' Choir. I readily accepted, but soon began to wonder why she'd thought I was good enough for the job, as she would sometimes shout at me with disapproval during rehearsals. But playing for the choir was a wonderful experience for all that, and I had the privilege of accompanying the choir for several live broadcasts, after which I would sometimes receive the comment 'Well Geoffrey, at least you didn't ruin the singing!' Wow, as far as Beryl was concerned, that was praise. And what is more, I was even allowed to train the choir in her absence!

Stockport Town Hall was a place to remember. The hall was packed; the Maia Choir was on the stage ready to begin the concert, when a light bulb exploded in the chandelier just above the piano, covering the instrument with broken glass. I went to the piano, using my handkerchief to clear the glass from the keyboard. So far, so good. But then I felt a sharp stab in my bottom, and stood up to clear the glass from the stool. My handkerchief performance received massive applause - most embarrassing!

But my feeling of fame was short-lived and was completely wiped away at my next piano lesson when I received an equally massive telling-off. "How dare you make such a spectacle of yourself? It was completely disrespectful to the choir, and to me personally!" Oh dear!

My escapade wasn't the only unexpected happening in the Town Hall that night - it was quite an eventful evening. After the interval, Beryl (who was a well-known accompanist) came to the piano to play for a cellist, who was giving a short recital. All went well until the encore. We were about to hear 'The Swan' by Saint-Saëns when it was discovered that the sustaining pedal had somehow become disconnected. But help was at hand, as someone was found in the audience who was willing to crouch under the grand piano, with a spare copy of the music (which was miraculously produced), and operate the pedal shaft by hand. The gentleman who performed this feat received a huge ovation, and much praise from our Beryl. Mind you, I think he well deserved the applause and the praise. But when I got a ticking off for my own feat of dexterous glass removal, I thought, 'It's all right for some!'

One year, Beryl Dallen entered her choir for the Llangollen International Eisteddfod. This necessitated a coach trip, but before we set off I was warned not to get too friendly with any of the girls. "And just remember that you're here as an accompanist, and that is all!"

The return journey from Llangollen was a journey of triumph. We had won! Miss Dallen was quite excited, but her pleasure turned into great displeasure when she discovered that there was no civic reception planned for us. We were mentioned on the radio, with extracts from our performance being played, but was the Mayor of Stockport entirely unaware of our success? If so, he wasn't unaware for very long, not with our Beryl in fighting mood, and within a week, a celebration meal was organised for us. You don't ignore Beryl and get away with it.

Miss Dallen was without doubt a formidable woman. Pupils and parents alike did as they were told. Dad was rebuked for allowing me to practise on what she deemed to be a below-standard piano. He was instructed to buy me a grand piano. Well, he DID buy one, but not immediately - I had to wait for my twenty-first. Nonetheless, thank you, Miss Dallen.

As I was no longer at school and not yet in employment, Miss Dallen taught me during early afternoons, and gave me very long lessons, as long as needed. Here was a teacher with a huge zeal to do her best for me. Dad, of course, paid for my lessons, whilst my part was to practise and do some of my teacher's household chores. "Geoffrey, while you're waiting, just go into the kitchen and wash up!"

And although I was in love with playing the piano before I met Miss Dallen, it was she who made me aware of the vastness of music. It's as though she'd opened a door to the universe and let me in. Despite her reprimands, she always nodded with approval when I allowed my feeling to be expressed through my fingers, and I no longer felt embarrassed when I showed emotion in my playing.

I remember Teacher No. 4 with thankfulness and I owe a lot to her. A few years earlier, her rather severe manner would have squashed me flat. But somehow she actually helped me to grow in confidence as a person, never mind as a pianist. She also lifted me from a merely technical approach to playing, and showed me the poetry and freedom of music. And that is only part of the help she gave me, so unstintingly. I can say with certainty that it was Beryl who encouraged me far more than anybody else I had known, and that's quite apart from her help with music. She was very interested in my life's story and was the first person to urge me to write a book about my experiences. I'm now doing as she said, albeit sixty years later!

Round about this time I started teaching piano to children in the neighbourhood. One of my pupils came to me through rather unusual circumstances: Dad once asked an odd-job man to do some tidying-up in the garden, but this man did a bit too much tidying-up, in that he climbed over the fence and chopped down a conifer in the neighbour's garden! Our side of the tree seemed to be dead, and it was certainly brown, and our 'gardener' thought it was an eyesore - in fact, he was doing us a good turn! The next day an angry letter arrived, prompting Dad to call round to try to placate the neighbour. He returned home entirely successful, carrying the gift of a jar of home-produced honey, plus a request that I teach the daughter piano. The little girl's name was Felicity Adams, giving rise to a new mnemonic for learning the spaces in the treble clef. She had been ill, and had a sore throat; her mum wanted her to gargle, but she just couldn't do it. So the mnemonic became 'Felicity Adams Can't Even Gargle', representing the notes F, A, C, E, G. Well, that did the trick - she learnt the notes, and to defy me, she also learnt to gargle!

Twice, when my parents went away for the weekend, I held a Saturday afternoon Piano Party for my pupils. Mam was quite amused when I invaded the kitchen and made cakes and a trifle for the occasion, but she preferred not to be around on the actual date. I had about seven pupils, and come party-time, they played for each other, and then afterwards we played a few games followed by our 'eats', with drinks of lemonade. It was such good fun.

Music was yet to play a much bigger part in my life, but we'll leave the story there for the time being.

M for MATHS

Having fled from Altrincham Grammar School as a complete misfit, it wasn't long before mathematics took off in a new direction. But first, there was a brief parenthesis in my life, which I'll now explain:

I considered taking up art, of all things! It was absolutely out of the blue, thus taking me on a completely new career path. Perhaps it was a knee-jerk reaction after the maths fiasco at the Grammar School. But why art? If anyone should have studied art it was Mary, the girl whose party I'd attended just a few months earlier. I was nowhere near Mary's standard, but at least I had a distinction in School Certificate, so I applied to the Manchester College of Art, and was granted an interview with the Principal. I took my portfolio of drawings and paintings to show him, and was soon to experience a humbling rebuke. The Principal had a massive desk in his office and I sat behind this desk, alongside 'The Presence'. He opened my portfolio and I watched him turn the pages very, very slowly. Time went by, not a word was spoken, and the silence became so unbearable that I just couldn't stand it any longer, and I blurted out my never-to-be-forgotten comment: "I know they're not ALL good, Sir!"

Immediately Sir swung round on his chair, and looking over his glasses he glared at me and said "So you think SOME of them are good, do you, Smales?"

With my head bowed, I meekly answered, "No, not really!" Nevertheless I was soon to receive a letter offering me a place on the architecture course, but I decided not to proceed. The parenthesis is now closed!

Back to important matters - my exploration in the world of mathematics! William Angling once said, "Mathematics is not a careful march down a well-cleared highway, but a journey into a strange wilderness, where the explorers often get lost, or even discover more than they thought possible." Well, that just about sums up my whole life, never mind the purely mathematical part of it!

Anyway, let's begin my journey into this strange wilderness. It all began with my decision to study actuarial mathematics. Grandpa (the posh one) and Dad were to 'blame' for this new venture!

Grandpa used to be a coal miner, a real man's profession, but after a few years he left the pit and became an agent in an insurance company. Little by little he climbed the promotion-ladder and reached a high position from which he hoped to become a director of the firm, but it didn't happen. Dad followed in his footsteps, and became the youngest person to reach this same high position. He also hoped to become a director, but it didn't happen. It was Grandpa and Dad's wish that I would go into the same profession, and maybe at the third attempt there would be a director in the family, but it didn't happen.

However, because of their hopes, I decided to study actuarial mathematics, with a view to becoming an actuary. At the time there were very few actuaries worldwide, with all their names being listed in one small handbook. Most of them were employed in the insurance world; so was there still the thought that I might eventually become a director, but by a different route? After all, there was already an actuary on the Board of Directors.

I studied at home with the help of a correspondence course. I had a lot of hard work ahead of me, as it was a very tough exam, and at the time, exemption could be claimed only if I had a first class honours degree in maths, so that ruled me out! But never mind, here's a subject I enjoy, so let's start the exploration in earnest.

Actuarial maths was most exciting. On one occasion, Mam and Dad went out for the day, having invited me to join them, but I preferred studying maths to having a day out. When they returned later that evening, I was still engrossed in my maths, but after a while they interrupted me and asked me what I'd had for dinner and tea. Oh dear, I'd never given food a thought!

The mathematician Paul Eros once said that 'maths is a device for turning coffee into theorems!' But my theorems seemed to turn me off coffee, off eating altogether - well, for that particular day! Mind you, I was in good company with absent-minded Beethoven who once went to a tavern for dinner, but got so engrossed in composing that he dismissed the waiter's repeated visits, and having eaten nothing, he eventually went to the bar to ask for the bill!

But not everything in my exam preparation engrossed me. Why did officialdom decree that essay writing should be included at this stage of mathematical advancement? I dreaded this part of the course, because of my limited general knowledge. There would, it is true, be a choice of essay subjects, but none of the simpler subjects were ever included. An essay on Happiness or Holidays would have been fine, but such topics as the Industrial Revolution, or the History of the Locomotive were more likely. I know that London is the capital of England, I know the name of the Prime Minister, but don't push me too far! I can think thoughts, but I don't know facts. I'm quite extreme in this dichotomy.

My maths progressed well. But with the exam date just around the corner, and bearing in mind my fear of the essay, I went into *Sherratt and Hughes' Bookshop* in Manchester, rather belatedly. I looked around aimlessly, and after some hesitation I bought a book called *Coal Mining in Russia*. Why did I buy this book? Why did I read it with such urgency?

By now it is almost expected that unusual, improbable and even impossible things happen in my life, and now for an almost impossible. On exam day, one of the essay topics was 'Discuss coal mining in Russia'! There was no holding me back, I could hardly write the words quickly enough, and I felt extremely excited. Was the essay subject just the luck of the draw, or had God guided me in choosing the perfect book in the first place? And what about my French exam? Was it God who gave me the French word for 'skater'? If so, have I actually cheated in both exams, but with divine help? I simply ask the questions, but I have no answers.

I was obviously on a high about my essay, so perhaps that's why I had a strange mental block when I reached the last page, with not much time remaining. My essay finished with about half of the last page spare, but on the last line I'd written the word THEIR and in a state of confusion, I decided that the spelling was wrong, that it should have been THERE, so I changed it. I then decided my first spelling was correct, so I corrected my correction. This alternation of spellings went on to the bottom of the page - their, there, their, there, their... What panic! I can still visualize the column of words.

Anyway, I passed my exam and thus gained membership of the Institute of Actuaries. Humble Grandma told all her friends that I was studying to be an ESTUARY!

The first stage was now over, so on to the next actuarial exam. However, in total contradiction to my previous manner of studying, I did no work whatsoever, absolutely nothing. I was completely overcome, once again, by my bewilderment concerning the meaning of life. I read books on all sorts of spiritual subjects, but none of them convinced me. I had no problem with simply believing in God, or in acknowledging that He had looked after me way beyond human resources, but I could get no further. Day after day and night after night the questions kept coming, but not the answers. And so I had no hope of passing my exams. I had no correspondence course for this exam and so there was no tutor to question my lack of work.

Not surprisingly, I didn't tell Mam and Dad what was happening, or rather what was NOT happening, so they assumed I'd pass quite easily. I'm ashamed of my silence, and yes, the fact that Dad had paid quite a lot for me to take the exam did concern me, but regrettably fear had a greater grip on me than honesty.

Come the exams, I wrote poetry throughout them all - well, I had to do something! Of course, everything was collected afterwards, including rough paper. Think what poetic gems I might have lost! Anyway, these verses were my considered answers to the maths questions! What with 'their, there, their...' in the previous exam and now loads of poetry in this exam, I wonder what the examiners thought about me. I can but guess! And so, of course, I failed! I also failed my driving test round about the same time, my first of five attempts!

But at least, as a member of the Institute of Actuaries, I was in a good position to find employment, and soon I became the Statistician, not as yet of an insurance company, but of the British Road Services, in Manchester. Statistician? What a high-sounding title! In fact I was merely a filler in of forms, with no mathematical skills needed, apart from adding and subtracting! Almost immediately I had some doubts, wondering whether I was on the right lines career-wise. Having a boss who was usually drunk made things worse - he just couldn't manage the word 'statistics', and after several attempts, Mr Spink would always resort to a stuttered 'Fetch me the figures, will you!' I had to go into the smoke-filled drivers' room every week to collect the logbooks. The drivers regarded me as an unnecessary evil, and I dreaded my visits.

It's all very well trying to find a career to please Dad, but by now I had several aspects of my life clamouring for my attention - mathematics, music, and whatever you call it in the spiritual line. I was passionate about each, but not about sitting at a desk filling in forms. It seemed as though the road ahead was about to be closed once again, by reason of my doubts about my present employment.

I loved the poetry and freedom of music, I was excited by the precision and logic of mathematics, and I could not move away from my spiritual searching. Perhaps these passions were signposts. Should I try to please Dad or try to follow the signs? But which sign should I follow?

My music in this period of my life ended with success, my maths with failure, and my statistical employment with doubts. But maybe it's time to leave all this aside for the moment and see what happened in the so-called spiritual area of my life, in that part of my life which has consumed my thinking for many years.

M for METHODISM

I'll go back to the day I received my School Certificate results, and Dad decided we should go to the Methodist Church as a thanksgiving to God for my passing the exams. I wondered how going to church was the way of saying 'thank you'. Maybe it implied that we acknowledged that God had been good to us concerning my results. But couldn't we have been thankful at home, without all the fuss of getting into the car, and going somewhere else to express it? But quite apart from the car journey, here was a brand new experience for me to consider.

Church? Whatever is it like? What happens? Will I get any help in understanding the meaning of life? Will I learn more about God as I sit in that pew? Will I discover that God really IS all-powerful and all-knowing? Or are these descriptions of God no more than mere words?

The advance of science together with the horrors of war had already made me very much aware of MAN's knowledge and MAN's power. Man had not yet landed on the moon, but the goal was already set, a goal which was eventually achieved nearly twenty-five years later, in 1969, 'and now nothing will be restrained from them, which they have imagined to do.' (Genesis, chapter 11)

Nothing seems restrained from men
That they begin to do;
See their wisdom, skill and power,
And hear their much ado!
Progress is a nation's pride,
'Tis boasted day and night;
Each achievement seems to prove
That men are gods of might.
Sailing round the watery globe,
Or flying far and wide,
Diving to the ocean's depth,
Or scaling Everest's side -
This is almost of the past,
Today we seek new thrills:
Lethal gases, nuclear bombs,
Or anything that kills.
Even when in saner mood,
Exploring into space,
Landing on the barren moon
What is it but a race?
Rockets poised towards the sky,
Who'll be the first on Mars?
Discontent with even this,
'Tis then to distant stars.

Yes, man's power amazes me. But what about GOD's power? I believed I'd seen His power at work as He'd lovingly cared for me, and helped me again and again. What about Mr Sparrow? What about that night when Jesus stretched out His hand and gently touched me? Maybe these are just small tokens of His power, but what can I say about God's universal power? What about His kingdom and His glory? Perhaps I need to stop asking questions, get on with my life, and maybe the 'big' answers will just come. So that's what I'll do!

Soon, and still a teenager, I was asked to be the secretary of the Sunday School. And so, with my new determination to get on with life very much in mind, I accepted the position. Mind you, I was very experienced in the ways that Sunday Schools are run - after all, Derek and I had actually been to one, so we should know!

About 200 children attended each Sunday (rather different from today's Sunday Schools), and my job was to sit at a table during the whole proceedings and deal with the big register. The teachers ticked small registers, which were for individual classes, then handed them to me to summarize, and enter into the 'big book'.

I also had to arrange the Sunday School outings, which meant booking several coaches, and calculating how much bread, etc. would be needed for sandwiches. Now, at last, I'd found some practical use for my maths! Things were rather formal in those days, and so a building had to be booked at our destination, so that we could eat our meal at tables! And somewhere had to be found to play outdoor games.

In addition, there were business meetings to arrange from time to time, and minutes to be taken - all good experience for me.

And here's another addition - I became one of the teachers, so now the 'big book' had to be filled in after everybody else had gone home.

I've always been somewhat absent-minded, living with my head in the clouds, but one Sunday this fact was brought home to me sharply: I'd walked to Sunday School to teach my class, holding a picture I'd drawn as a visual aid, plus a letter to be posted. The children were now all seated around me, but where was my picture? And how come I'd got a letter in my hand? The children were very disappointed, as the previous week I'd promised to bring the picture - not the best way to impress my class!

With my head in the clouds,
I can't see the ground;
And I can't see the crowds
Who are milling around.

I fell flat on my face -
Just to add to my woes.
Yes, I'd fallen from grace;
So what next? Who knows!

But I didn't have to wait very long to know what came next in my list of jumbles and tumbles:

The father of one of the children in the Sunday School was seriously ill, and as Secretary I arranged for two children to take some flowers to the home. They soon returned, minus the flowers, but told me the sad news that 'Johnny's Dad died yesterday'. So I sent a letter of condolence to the family, but alas, the poor man had NOT died! It seems that Mum had explained to the visiting children that her husband had 'gone' - but he hadn't gone to heaven as my emissaries thought, but to hospital, where he eventually recovered!

Later on my responsibilities were widened further. I was now the secretary, a teacher, AND the pianist. The latter necessitated my practising every hymn in the hymnbook before the following Sunday, though I still experienced a few awkward and embarrassing pianistic moments, to humble me. But maybe I had a bit of an excuse, having only been learning to play for a few months.

Time went on, and although I learnt quite a lot about taking responsibilities, it was, in one sense, peripheral learning. At the centre of the circle was my desire to understand more about God. The sermons were boring, and seemed to be as peripheral as my Sunday School duties. True, important matters were mentioned concerning practicalities, and rules for living an honest life. Jesus was shown as a good man who exemplified all these practicalities of decent living. But I thought that I didn't need a sermon to tell me these things, as they were merely matters of common sense. What about the reasons for our existence? The 'big' answers were just not coming, and so I felt quite justified in spending sermon-time playing games with the numbers on the hymn board, and (when my piano playing got more advanced) playing Liszt's Transcription of Rigoletto in my mind - a feat which could be accomplished twice in one sermon! Methodist sermons take twenty minutes!

So although I was attending church, I still felt to be alone with my searching, hence my year-long maths blackout which caused me to fail my actuarial exam. I just had to forget my resolution to stop asking questions - and so instead of studying maths, I was busy reading books, some of which were certainly not prescribed by Methodists!

However, I met Dudley at the church, and it seemed we were on similar spiritual wavelengths. He was studying to be an optician AND he'd passed his driving test, which was far more important! We often went by car (Dudley's dad's) into the nearby countryside, found a scenic parking place, and just sat and talked about life. We talked without any restraint, without fear of offending each other. The freedom we experienced in our discussions seemed better by far than the protocol of the church.

We found there were others in our age group who wanted to talk things over, and so we obtained permission from the minister to meet in the vestry on Saturday mornings, simply to exchange thoughts. It was so helpful. But all this came to a sudden end when the minister changed his mind and told us that our get-togethers must cease, and that we must be satisfied with the meetings already on offer.

Despite the minister's discouraging ban on our Saturday morning meetings, which I thought was enough to stifle any spiritual interest, I asked him about the possibility of preaching in the church. All at once it happened - I became one of the MLPs, as we were called. And so, at the age of twenty I began visiting churches in the area (or circuit, as it was called) to take the services as a Methodist Local Preacher.

I didn't know all that much about the Bible, but at least I was certain of one thing - my belief in God. And I knew that God had helped me through difficult times. But wicket gates still left me guessing. However, that didn't mean that there was nothing left to preach about - but what? It was probably a collection of my own thoughts, illustrated with Bible verses and stories. Maybe that was the wrong way round, but that's how I seem to have begun. As for understanding deep Biblical doctrines, I was muddled and could only manage a 'simple' sermon!

Perhaps I was in one great big mix-up about everything, just as I was as a child when, as a muddled green bottle, I fell down two bottles too soon, amidst the laughter of the audience.

But now for a more recent and seemingly trivial picture of my muddles and fuddles – I simply lost my camera! Wherever could it be? Maybe it was stolen from my saddlebag when I cycled to the grocers earlier that day. So off I went to the Police Station and reported the theft. Well, over sixty years later, I expect the Police are still searching for my camera, because I never dared tell them I'd found it – in the oven! Yes, it really was in the oven. Unbelievable! Whatever is the explanation? How on earth...?

This 'camera' saga seemed to represent all my other unanswered questions. My camera in the oven? The impossibility of finding an answer seemed to be on a par with asking why there was so much suffering in the world, or why God allows all this suffering. Years later I was told that the Bible answers the question perfectly; just look at verse so-and-so, and you'll understand. But it all seemed more like solving a mathematical equation to me – QED and all that! As schoolboys, we changed 'Quod Erat Demonstrandum' into 'Quite Easily Done', and that seemed to describe the glib way my 'advisors' trotted out their answer, telling me that 'suffering is all because of Adam's sin'. Try telling those who gazed in disbelief at the devestation and loss of life after the 2004 Indian Ocean tsunami!

Puzzling mini-events continued to haunt me, such as the time, many years later, when I lost my Bible the evening before I was due to preach. I searched the house in vain, but the following morning I found it whilst having breakfast. Believe it or not, it was in the cornflakes packet – it was mind-boggling; it seemed to be totally impossible! And it was yet another example of my plethora of unanswered questions. I almost entitled this book *A Bible Among the Cornflakes*, but thought it might sound a bit irreverent!

Yes, there were many 'impossible' questions which obviously I couldn't begin to answer, but there were also some easy questions which I refused to answer, as I will explain:

To be fully fledged as a Methodist Local Preacher it was necessary to take exams, so for the time being I was 'on trial', or 'on note' as they said, but I refused to take these exams! My previous refusal to do something was seven years earlier when I'd said 'no' to a game of Monopoly, but my exam-refusal got me into the minister's black books. I'd decided that thinking things out was more important than writing things down in formal exams. But I was taken aback when the minister told me that all I had to do was SIT the exams, and that when the results were known I would be fully accredited, whether I'd passed or failed! It was an offer too good to refuse, but I did refuse!

Having admitted that I had many unanswered questions about my beliefs, I explained this to the minister, asking whether it was right to continue preaching. He gave me an unequivocal answer: 'It doesn't matter if a preacher has uncertainties - what matters is honesty.' But at least I believed the Bible to be the source of truth, even though I failed to grasp much of it, and so I continued to preach. In any case, might it be that the minister had a point?

My early sermons were written on good old-fashioned foolscap paper - with the full script in front of me in the pulpit. I didn't read the script, but would have felt unsafe without it. However, a certain event changed all that - I was preaching in a big church, and was enclosed in a tower of a pulpit, which necessitated climbing many steps to reach the dizzy heights, but when I began to preach someone unexpectedly opened a door, and what seemed like only a slight breeze attacked my sheath of papers. The whole lot floated down from my tower and spread all over the floor, with my confidence falling to the floor at the same time. I stood in shocked silence for ages, glued to the spot! Nobody came to my rescue. These days I would have said "Oops, just wait a mo!" Never again did I have such full notes. The experience turned out to be a big help, because I'd made the discovery that I wasn't dependent on notes after all. Life's mishaps can often become stepping-stones.

Despite my spiritual muddles, at least I was busy in the church - Local Preacher (on trial, with a thousand unanswered questions), Sunday School Secretary and teacher, Sunday School Pianist, and by now, Church Organist.

What a huge turn of events! After years of being frightened and alone, it was a new experience for me to do things in front of others. And then to dare to refuse to take the exams ... words fail me! Was it all a dream? It was as though I'd been lifted out of one life and dramatically placed in another!

Thinking of my experience with the number 3,333,333,333 sometime previously, and the debating events which followed, I decided that this must have been the point in my life where the past and the future met. Certainly changes began to happen then, but now the changes seemed to multiply and I did find the whole metamorphic experience rather confusing, and I suppose I felt a bit lost.

There were also lesser events in my life to punctuate the bigger events, things that were amusing and humbling - 'green bottle' experiences! There was the time when I fell down in the pulpit with my feet high in the air. I'd tried to sit down after I'd preached, but someone had removed my chair to give me more room! And another time I preached about Jonah, but when I tried to do the reading, the two-page book of Jonah seemed to have gone missing from my Bible! I fumbled for ages, not daring to look at the index - after all, that's not what preachers do!

Some of the churches where I preached used the Lord's Prayer and some didn't. Once, when I enquired about the prayer, I was given the go-ahead, and so I went ahead as instructed. "Our Father who art in heaven ..." but unfortunately, no one joined in, and after a few more words on my own, I just couldn't think what came next, and the prayer disintegrated!

I'm reminded of Dorothy, an elderly friend, who was suffering from dementia, and living in a Nursing Home. Two of the carers were giving her a bath when she began to say the Lord's Prayer - but she stopped abruptly and reprimanded the girls for not joining in. The prayer was started all over again, this time as a threesome, all amongst the soapsuds and splashes! So, perhaps I should have likewise reprimanded the congregation and told them to start all over again, and join in this time round!

Playing the organ had its embarrassing moments too, such as the time when I decided that the last verse of a hymn should be played fortissimo -

so at the appropriate moment I pulled out all the stops and filled the church with everything the organ could give. Alas, the hymn had already finished!

Another time I was given the hymn numbers, and obediently played the tunes in the order given. After all, there was no need to listen to the minister all that carefully when I had my infallible list in front of me. Unfortunately for me, he'd changed the order without telling me, and when the second hymn was announced I simply played the second number on my list. There was a valiant attempt to sing one whole verse to the wrong tune - a tune with different metre. Oh dear, what an appalling cacophony!

Well, after those bits of trivia, here's something more serious - other facets of my music were becoming useful in the church. For example, I was asked to train small choirs of children for church concerts - which was a great challenge. I also enjoyed accompanying various singers, *Annette* in particular, though it always amused me that she could only sing barefoot!

Now *Annette* was a girl in the church who broadcast as a member of the BBC Northern Singers. I accompanied her for her other engagements, which was very rewarding musically, though I was in a spot of trouble on one occasion when a piece of stray sellotape attached itself to one of my fingers during a concert. Imagine the scene as I tried to remove it whilst still playing, only to find it had stuck to my other hand, and then back again, left, right, left - a pianist's nightmare!

Unfortunately, because I saw *Annette* quite frequently, some jealousy arose - and poor old *Dennis* began to wish he'd learnt to play the piano!

Why *Annette* kept asking me questions about what appeared to be merely hypothetical moral situations, I didn't know. But one day, I'd caught the bus to Wilmslow for my piano lesson, and whilst walking through the town I saw *Annette* who, to my surprise, ignored me. I carried on walking towards Miss Dallen's house, but suddenly there was a frantic shout. "Geoffrey, stop!"

Annette was running towards me, almost screaming. Eventually we found a bench in a nearby park, where we stayed for a couple of hours, as she sobbed her way through the story of her affair with the organist of the Parish Church (her singing teacher). He'd promised her he'd leave his wife and family, and had in fact already rented a flat in Wilmslow, and on this particular day the plan was to move in together. When I saw her, she'd just left the flat, having found a note explaining that he'd changed his mind.

This was the first time I'd had the privilege of listening to someone in such trouble, and I felt it to be a very important experience, and a big responsibility. Most of the time I simply listened, but when I spoke, the words just came from my heart, and I made no reference to the Bible. To be honest, maybe my only help was to 'be there', even if nothing I said relieved the situation. Clay Harrison writes:

Often in times of trouble
We don't know what to say,
So we choose to say nothing,
And sometimes run away.

When friends are really hurting,
We don't know what to do,
So we offer weak excuses
Or say we're hurting too.

But it really doesn't matter
What kind of gift we bring;
We only need to be there
If we never bring a thing.

However, 'being there' with *Annette* didn't make things all that easy for me when I returned home, having missed my piano lesson. Dad was not at all pleased, especially when I told him what I'd been doing. "I've been talking to *Annette*, and she told me she was pregnant." You should have seen Dad's face! Perhaps I could have made my explanation a little clearer, but seeing his look of horror, I quickly added, "It wasn't me!"

The church knew nothing about *Annette* - she just vanished! And by the way, I don't think that poor old *Dennis* would have stood much of a chance!

The following week I had to face Miss Dallen, after missing my piano lesson. Dad had already phoned her, though I'd no idea what he'd said. I went to my lesson with some trepidation and was met with, "Well done, Sir Galahad, for helping a lady in distress!" Phew, I think I got away with that one! But she had more to say: "You must never let this happen again. Nothing must stand in the way of your lessons!"

Talking to *Annette* on that bench made me think hard, and led me to believe that troubles are still troubles and pain is still pain, whether you've acted with high moral principles or not. This opinion grew into a conviction. It was to me a fundamental truth, and something which became of increasing importance to me in my attitude to others.

There is a short paragraph in the book *The Problem of Pain* by C S Lewis -

just two words, 'Pain hurts'. And please, Mr Lewis, allow me to add that it hurts whatever the cause, and whoever the victim.

But back to the church - one day a young lady came to one of the services, seemingly from nowhere. She came again, and yet again, and soon she was attending regularly. But she had a pram! Eyebrows were raised, questions were asked and rumours were rife. What, an unmarried mother coming to our church? Oh dear, that's not what we want! Our young lady was several years older than I was, but we became quite friendly, and sometimes we went for a walk, plus pram. What did we talk about? Well, mainly about how her life had gone wrong in so many ways. Of course, I was teased about my new girlfriend with a ready-made family! But they were all wrong. I simply had an affinity with her, and felt at home with her in her troubles. My problems had obviously not been the same as hers, but did that matter? No, pain hurts, whatever the cause.

I felt particularly drawn to those who had problems, or who were unpopular. I felt at home with them and thought, 'I know how it feels, I've been there'. My background of illnesses, bullying and failures actually proved to be a big help to me.

I look back on pain, on troubles and such,
And count it all gain, as it's taught me so much.
They shout and they jeer, and they push me around,
They fill me with fear as I'm thrown to the ground.

But because of it all, I know how it feels
When I see those who suffer a thousand ordeals.
I feel that I know them, and try to draw near -
If my words cannot help, I'll just offer a tear.

Even to this day I don't claim to do any of this 'drawing near' very well, but at least my background has given me a good start. Perhaps I'd now gone through some sort of wicket gate in my relationship with others. It wasn't THE wicket gate, but it was certainly a gate to something or other. Maybe these experiences were indications that I needed people in my career and in my life, rather than papers. But in what way? Turning a doubt about my present career into a decision was not easy.

Soon I had my twenty-first birthday meal at Parker's Café in Gatley, and this was the first party I'd ever had. I was of course living at a time when there were just two significant dates in a boy's life - the first was when he was allowed to wear long trousers for the first time, round about the age of fifteen. And the second was his twenty-first birthday - eighteenth birthdays meant nothing. These were the days when schoolboys wore nebbed caps, which were raised when any lady approached. But by the age of twenty-one I was promoted to wearing a trilby hat, which was more difficult to raise. So I arrived at the café wearing my best suit and trilby. How different life has become!

My twenty-first was a very special occasion because I'd just discovered that the consultant had warned my parents that it would be unlikely that I'd reach the age of twenty. So my childhood conviction about the 'twenty' deadline had been almost prophetic. But here was an occasion for rejoicing, because my childhood prophecy and the medical prognosis were both wrong! I gave an after-dinner speech of thankfulness to God and to my parents - but it was difficult to express myself because of the emotion in my heart, and also, more practically, because once again I had no teeth. I was toothless and denture-less for about a year, but this time round I somehow managed to pronounce that dreaded 'th'.

So here I am at the age of twenty-one, preaching with no teeth, playing the piano with no aim in mind, meeting people with no solutions to their problems, and working as a so-called statistician, but with no enthusiasm. Perhaps I'm in a position of stalemate. Or is there by any chance another move available on life's chessboard?

Annette was a good pianist, as well as being a singer

Two girls at a Piano Party. The expert at gargling is at the piano

Chapter 7

Kicking the Chessboard

I was no longer interested in winning the game. I had no desire to get my pawn to the other side of the board in exchange for a Queen. I was confused, and seemingly on impulse, I put an end to it all by kicking the chessboard off the table, with all the pieces flying in every direction. And that was the end of the game!

I wasn't coping with my multiplicity of aims, with my uncertainties, and my seemingly pointless employment. So one day, after work, and before catching the bus home, I phoned Mam and Dad to tell them I was at the end of my tether, and that I'd just got to do something about it! I knew I could express myself much easier if there was no eye contact, and a phone call solved that problem. "Hello Dad, there's something I want to tell you!"

And having begun I just had to continue somehow! "And what do you want to tell me?" I had to force the words from my lips, explaining that I'd just handed in my letter of resignation, and intended to take up music as my career. That was met with stony silence! 'I've given a month's notice' I continued, 'so I've got a little time to plan things.' Oh dear, it was a strained phone call!

Anyway, that was the first step. The second step was to catch the bus home and talk to my parents face to face, and that was far from easy. There was now no hope of having a director in the family 'at the third attempt'. There wasn't even an attempt being made any more.

However, when Mam and Dad had recovered from their shock, they were most understanding and gave me all the encouragement I needed. Three cheers for Mam and Dad!

After all my struggles, it was dawning on me that my career should not be settled on the basis of trying to please someone. Surely any skills and desires inside me make a better basis for choice of career than looking outside at my parents, or even at my prospects. The expectations of others could easily hide my own inclinations, and send me off in the wrong direction. That's what I thought, anyway! And that's what I acted upon, with all haste.

Yes, this was another roadblock, but I had no doubt about what detour to take. I practised the piano for twelve hours a day, under the guidance of Beryl Dallen, and then applied to the Royal Manchester College of Music (now the Royal Northern). My audition with Harold Dawber was lengthy, and half way through, he called in others to 'inspect' me! I felt apprehensive about the outcome; nevertheless, I was accepted.

I began my three-year course a couple of months after leaving work, which gave me time to build up my piano technique. It turned out to be perfect timing for entering the college, as a degree course was on offer for the very first time. I was accepted for this and felt impatient to begin.

I was placed under Gordon Green for piano tuition, much to the dismay and annoyance of Beryl Dallen, who claimed that I couldn't have gone to anyone worse! He was one of the two most respected and longed-for tutors in the college, and it was a privilege to be under him. So why did our Beryl lift up her hands in holy horror? The fact is that piano teachers have different opinions on technique, and Beryl and Gordon were the perfect exponents of completely contrary viewpoints. As far as I was concerned, it was extremely helpful to see these two methods stated so vigorously, and both with a thousand success stories to back them up. What a help to me in my future teaching to have seen both sides. Beryl taught the waving-arms-about technique, whereas Gordon said one should play mainly with the fingers, though that's somewhat of a simplification!

For many weeks, pupils under Gordon played no pieces whatsoever, only finger exercises, day after day. He used Oscar Beringer's prolific supply of finger twisters in order to torment us! 'All your previous experience is discounted,' he said. Our Beryl was hopping mad!

Before the playing of pieces of music was banned, Gordon asked me to play my audition pieces, which I played from memory. This made him insist that everything else I played in future must be memorised. Although he encouraged me so much, he gave me one word of discouragement - he told me that although he was pleased with my playing, he had his doubts about my progressing much further seeing that "you began having lessons too late."

Mr Green was the only piano tutor who gave a group piano lesson each week. We all had a weekly individual lesson, but in addition, about six of his students at a time had a lesson of considerable length, so that we could watch him teach others and actually help in the teaching. Here I met Alan, and we became good friends.

Alan was a pianist with enormous talent. His playing was absolutely breath-taking - but he was a non-academic. He gained entrance to the college for a diploma course, just on the strength of his performance skills. My friendship with him lasted a year, during which time he lost weight with worry, and failed all his academic exams. He felt ashamed of his failures, and also of his poor diction and grammar. He paid to have elocution lessons, thinking that a concert pianist needed to be able to speak 'proper'. It was a close friendship, which seemed to make our different backgrounds and abilities insignificant. I recalled my friendship with Lionel, and realized that like doesn't necessarily have to go with like in true friendships.

I remembered the time, a few years earlier, when I was told that I could become a fully accredited Methodist Local Preacher merely by sitting the exams, pass or fail. The story was repeated with Alan when the Principal urged him to stay at the college: 'It doesn't matter if you fail all your exams, you'll still become a famous pianist'. Alan declined, and returned to his old job - selling ladies' underwear!

Yes, Alan and I got on very well, and I missed him very much, but I was about to gain another friend. Little did I know what awaited me concerning this new friendship. So how did it all happen?

When I returned for my second year, an encouraging surprise awaited me, as I was placed in the third-year piano class! The other third year students were not too pleased when a mere second-year chap arrived on the scene - though they soon forgave me. Perhaps Mr Green had repented about his statement a year earlier that, "you began having piano lessons too late."

In this third-year group was a girl by the name of Mary. This was not Mary the artist, but Mary the pianist, a brand new Mary from Huddersfield. And we soon discovered that we had a common interest, besides music.

So what was special about this Mary? Well, she was a Methodist for a start, and held strong evangelical beliefs. I was also a Methodist, and a Local Preacher. But I'd certainly never thought of calling myself an evangelical - it wasn't a word I was accustomed to hearing. Mary was certain, whereas I was still asking questions. So I must say that our interest in spiritual matters wasn't exactly SNAP, but it seemed to be a reasonably near-match. The only perfect snap was that we were both proud to come from Yorkshire. What more could we want? Oh, and by the way, I have to admit that she seemed very nice! And to cap it all, here was a girl who didn't collect shoes!

66

Little by little, Mary and I became quite friendly, but nothing more. So I was a bit lost for words when I was invited to her twenty-first birthday meal, after only knowing her for three months. It was a get-together of her student friends, in a restaurant in Manchester. I bought her a present - a fountain pen and propelling pencil in a case! But Dad thought I'd spent too much, and wondered if there was more to the gift than met the eye! He would!

Now Mary's birthday meal was early in December, so it was an even bigger surprise to be invited to her home in Huddersfield two weeks later, to stay for Christmas, but I accepted. Soon I was to meet her placid father and her formidable mother. However, her mum was most impressed with me (for a while). She was delighted to meet a friend of Mary's who was a musician, who had qualifications in mathematics, and was a Methodist Local Preacher to boot! As we parted company at bedtime on the first night, she said to me at the bottom of the stairs, "You know you won't be able to get married just yet, don't you?" That was a bit of a shock. After all, Mary and I were just friends.

It certainly forced us to talk about her mother's arresting comment. But we felt we were being pushed along, way ahead of our present relationship. Of course, I would have to wait another eighteen months before gaining my degree, which meant that I was not a financially viable candidate for marriage just yet. So Mum was right after all!

But despite this Mary-diversion, studying was the urgency of the moment! I enjoyed most of the lectures and passed the exams, both the diploma and the degree exams. There were however a few interesting stories to tell along the way.

Dr Williams gave lectures on Psychology in Music. He was boring times ten, and so I decided to do something about it and went to see the Principal, asking to be excused from these lectures! He said, "You've got a nerve, Smales, but I've decided to excuse you!" It was obvious that the Principal agreed with me.

I was absent from those appalling lectures, with papal dispensation, for a few months. Other students envied me, but eventually it was *Dr Williams'* turn to see the Principal, and the following week, there I was, back in my place. *Quel dommage!*

We all liked and respected Dr Andrew, and he was particularly encouraging to me. So I wonder why I did no work for him until the week before the exam – it was just another of those puzzling contradictions in my life.

His subject was Form in Music, the important subject of how music is designed. The exam was at the end of the second year, and it would be quite handy, I thought, if I could be ill on exam day, and then take the exam (as was allowed in the case of sickness) at the end of the third year. It was tempting!

Happily, on the morning of the exam I actually felt a bit groggy, and with the help of a little bit of exaggeration, I could easily declare myself to be ill, which I did! I'm not proud of this decision - far from it. The long-distance runner Paula Radcliffe also committed this sin in order to avoid a school test, but then she was only ten at the time.

Unhappily, when I went to college the next morning the Principal called all the second year students into the hall and explained that as there had been some cheating in the exam the previous day, a new paper had been set which we were to take in the afternoon! Paula's plan also failed, as she discovered to her dismay when she returned to school.

I didn't write poetry during this exam as I did during my actuarial exam, but just tried my best to keep on writing - surely I could invent something! Somehow or other I passed with distinction. Well, that saved a year's work ahead of me! But I wonder whether my paper was ever marked; might it be that a mere estimation was made on the basis of previous results? After all, the examiners might well have been tired, as they had already marked a good proportion of the previous day's papers, as a result of which the cheating was discovered.

Another surprise that came my way was being asked by Dr Andrew to give some lectures. He couldn't have known that I'd done no work for him, otherwise he would never have given me this opportunity. But why me? I never knew the answer to my question, but the fact remains, I was the only student to be given this task.

Soon other lecturers gave me openings, and I gave lectures on teaching piano, the history of scales, the history of the keyboard, the theory of discords, and a few other subjects. What a good thing that Mr Reverend had started me off a few years earlier with my talk on the virtues of gambling! Anyway it was all very enjoyable, and a plus in my experience.

On a lighter note, visiting the toilet had its problems. There was a shortage of practice rooms, and so students searched for alternatives, including the toilets. Cubicle 1: trombone, cubicle 2: violin, and so on. The total of all these sounds was a discordant and horrifying pandemonium!

Mary gained her diploma and was accepted at a secondary school in Huddersfield to teach singing throughout the school, and also general subjects to a class of D-stream leavers. Mary didn't find the latter an easy task, but she somehow endured to the end of the school year. She was more than happy to be off school for six weeks, all because of her appendicitis!

Meanwhile I was completing my diploma and degree studies, and becoming much clearer about my career. I think my personal background of illness gradually became the foreground, and gave me my increasing desire to teach disabled children. So, in my third year (in which teaching practice was organized), I asked to be placed in a Special School, and that turned out to be Henshaw's School for the Blind. How I enjoyed it all, and when I compared this work with sitting at a desk pretending to be a statistician, it seemed that this, at last, was something real and worthwhile. It confirmed my desire to teach children with problems of some sort.

At Henshaw's, I taught singing and musical appreciation, and when in my explanations, the words 'Do you see?' slipped out, I wished the earth would have opened up and swallowed me, but I soon discovered that I could speak normally without having to check my every phrase. I learnt Braille, but not surprisingly, I could only read by sight. Mary also learnt some Braille so that we could correspond using our secret code, but years later when we found these letters, we couldn't decipher them!

Teaching blind children was very interesting and challenging, especially having to restrict all my explanations to voice only. Hand gestures were only for my own benefit. But what a rewarding response from the pupils! I really admired them.

Soon it was the end of the third year and now all my exams had been taken and passed, both for the diploma and the degree courses - but I was about to have an enormous shock! Imagine my disappointment and frustration when I discovered at the very end of the degree course that the Ministry of Education had decided, at the last minute, that the college hadn't fully met all the degree requirements.

So after all the work I'd done over three years, there was no degree for me, nor for several others. Quite devastating! Those students who began the degree course the year after me were saved from this trauma, as the college managed to make the necessary adjustments the second time round. So much for my perfect timing for entering the college!

But what had been happening with Mary and myself during the last few months? Well, we became friendly enough to be mutually cheeky, and we would call each other Wazzock, a word well known 'up north', a word that has the same meaning as Wally. But bit by bit we changed Wazzock into Wazzy, and then into Wizzy, and there it stuck. Mary was Wizzy, and I was Wizzy as well, and that's how we've addressed each other ever since - the two Wizzies!

By now I was getting to know Mary's Yorkshire relations. Some of them had the ultimate Yorkshire accent, and I couldn't always understand what they were saying. Cousin Sararna had heard a rumour that a man in the village had died, but she began to think that maybe the rumour was untrue. Why was that? Simply because 'never nubdy said nowt namore' - not the sort of thing to impress Mary's mother!

Before long Mary and I had got quite a bit of history behind us, with a sequence of events which eventually led to our marriage. The story went something like this:

We met as mere students in year '54.
Someone from Yorkshire? What could I wish more.
Well, Mary seemed nice and I liked her a lot,
But would Mary like me? I thought 'Probably not!'

But I hoped that one day she might be my wife,
Though to ask was the scariest thing in my life.
But at long last I dared: 'Will you give me your hand?'
Oh dear, woe is me, it didn't go as I'd planned!

I'd hoped she'd say "Yes, come along, let's get wed!"
But she thought for a bit - and guess what she said?
'I'll consider the matter, but just make a note,
I'll only consent if you BUILD ME A BOAT!"

By now my nerves were all twisted and tense,
But I quickly said 'yes', to end the suspense.
On the strength of my promise I bought her a ring.
Well, that was OK. But the boat? Not a thing!

And it wasn't a model that Mary wanted; oh no, it was a full-sized rowing boat! Nearly sixty years later, there's still no boat, but despite my gross failure, Mary remains with me! Yes, Mary DID ask me to build her a boat if she married me, but do you think there might have been a very slight exaggeration in my description of her demand? But would I do that? Surely not!

Never mind the boat for now, the fact is that Mary said 'yes' to my proposal, but it was necessary to gain formal permission for marriage, and have an interview with my future father-in-law, who chose to take me for a ride in his car for the purpose - I think it was to avoid eye contact. However it was a silent journey as neither of us dare open up the subject, and so it all happened at the end of the journey - in the drive. What a wasted journey!

His main concern was money. Had I enough? Would I earn enough? These were really Mary's mother's questions. But to cut a long story short, I was accepted. Formalities over!

Buying our engagement ring was a difficult occasion, and far from romantic. That's because Mary's Dad came with us! He had arranged for us to see his Masonic jeweller friend in his home. But we were only given a choice of three rings, and I daren't ask if there were others. He didn't seem to be much of a jeweller to me, and I felt trapped and thought I'd better choose the most expensive of the three! But who is to say to what financial lengths I would have gone, had we been left to our own devices?

A few weeks into our engagement, I suddenly clasped my chest because of heart pains, with Mary's mum watching the entire proceedings. Whilst I was still enduring the pain she told Mary, in my hearing, that our engagement must be broken off. She was obviously concerned about her daughter's future happiness, and it was understandable that she panicked. Why couldn't my chest pains have waited until Mum wasn't around?

No, Mum didn't approve of my health - nor of my handkerchief, for that matter! Once I dropped the latter on the floor, but didn't notice. Unfortunately it was Mum who found it, and in a voice of utter horror she told Mary that she'd managed to 'kick Geoffrey's dirty handkerchief into the spare bedroom.' Ugh!

Staying with Mary's Mum and Dad was never easy. It was the middle of the night, and I was awakened by loud sobbing. I got up, went out of my bedroom, and there was Mary, already on the landing. We stood there for ages listening to Mum as she sobbed, and as she opened her heart to Mary's dad - complaining about me and my many shortcomings!

Soon Mum had another sleepless night, mulling over my various failings. Come the morning, she charged into my bedroom before she'd finished getting dressed. She was angry with me. I shouted out, "I refuse to be told off by a semi-naked woman!" The words just came out before I could stop them. I felt worried, but it was too late - 'that moving finger writes, and having writ, moves on.' The upshot was that she fled in haste. Oh dear, I wasn't doing very well.

On another occasion, when I gave Mum a kiss, she told Mary afterwards that it was a traitor's kiss! Was there nothing I could do right?

Out of the blue, Mary's dad arranged to come to Manchester by train to have a word with my dad, but the poor fellow was obviously working under orders! He came to explain how I'd failed over and over again. Dad was very cross and fully defended me. I think Mary's dad must have had a difficult life - in fact he once confided in me about his lot!

Despite all the tensions, our parents actually urged us to get married soon. I wonder why. The wedding took place at Park Road Methodist Church, Huddersfield, in August 1955, with Dudley as my Best Man. Mary and I wanted something much simpler, but Mary's mum had other ideas.

Oh yes, we wanted to get married, that wasn't in doubt. It would have happened anyway, but we would have preferred to decide on our own time, and to arrange the wedding in our own way, at least to some extent. A compromise would have been fine, but having so little say in the matter was not what we wanted. Mind you, as I've already mentioned in verse, it is possible that the only reason Mary accepted me in the first place was because of my promise to build her a rowing boat - but I think I got away with it quite well by never telling her WHEN I'd build the boat.

Years later she thumped, "And where is my boat?"
But who says my promise was not kept afloat?
Yes, I did say I'd build one, but I gave her no date,
Oh Wizzy, I'm sorry; you'll just have to wait!

But hold on, it's not 'years later' yet! As for now, not only was there a wedding to arrange, in accordance with orders from on high, but there was also employment to be found. I applied for music posts in schools for disabled children, but made no headway as 'you lack experience in this kind of work'. Actually I had more experience in this kind of teaching than any other. But I had to be patient and just be satisfied with applying for a music post in any school.

Eventually I was accepted as Head of Music at Holly Lodge Grammar School for Boys, in Smethwick, (though I'd no experience whatsoever in teaching Grammar School boys!) and Mary found herself a job in a nearby Junior School with scope to teach some music. We also found a small flat to rent.

So, having kicked the chessboard off the table three years earlier, sending the pieces flying in every direction, I have now gained a diploma in music, decided on my career, found a job, got myself a boatless wife, and found somewhere to live. So, maybe things will settle down now. Some hopes!

On our wedding day

Mam and Dad

Dudley, the Best Man, making adjustments

Mary's Mum and Dad

Chapter 8

New Horizons

Wizzy and I spent our honeymoon in Tintern. We'd booked for a whole week, leaving ample time to get ready for my new teaching post the following week. We'd assumed that Mary's school term would commence on the same date as mine, but no - her term began the week before mine, and so we had to pack our honeymoon bags and go - four days early!

We returned to our flat in Smethwick, and I took up my post as Head of Music, but as it turned out, I was the only music teacher there, and with insufficient music teaching to fill my week, I was drafted into the Maths Department for half my teaching periods. Head of Music indeed!

Holly Lodge was a non-posh school trying to look posh, and so we had to teach in academic gowns. Mine was big and flowing, and frequently got caught in the self-closing door as I walked briskly into the classroom, thus dragging me back abruptly! Why didn't I hold my gown to myself on entering the room? But at least it amused the boys, earning me the long-winded title of 'The Absent-minded Professor'! As far as nicknames go this one was not too bad, and was far better than the one I had as a boy when my surname Smales was changed into Smaley, and not surprisingly Smaley was soon transformed into Smelly, and there it stuck for years!

My first year of teaching was marred by health problems. Hence I got to know Sulky Solomon quite well - he was my GP whose actual name was Dr Sudki Salomon. Sulky used to send me on errands to buy fags for him, a task which I heartily disliked. However, during ensuing years and despite many pressures of work, my health greatly improved.

Sunday by Sunday we attended the local Methodist Church. Mary's certainties and my ongoing questionings were not exactly snap, but we had a perfect snap in our negative opinion the church, and so, for a while, we became non-churchgoers.

As a teenager, Mary had known a sudden conversion experience - one moment she wasn't a Christian, and the next moment she was. And there she was, someone who had gone through that wicket gate, the very gate where I seem to have stumbled when I'd read *Pilgrim's Progress* as a boy. Sudden conversion? That's an experience I'd never known.

One night, in bed, I decided I'd ask Mary to explain her experience to me. How can it all happen so suddenly? What does it all mean? I listened for ages to her words of certainty. This IS what happened to me. This IS what it all means. The word 'maybe' never came into her vocabulary. This is not something to doubt or debate, but to declare! Wow, quite a bedtime sermon! I must say she seemed to know all the answers, and I began to ask myself, "Who IS this woman I've married?" Mary has now no recollection of the occasion, but her words had a big impact on me. But to be frank, I found her sermon just as baffling as John Bunyan's allegory.

I already knew that I trusted in God, but I still had many unanswered questions clamouring for attention. I'd spent all those years not knowing - just searching, thinking, reading, and even failing a maths exam because of it all, seemingly to no avail.

But come to think of it, I suppose that if I can use a light switch, and suddenly there is light in the room, maybe that's all that matters - perhaps it isn't necessary to understand electric circuits and all that. Could it be that I don't need to keep on trying to understand the complexities of conversion, after all?

Where reason fails
With all her powers,
There faith prevails
And love adores.

So said Isaac Watts, and I think he was right.

I didn't feel to go through any wicket gate that night, but from that point onwards it seemed that I'd taken a step forward. It was the night when I decided that trying to sort it all out was in the same category as trying to understand electric circuits, and it just wasn't necessary. When I'd read the Bible as a boy, I think that this was the time when my faith began.

And surely that must have been the time when I really knew that God loved me, and that 'He gave His only begotten Son' not only to help me today, but to give me everlasting life 'tomorrow'.

I now knew that my many books and many lines of thought could disappear, and my answers could all be found in ONE book. Segal's Law states, 'A man with a watch knows what time it is, but a man with two watches is never sure.' Likewise a man with one book (the Bible) claims to know what he believes, but a man with many books is never sure. So it seems that my investigative thinking was now asleep. What a night for me to remember, even if Mary's mind has gone completely blank about it!

Soon we were to experience another night to remember, a night which we both remember, but this time it was of no lasting importance. It had been pouring with rain for hours, and we went to bed with the sound of heavy rain pounding on the bedroom window. Suddenly Mary sat up with a start. "Whatever's that massive bulge on the ceiling?" she asked. We stared at it for ages, and in the end we decided to investigate. I cautiously prodded this bulge with a stick - and whoosh, down it came – water everywhere! We were drenched, and so was the bed, and we weren't too pleased when the landlord showed little interest.

So we moved to another flat - a better one with a decent roof. But after only a few weeks we were told to leave, because 'you are dirty,' explained the totally blind landlady! What an expense - paying to have the grand piano moved into the flat, and then a few weeks later paying to have it moved out! Eventually we discovered that the landlady wanted us to move out so that her nephew could move in. So maybe we were not all that dirty after all.

But whatever earthly mishaps we experienced, after 'that night', it meant that we could look for a new church with one mind.

Eventually we 'tried' the local Elim Church. We were most impressed, because every time we asked folk spiritual questions, they never said 'maybe' but simply referred to the infallible Bible, giving us the 'correct' interpretation as well. I was convinced that living by the Bible was the only right way to live. Soon we became members of the local Elim Church, and the door suddenly opened to a new world of Pentecostal belief. And in our boldness we believed that we'd got it right!

We were bold enough to quote the Bible to our parents. Once, in quoting a verse to Dad, he forbade me ever to mention the Bible again. Wasn't this the Dad who had given me a Bible in the first place? Nevertheless, soon after making his new edict, he asked me to pray - but was he trying to antagonize me? There had been some tension in the home, and he shouted at me explosively, "You're supposed to be a Christian, aren't you? So pray NOW, and we'll just see what happens!" I didn't obey him. "Come on, do it!" he shouted angrily. But I still didn't. I couldn't. And not surprisingly the tension worsened!

On another occasion when we quoted a verse from the Bible to Mary's mum, she replied heatedly, "Just leave me alone with my simple faith!" That is a comment which today I consider with much sympathy.

But I'd better come down to ground level. Towards the end of my first year of teaching at Holly Lodge Grammar School for Boys, I applied for posts in Special Schools. My first application was for a post in an Open-air School. I was invited to be interviewed, and was in fact the last of the applicants to be seen. When my interview concluded and just before I left the building, the chairman came chasing after me to tell me that they were all very pleased with my application, that I'd got the job, and that there would be a letter of confirmation in the post. I was extremely happy. Sure enough, the letter arrived, but it read 'You have not been successful on this occasion.'

To be told YES one day, and NO the next day was, to put it mildly, rather confusing. So I wrote a letter to the Chairman marked 'private and confidential' to ask for some explanation. It wasn't long before an embarrassed Chairman came to visit me and gave me the reason for the contradiction. "After we had interviewed you," he explained, "we agreed amongst ourselves to accept you, but then we began to have second thoughts, and decided that maybe you were too enthusiastic." He then asked me whether I was trying to run away from something, and gave me advice on how to approach future interviews: "Just keep your enthusiasm in check!" But I've never heeded his advice. I cannot hide enthusiasm!

My second application was for a teaching post at Lingfield Epileptic Colony. What a disaster it turned out to be! I was granted an interview, and on the appointed day I arrived early at the train station ready for my journey to London. Just before the train arrived, Mary unexpectedly appeared on the platform, with a letter which had just come from Lingfield a few minutes after I'd left home, explaining that my interview time had been changed, and that it would now be two hours earlier than planned.

What panic! However I caught the train and then travelled from London to Lingfield by taxi - what else could I do? I arrived after all the other interviews had concluded and was refused an interview, and I was also refused all my expenses! My attempts to find a suitable post seemed thwarted.

You never know, I might have been accepted at Lingfield, but my time there would have been brief, as the school was closed a year later due to falling numbers. So having no interview might have been the best option - except for the expenses bit!

However, I kept on applying, and it was third time lucky! I was accepted at the Wilson Stuart School for the Disabled, in Birmingham, and we bought a semi-detached house near the school. Moving to our new house turned out to be the easy bit, but having tried to understand the Smethwick lingo for a year, we now had to undertake the task of learning the Brummie lingo, and that took time! When travelling by bus, the conductor always shouted out the name of one of the stops as 'Pork Pies', which was rather puzzling to us. It seems that we'd reached a place by the name of Pype Hayes! We thought 'Why don't they speak proper?' But we were quite pleased with our lovely new Brummie names - Mr and Mrs SMILES!

Not everything was lovely about our new venture, as my new appointment was unexpectedly delayed for a term. The school was moving into new purpose-built premises, but the contractors were behind schedule. Why I couldn't have taken up my new post in the old building, I don't know. But whatever the reason, I had no job awaiting me. However, the Education Committee was helpful and gave me a temporary post in a Junior School.

There were nearly fifty children in my class, including Margaret, who often brought an 'apple for the teacher', in the form of a box of *Lyons* Jam Tarts! I accepted the 'apples'. Was I naughty?

The school's rule regarding the use of toilet paper was rather odd, as a result of which, the following scene was enacted on a daily basis:

Pupil: Please Sir, may I leave the room?
Teacher: With or without paper?
Pupil: With paper, Sir.

I then opened the typical old-fashioned teacher's desk and dispensed a single sheet of toilet paper, all according to the rules! I thought it was bit a mingy, and if I'd been the pupil, I'd have said 'with paper' every time and done a bit of stockpiling.

One term later I took up my position at the Wilson Stuart School. It was my dream-come-true! Fortunately I had, at the time, no way of knowing that this was going to be another rise-and-fall experience. Needless to say, I took up my post with unhidden enthusiasm, and was given a class of older pupils in the A-stream. I now found myself teaching general subjects, which I really enjoyed despite my lack of general knowledge!

Having begun to teach these disabled youngsters, it soon became clear that although my teaching qualifications got me the job, they did not equip me to teach. All the notes I had taken on psychology and teaching methods seemed of little avail. Here was a new situation, with particular needs, and I had to find particular solutions. Generalities will help me no more. Come on Mr Smales, get thinking for yourself!

In my first few weeks at this school I had an unfortunate experience when I saw Barbara fooling about in the corridor. I must have spoken to her somewhat over-forcefully, so much so that I spewed out my dentures! However, with great dexterity I managed to catch them in my hand and then continue my toothless reprimand. But Barbara seemed to give me a knowing smirk every time I saw her afterwards. It wouldn't be long before the whole school would have known that the new teacher had no teeth, but fortunately, this universal knowledge never seemed to have done me any harm.

It took me a long time to know all the pupils by name. I might have had some excuse if they had worn uniforms, but they wore what they wanted, and that should have made things easier, but not for me! One of the younger girls wheeled herself up to me. She was wearing a red dress. I thought I knew her name, so out it came.

"Hello, Jill."

"No, Sir, that's another little red girl."

I was quite amused by her answer, but it was also another 'oops' experience for me! Anyway, maybe there were lots of little red girls in the school, and red girls brought back memories of green bottles.

Not long after I arrived at the school a boy in my class died. He was a lovely lad by the name of Colin. He suffered from arthritis, and although he could walk, it was half inch by half inch. He was treated with high doses of steroids, which seemed to have drastic side effects. I represented the school at his funeral. Oh dear, it was so hard. Pain hurts!

I felt at home with these young folk, though at first tears would come to my eyes when I saw them having difficulties in moving around, or in engaging in relatively simple tasks.

Despite my tears and a few mini-problems, things couldn't have gone better, because as well as teaching general subjects, I was able to develop the music at the same time. The interest in music shown by these disabled youngsters was most encouraging, and way beyond my expectation. I gave piano lessons in the dinner hour and trained two groups - the recorder band and the choir, both groups winning trophies at music competitions.

On the grounds of these successes and the huge interest shown in music, Birmingham Education Committee agreed to my request to teach music full-time, and so I became the only specialist teacher.

I sometimes organized morning assemblies. On one occasion I asked teenage *Marion* to read some poetry - but I hadn't realised that I should have reminded her to visit the toilet immediately beforehand. She read very well despite a certain problem which occurred, presumably through nervousness. But undeterred, she continued to the end! Nobody seemed to notice the puddle, and if they did, nobody looked concerned or embarrassed, not even the girl herself. However, I felt guilty, sad and tearful.

These youngsters loved their music, and they even enjoyed taking theory exams! It was difficult finding time to teach groups of pupils who were soon at different levels, but I resorted to the help of one of those very heavy reel-to-reel tape recorders, which came with me daily as I walked to school. Phew! The lessons I'd prepared on tape were given to one group, while I taught another group. And it worked well. It's amazing what can be done by speech only. Well, speech was my only tool when I taught the blind children, so I'd had some grounding.

About twenty at a time took the lower grades of the 'Rudiments of Music' exams. One such occasion was in the centre of Birmingham, when I had to get all these youngsters up two flights of stairs - and some of them had to be carried! The Examining Board had arranged for a chair to be placed on the landing, so that I could have a rest on my journey.

I must say that carrying Evelyn (who had muscular dystrophy) was a frightening experience. She was quite a lump, if I may say so, and although she put her arm round my neck, she couldn't cling on to me. I felt she was going to drip though my fingers, like water. What would today's Health and Safety legislation have to say about my carrying Evelyn up all those stairs - a teacher with a history of heart trouble? Shirley had muscular dystrophy too, and she sat in the passenger seat on the journey to the exam. Suddenly I noticed a heap on the floor - it was Shirley! I had braked slightly, and of course there were no seat belts in those days, and down she went! I still had a lot to learn.

At venues for exams or whatever, toileting emergencies sometimes arose with the children in wheelchairs - entering a cubicle was certainly not easy for them. As for the girls, I just had to forget all about embarrassment and simply be prepared for anything! Sometimes I wondered whether I dare approach some poor unsuspecting woman with a request, "Would you mind carrying Hannah into the toilet for me please?" The fact that no other member of staff came with me wouldn't be tolerated today.

Back in the school, the choir was a huge success, with impediments of speech often vanishing when the words were turned into song. We sang in two parts and there was a real sense of unity and much sensitivity in the singing. The competitions? They were a big incentive. Having Mary as the accompanist was ideal, and in arranging the music, I was confident that whatever I wrote she'd be able to play. Good old Wizzy!

I enjoyed teaching recorder. The group entered competitions and won, despite the fact that one severely handicapped girl could only play the note B! So what? She'd joined in, hadn't she?

Several pupils had individual recorder lessons, taking exams up to Grade

6. When I began preparing Evelyn for this exam, her doctor had a word with me and told me not to allow her to play a long passage in one breath. Obviously I obeyed the doctor and never taught her one of the exercises with long phrases, explaining to Evelyn that we'd just have to put up with losing a few marks. But she was having none of it, and learnt it on her own, never telling me her secret, which was only revealed when I read the examiner's report.

Teaching piano was exciting. Robert was a dwarf. I remember how he used to walk under the table as a short cut! In common with many other dwarfs, he had six fingers on each hand, and so, with tiny hands and a total of twelve fingers, the pathway to pianistic success was not along normal lines. Playing scales was good fun, using such unusual fingering. He eventually became the smallest pageboy in the world, in a hotel in New York.

Another piano pupil, Gerald, as well as having a conical head (oxcephaly), had hands which were unbelievably disfigured - his fingers merged together (syndactyly). Both his hands were worse than the one shown in the picture, in that his little fingers were also unusable. When he played, I placed a small table at his side on which were a few wooden tools which I'd made, replicating the fingers in different chord shapes. These wooden 'fingers' were covered in felt so as to make smoother impact with the keys. Gerald either used the side of his hand, or chose and clutched a tool appropriate to the needs of the music. He managed to perform quite acceptably, even though the music had to be modified to a 'hugely huge' extent. He even played hymns for assembly now and then. Of course, there was no hope of progressing far, much less of taking piano exams. But what he could do, he did well, and with much enthusiasm. I call that a success story.

Others had paralysed legs, and therefore their piano playing was hampered by being unable to use the sustaining pedal. But problems are meant to be overcome, and soon two varieties of pedal gadget were in use. One sort suited one handicap, the other suited another handicap, but both types included a girdle to be worn around the waist, and necessitated that the pianist had the physical capacity to move the back slightly. I managed to devise one of these gadgets; the other was the invention of Percy Prole from Bath, who had already produced such a contraption for Pauline Maze (a disabled pianist who broadcast at the time, from her wheelchair).

These contraptions enabled pianists to use the sustaining pedal just as successfully and as easily as anybody else. They were perfect substitutes. Percy's gadget was very expensive, whereas mine was of minimal cost, but Percy's seemed to suit a greater number of pianists. However, my version gave easier access to the keyboard (see the photographs). Incidentally, we just had to say good-bye to using the soft pedal; there was no way I could have devised a gadget for using both pedals.

To my amazement, the Examining Board which I'd planned to use refused to examine my piano pupils, because 'their gadgets give them an unfair advantage' - unbelievable! And so I wrote to the Trinity College of Music and received a wonderful reply, "We will judge by what we hear, and not by what we see." The problem was solved.

It was rewarding to find that the introduction of piano lessons was met with such huge enthusiasm and success, with at least twenty pupils taking piano exams (from grades 1 to 6) every year. During my seven years at the school, no one failed an exam. Mavis gained the minimum pass mark, but the majority managed to gain distinctions, including Yvonne who was my most advanced pupil - she was way beyond Grade 6 standard, and played Chopin Waltzes with much sensitivity. Because of her disability, Yvonne had to use her left foot to operate the sustaining pedal - not much of a problem, though.

I began having invitations to give lectures on music therapy at universities and music conferences. Sometimes I was the only lecturer, and at other times I was part of a team. We were often asked for copies of our scripts, and to my surprise, the other team speakers complied, but I had to admit that I hadn't got a script, so perhaps it served me right when I was sometimes wrongly reported. Once in the Times Educational Supplement, I was actually quoted as saying, "Poor teaching doesn't matter" - I guess the reporter enjoyed including this sentence in his article. Oh dear, what I'd said was that enthusiasm is more important than correctness of teaching technique.

At some of these lectures I demonstrated Percy's pedal gadget, and so I had to get permission to drill two holes underneath the piano keyboard, and to fasten the gadget to the piano by means of a couple of screws. Yes, I have drilled holes in several Steinway pianos!

I was never in doubt that music can play a big part in helping the disabled, but other lecturers went further, almost implying it was some sort of panacea. By comparison my words seemed weak, as I would only say that music helps.

Once I was co-lecturer with Cyril Scott, and I caused a bit of a stir by complaining about this well-known composer! He was heavily involved in the occult, and was in fact a psychic who claimed to be in contact with the Great White Brotherhood, who gave him inspiration for his compositions! There was a bookstall at the conference full of his books on the occult. I claimed that this was a MUSIC conference, and managed to get the books removed! By now I was a keen evangelical, and the thought of having such books on display was an abomination!

After a couple of years at the school, I asked the Head, *Miss Bruck*, for permission to start a Christian Fellowship in the dinner break. I approached her with some diffidence, as she was no longer happy with having me around the place, all because of an unfortunate incident with Father Christmas a little while previously! Furthermore she was Catholic, and I wondered whether that would make her hesitant about my request. However, she told me she would give the matter some thought, and would let me know later in the week.

It seems that *Miss Bruck* consulted with her priest, who told her that it was unlikely my venture would succeed, that it would soon die out, so 'let him do it', with the proviso that no Catholics were allowed to attend the meetings.

At least thirty pupils came each week, with Martin (a Catholic boy in his wheelchair) listening in on the other side of the door! We sang choruses, which I accompanied on my piano accordion, and there was a short reading, a prayer, and a talk. And that was it! These meetings continued for a few months, until *Miss Bruck* consulted her priest again, and the meetings were suddenly stopped!

Mind you, despite *Miss Bruck*'s dwindling opinion of me, I came in quite handy at nativity plays. With no prior warning, I would suddenly be awakened by the words, "Mr Smales will now lead us in prayer!"

Back to the matter of the cancelled Christian Fellowship, I was surprised to find that these youngsters had met together to discuss the situation! As an outcome they sent two representatives to see me, pleading with me to find a way to start the meetings again, "Somehow, Sir!" I was dumbfounded by their sense of urgency, and knew that I must consider their plea seriously. But it seemed that I was travelling down the cul-de-sac of impossibility.

Despite the apparent impasse, a way was actually found - but not on school premises. I guess *Miss Bruck* wasn't too pleased with my suggestion, but any displeasure on her part was hidden, at first, by her verbal acknowledgement that this move was acceptable as the meetings were no longer under her auspices. But behind her veneer, I think there was a feeling of defeat.

So the meetings resumed, and at the same time, the number of youngsters attending doubled!

But how did this happen? Well, first of all, we bought a second-hand minibus for £345. We then hired a hall which was used by a Social Club, and with the help of a few sympathetic friends with cars, we went to various parts of Birmingham on Thursday evenings, and picked up the disabled youngsters. But soon they began to bring along their non-disabled friends, and so the numbers attending doubled. We couldn't really afford to buy and run a vehicle, and would not have done so but for the demands of the new meeting.

Yes, there were times when our venture gave us financial problems, but we still believed we'd done right, especially when the unexpected began to happen. For example, one day when I was doing some shopping in *Woolworths*, a man approached me with the words 'I know I've got to give you this!' He then gave me an envelope containing £10 notes, and off he went! But who was he? I will never know. Cash was sometimes put through the letterbox, just at the time when it was needed most. Once, when we owed some money, we were puzzled as to why we were never asked to 'cough up'. I discovered that someone had already paid - but who?

Would anyone dare to say that these multiple events happened merely by chance? Personally, I believe that God came into the picture.

In contrast with my smile of thankfulness about the Lord's provision was *Miss Bruck*'s frown. Mind you, I could well understand how she felt, but having put my hand to the plough, it seemed there was no turning back - and wasn't the Lord confirming our venture, anyway?

Mary and I played our accordions at the meetings, and that was a big help to the singing. But there was also the opportunity of getting to know the parents, through fetching the youngsters from their homes. I soon became involved with several families, many of them with financial and other worries. Life's horizon had unexpectedly widened, and I felt a growing affinity with these folk, which was coupled with a sense of enjoyment. And of course, there was an important gospel message to bring to them!

Once, when we held a Christmas meeting, we invited the members of the Social Club to join us. They happily agreed and offered to provide us all with refreshments after the meeting, with homemade cakes. I brought my projector and a screen ready for my visual presentation. However, the members of the club had prepared much more than refreshments, as the hall was decorated with streamers galore and a thousand balloons. I kept having to duck my head as I walked to the front, as the decorations hung down very low. So much for my visual presentation, which was now an impossibility! I had to conjure up another idea within minutes.

Things went smoothly with our meetings, but not for long. Suddenly *Miss Bruck*'s dislike of me took a turn for the worse. She went on the attack regarding my relationship with the girl passengers on our journeys to the meetings: 'You're not to be trusted with these girls,' she shouted. What, with Mary sitting next to me? Is that likely? To say the least, this was an inconvenient allegation, as thereafter Mary and I decided that we'd better pick up a boy first and drop him off last, so as to avoid having a girl in the vehicle on her own. It meant that our journeys were rather zigzag and petrol-wasting.

The accusation was often repeated, but I ignored it, and apart from making some travelling adjustments, things just went on as normal. It was like hearing an ugly discord from time to time, a nasty buzz in my ears, and then it was quiet again. The minister of our church was incensed and pleaded with me to let him see *Miss Bruck* and tell her a thing or two! But I declined.

Despite all *Miss Bruck*'s accusing words, nothing was ever investigated and no questions were ever asked. Why not? Surely it must have been because *Miss Bruck* never doubted my behaviour in the first place, but simply decided to try to hinder me with her accusing words. And for good measure, she also thundered at me, "You've got a warped mind!" Ah well, at least I've got a mind!

I didn't teach Joan, who suffered from spina bifida, but through the meetings we came to know her quite well. And in visiting the home we soon came to know her brother Leslie. One Thursday it was planned that Leslie and Joan should come to our house for tea, before going to our meeting. Leslie was to come by bus, and I was to bring Joan back with me from school. Joan's mum sent a letter to *Miss Bruck* to explain the arrangements, and to say that Joan would therefore not be coming home by school bus.

School was now over, but where was Joan? One of the teachers told me she'd seen *Miss Bruck* taking Joan on to the school bus. I learned afterwards that despite Mum's letter, *Miss Bruck* had instructed the driver that on no account should he release Joan to me! I had to drive to the other side of Birmingham and back in order to rescue her. I was furious, and so was her mum! The following morning, I took the initiative and went to see my beloved Headmistress, who immediately detonated. She shouted and raved at me, accusing me of almost everything under the sun. I walked out during her explosions and left her shouting into thin air, but feeling at peace within myself. This encounter was never mentioned again.

But things got worse. There were three troublesome boys in the school, who despite their disabilities, could walk normally. These boys decided to attack the houses of teachers who lived near to their own homes, damaging three houses in the space of one month. Our house was the last to be attacked. Teacher George had his new garage doors ripped off their hinges and smashed, but in our case they simply threw a brick through a window and on to our dining table, scratching the table quite badly. It was decided that enough was enough, and that the time had come when these incidents should be reported to the Chief Education Officer. Soon I was summonsed into his presence, but the other two teachers were not.

It was a difficult interview, because from the start I was regarded as being to blame. The Big Cheese told me that he could look at the incident from three points of view - the parents', the boys' or the teacher's. "But I've chosen the viewpoint of the boys," he said, "boys who you have obviously antagonized." He completely ignored the fact that I'd never taught them, that I only knew them by sight, and that they were already in trouble with the Police over other matters. Not for one moment did he listen to what I had to say - it was all one-way. The three boys all got off scot-free, and I was dumbfounded.

Anyway, a month later a 'letter' arrived at the school, addressed to me - it was a report by the Chief Education Officer about me. There was no covering letter, and it remains a mystery as to why it was sent to me. Was it sent by mistake or was someone trying to be helpful by warning me? The report told of my harsh approach to the pupils, and of my doubtful relationship with the girls. So it seems that *Miss Bruck* must have reported me to the Chief Education Officer! But even now nothing was investigated. In fact all the accusations ended with a big full stop; nonetheless I wondered, how much longer I could last, and would I ever be able to find employment again?

Accuse as you will,
And lie as you please -
Your words cannot kill,
And my heart is at ease.

Yes, despite the accusations, I still felt at ease. Nonetheless I was aware of being in a rise-and-fall situation, though it was more of a slow decline than a fall, as I remained at the school for several years after this, still loving the challenging work, but knowing that I was a mixed blessing to *Miss Bruck*. She couldn't help but be pleased with the music, but what a pity that I was the one who was in charge of it!

My problems at the school began long before all these events - it was when Father Christmas visited the school on the last day of the winter term. Each pupil received a present from Santa, but this done, it was the teachers' turn to receive presents, accompanied by applause and cheering from the children. But the response was more enthusiastic for some teachers than for others, which was rather embarrassing. I did well, and that was hard for *Miss Bruck* to accept, as her applause was minimal. From the jeers at my Grammar School as a boy to the cheers at Wilson Stuart School as a teacher, was quite a step-up for me. But paradoxically it was also a step-down, because from that moment onwards, *Miss Bruck*'s attitude towards me suddenly changed for the worse. Putting it another way, Santa had led me on to a slippery downward slope.

Quite out of the blue a letter arrived from Mother Superior at St John's, asking whether I'd be interested in giving some piano lessons there in the evenings. What IS this place called St John's? I had no idea. However, as I loved teaching piano, I phoned this reverend lady and an interview was arranged. We met, and it was agreed that I would go on Tuesday evenings to teach a few interested girls. As the interview was drawing to its conclusion, Mother Superior became very serious and said, "You do know what kind of a place this is, don't you?"

By now it seemed obvious that this was a Catholic boarding school for girls, so I gave an unquestioning "Yes, of course," to her enquiry.

The following week I went to St John's, rang the doorbell, and was greeted by a nun wearing a chain round her waist from which dangled lots of keys. On our long and silent walk to the Music Room we encountered several locked doors, but key by key we progressed. Reaching our destination I entered quite a large room, and immediately my nun left me, locking the door behind her. By now I was feeling quite disorientated, but on looking around I saw a piano, and a girl of about twenty sitting at it. And there we were, the two of us locked up together! What would *Miss Bruck* have thought about that?

Half an hour later, the rattle of keys drew near, and this heralded the replacement of Girl No. 1 by Girl No. 2. And so it went on.

These girls had been sent to St John's because of some serious misdemeanors, but once they were under the care of these nuns, they were rewarded for good behaviour with packets of cigarettes! In teaching them week by week, I had a burning desire to ask, "And what have you done wrong?" but I remained in ignorance.

Although I enjoyed the work, I felt a little uncomfortable about being locked in a room with a young lady, and eventually I asked Mother Superior whether it would be more appropriate if Mary were to take over my teaching, and after some discussion, she agreed.

One incident which happened at St. John's is worth recounting. It was during a Nativity Play, when a girl dressed as an angel managed to defy all the locked doors and absconded. Our naughty angel walked down the streets of Birmingham, eventually succeeding in finding some normal garments on someone's washing line. Changing her attire there and then, she just vanished!

Back at Wilson Stuart, the success of the music was a huge motivation. But motivation and excitement were never far removed from sadness. It wasn't just my own problems which distressed me - Martin, the boy who had listened to the Christian Fellowship meetings outside the door, suddenly died. He suffered from fragilitis ossium, and one day the helpful bus driver, in lifting him from the bus to his wheelchair, tripped and dropped him! Tragedies like this are not easily forgotten. I had also recently rescued Don who I'd found unconscious with his head in a gas oven - he was a neighbour who we knew to be desperately unhappy. What did I know about such depths of misery? Suffering such as I had seen, in or out of the school, was very humbling and made me ashamed whenever I began to complain about my own lot.

As I write this story, I feel surprised every time I turn up another difficult experience. I've almost forgotten about my own setbacks. My overriding memory of this period of my life is one of happiness. It was a rewarding time, and exciting to know so many brave children. I'll mention two of them.

Jayne had been having piano lessons at school for a few months when her parents asked me to teach her privately. Jayne suffered from spina bifida, and was paralysed from the waist downwards, and so obviously she couldn't walk. She was a joy to teach, and soon became adept at using her pedal gadget. "Aren't I lucky, Sir? What if I'd been born blind? That would have been far worse!"

I got to know the family very well. One summer Mary and I took Jayne on holiday with us for a few days. We went to our caravan, and although it was a big responsibility, it worked out well, but it emphasized the vast difference between being a mere teacher on holiday for a week and a parent, caring year after year. Jayne eventually married a lad who also was paralysed, their wedding photograph with both of them in their wheelchairs, appearing in several national papers. About a year later they both died. By now Mum has also died, but we're still in touch with Dad and with Jayne's sister Trish.

Janet, my most advanced recorder pupil, lived in her wheelchair. She was adopted, but only found out by accident when she was a teenager. This discovery brought her into mental confusion, from which she never really recovered. One day her mum asked me to take *Janet* to some holiday destination, and a week later to bring her back. I was happy to accept, so Mary and I took her to London, along with her large mother - it was a very happy journey. We helped *Janet* with transport several times, but I was soon faced with a tricky dilemma 'Would you take *Janet* to the theatre to hear Tommy Steele?' But unfortunately it was on a Sunday! What, Tommy Steele of all people? And on a Sunday too? Years previously I'd refused to play Monopoly on a Sunday - but did I still place a taboo on Sunday fun? What was I to do? Rightly or wrongly, I declined.

What a pity that in today's climate, individual help with various needy families could easily get teachers into trouble with the law of the land. Nowadays we have to keep our distance!

However, there was more to life than I've already outlined. Our new experience in the Elim Church was beginning to develop. Oh dear, Mary's mother didn't like it. "Geoffrey, you have no right to take Mary out of Methodism," she thundered. "Mary was brought up in the Methodist Church, and that's where she belongs!" But Mary and I were in total agreement, and we were fully committed to the church.

As far as I was concerned, finding Elim was like finding a resting place after all my years of searching and questioning, and I readily accepted Elim beliefs - after all, they were based on the Bible, weren't they? When the Israelites journeyed through the wilderness, they found rest and peace when they came to the place called Elim, with its twelve wells and seventy palm trees, No wonder they camped in this oasis (Exodus, chapter 15). I also 'camped' in the oasis of Elim. And as far as I was concerned, the word 'Elim' meant 'truth'! By now, resting had replaced striving, accepting had replaced thinking, and 'camping' had replaced journeying. I could not go along with André Gide's advice to 'believe those who are seeking truth, and doubt those who find it.'

We soon became involved in the work at the church. Once we took a party of teenagers for a day's outing to Tenby, with our minibus full to capacity. All went well until disaster struck on our journey home: suddenly the heavens opened and we had to cope with torrential rain, but after a few minutes, the minibus lost its grip on the road and slid towards a high brick wall. One second before crashing into the wall, there was a lesser jolt, and it had the appearance that we'd been pushed away from the wall. Was it a divine hand which pushed us? If that's the case, why did the divine hand push us into a ditch at the other side of the road? At any rate, it was a less serious accident.

All the passenger seats were torn from the wooden floor, and everybody was thrown to the back of the vehicle. Janice kept screaming 'I'm dead, I'm dead!' which proved to us that at least one of them had survived. A moment later Christine stood up amidst the heap of prostrate youngsters, and she kind-of reprimanded me. "Don't you think we should be praying?"

We were pulled out of the ditch by a tractor, and amazingly our vehicle still worked, despite some external damage. But unfortunately the radiator had been pierced and after a few minutes of driving, we ran out of water, and our helpful passengers had to search for a stream and produce more water for the radiator. This replenishment was needed many times on our journey home. In any case, I had to drive extremely slowly as the seats were no longer secured to the floor.

As it happened Mary's parents were staying with us at the time, and so I phoned them and asked Dad if he could contact the parents to explain the situation and let them know that we'd be very late home. I gave Dad the names of all of them, and details of where they lived, but Dad had misheard one of the names and thought that Ronald Guck was Donald Duck - hence

Mummy Duck never got the message. We travelled through the night, and got Donald Duck back home just in time for him to do his paper round - poor lad. And the minibus? Well, all the damage was repaired with no cost to ourselves. Money just arrived, and the bills were easily paid.

The Elim denomination, in common with many others, teaches baptism by immersion. It certainly seemed clear to us that baptism was not being sprinkled from a font, but being immersed, as illustrated in the New Testament, where we read of a certain man on a journey with Philip, who said, "Look, here is water - what prevents me from being baptized?" So they both went down into the water and Philip baptized him. Within weeks, Mary and I went 'down into the water' in the church baptistry. In my case I had some fear about baptism by immersion, as I'd had a previous experience of wading through cold water, which caused me to clasp my chest in pain, with Mary's mother watching proceedings once again! But there was something I didn't know until the very moment of entering the water - it was warm!

But then, there was the question of the baptism in the spirit. Oh dear, whatever's that? We were told that we needed to receive the Holy Spirit and speak in new tongues. New tongues? What's this all about? Things were suddenly getting rather complicated, and it was all way beyond my understanding. However, we were shown various Bible verses, and they really did seem to support what we were being told about 'waiting to be endued with power from on high'. As a 'waiting meeting' had been planned after one of the evening services, and as we were personally invited to it, we went along, though with some apprehension. Maybe it would be worth it though, as we'd actually been told that we'd play the piano even better after this experience. Mind you, it did seem rather odd that there was no mention of playing the piano in the Bible verses we'd been told to read!

The waiting meeting turned out to be quite a frightening experience - several men shouted out what seemed to us to be emotionally charged mumbo jumbo. It was bedlam! Two men were shaking violently and breathing fiercely, all of which added to the confusion. These men laid hands on Mary and myself, asking God to send His Spirit upon us, but nothing happened.

There was a Mrs Chadwick with us. They laid hands on her too, and something DID happen - she suddenly fell to the floor, screaming, and then went into a trance-like state. They claimed she had received the Spirit. Why was it then that after this experience she lost all interest in spiritual matters, and stopped going to church?

We always had an uneasy feeling about that night. I then recalled that other memorable night - the night when Mary had preached her bedtime sermon, the night when it dawned on me that maybe my simple boyhood belief was enough - but much to my alarm it now seems that it isn't nearly enough. Perhaps the peace of the Elim oasis was having a few disturbances.

Our query about the 'waiting meeting' was not our only one. Why, for instance, is there usually an 'appeal' at the close of the sermon? Why does the preacher have to urge people to come to the front in order to accept Christ as Saviour? Where in the Bible is the justification for this? It all seemed rather pressurized to me, and I thought it asked for trouble.

In our church, Fred always sat on his own, in his wheelchair. He felt embarrassed for the pastor if his appeals weren't going too well, and if nobody else responded, he'd always 'help out' by wheeling himself to the front. Jean Rees, in her book *'Danger, Saints at Work'* tells the story of another helpful man: the pastor had preached an emotional sermon on the parable of the sheep and the goats, followed by the inevitable appeal. At first there was no response, but the pastor didn't give up - no, he just kept up his repeated invitations. Suddenly a fellow stood up and came to the front, shouting out, "Well, just to give the thing a start, I'll be a goat!" Oops, the wrong animal!

Church life soon involved using our music. I arranged piano duets based on hymns and choruses, and Mary and I often played them as part of the service. In fact we became quite well known, and soon we were asked to play duets for conventions at Birmingham Town Hall, the Colston Hall in Bristol, and in several other big venues. So, as you can see, if a pianist has any hopes of playing to a massive audience, the first step seems to be to join an Elim Church!

Although the Elim powers-that-be were pleased about our musical contributions, some tension arose regarding the Christian Fellowship for disabled children. It seemed that every Christian activity had to be under the discipline of the church, and I'd gone against Elim protocol by starting these meetings on my own. So what with *Miss Bruck* and Mr Elim frowning at me, who WAS I pleasing? Maybe God? But certainly it was the children themselves, and that seemed sufficient for me. Protocol? No thank you!

Time went on, and our involvement with the church grew. My preaching opportunities increased, and I sometimes took Leslie with me when I preached, plus my piano accordion. Do you remember Leslie? He was Joan's brother. They were part of a family with whom I'd become greatly involved - a household with a multitude of troubles. Soon after I met them, their electricity was cut off through non-payment, and looking after two disabled children without electricity was a disaster! Once, when visiting them, I opened the door of their sitting room, and the sudden intake of air seemed to be the cause of a gas explosion - flames everywhere! How they suffered! Joan had spina bifida, but there was also a younger sister who was much more seriously handicapped. As for Leslie, he sang beautifully and so he became the vocalist at various church services which I took, and I was his accompanist on my piano accordion. We were a good team!

One Sunday morning, after the Elim service, a Mr Hewel asked me to stand in for him by preaching at a Gospel Hall in West Bromwich, but unfortunately he didn't know the address, and all he could tell me is that it was somewhere fairly near the centre of the town. I asked Leslie to come with me, and we got there very early and started looking for the church. We asked many folk the way, including a member of an open-air Salvation Army meeting, but it seemed that no one had heard of the place.

In the end we gave up, and as the appointed time had nearly arrived, we just popped into the nearest church to sit in the congregation. We explained our problem, but once again no one could help. Nevertheless they gave us a warm welcome, so we sat at the back of the church, and waited. However, the preacher never arrived! And even though they knew nothing about me or what I believed, I was asked to preach, and Leslie to sing. In conversation afterwards, we found that the absent preacher was called Mr Hewel, the very fellow who'd asked me to preach, but who had given me the wrong denomination of church, and had also failed to tell the church he'd found a substitute.

During my seven years of teaching at Wilson Stuart, the tension between Miss Brook and myself grew, almost reaching breaking point. But in addition, it seemed that the Lord was giving me a push. Was He pushing me into being an Elim pastor? Surely not another change of course! Doesn't the Lord know that I'm uneasy about a few aspects of Elim belief? But the push seemed very strong, and after all, I was more than happy about most aspects of Elim, and I loved the enthusiasm and urgency of the folk we'd met in the church. I believed this 'push' was not something in my imagination, but a direct intervention of the Lord.

Mind you, it is so easy to say 'the Lord guided me' or 'the Lord told me' as a cover for my own persuasions, but it all seemed so real - it was something which I couldn't just dismiss.

Quite apart from that, I was beginning to think that maybe my time at this school was fast running out, due to *Miss Bruck*'s worsening attitude towards me. I knew full well that if I were to leave the school, it wouldn't be easy. Except for my brief spell of teaching blind children, and a few other isolated instances, this was my first real experience of doing something which, to me, was fulfilling. It had been a wonderful experience - challenging, rewarding, and exciting too.

However, with the full backing and support of the church, Mary and I took the plunge, and applied to be students at the Elim College in London.

I needed two references, one from my place of work and the other from the minister. *Miss Bruck* said to me, "Write your own, and I'll sign it!" It seemed a good idea, and was a way of making sure that her lying accusations weren't included in my reference; however, I declined her offer. My worst fears weren't realized after all, but I did get a rather weak reference.

The minister hadn't a clue how to write testimonials - all I got from him was, "I have known Geoffrey Smales for seven years and have found him to be hard-working and honest." Ah well, better than being described as lazy and dishonest, I suppose!

Notwithstanding these poor references I was accepted, along with Mary, as a student for the two-year diploma course. Needless to say, Mary's mother didn't like the thought of this new venture. But since the first month of our married life, after Mary's bedtime sermon, we had been at one in our spiritual aims, and the opinion of others didn't matter at all.

As for myself, my query as to whether to become an Elim minister had by now become a conviction. And Mary? She was in full agreement, and was herself eager to learn more about Bible teaching. So, all in all, the future looked good.

A new experience was about to begin, but resigning from the school where I'd been so happy, and where the work was so fulfilling was a big wrench. Neither was it easy to close the weekly meetings and not to see most of these youngsters again. However, the decision was made, and now there were many things to organize.

We sold the house quite easily, and we lent most of our furniture to a newly married couple who attended the church. But what about the grand piano and the minibus? Simple! The Dean of the college said we could put the piano in the college common room, and park the minibus on the front drive. He even hinted that the minibus might come in quite useful! So, with everything sorted out, off we went!

Our journey to the college could so easily have ended in disaster. On the motorway, an oncoming car travelling at high speed skidded across the central reservation. I screeched to a halt. The oncoming car rolled over, coming to rest just in front of us. Several lorry drivers got hold of the wrecked car, turned it the right way up, and carried it on to the hard shoulder - most impressive! The driver emerged from the wreckage with no serious injuries.

Some people told us that this accident was obviously planned by Satan, who was endeavouring to stop us from doing Christian work, but that God had miraculously intervened and saved us. But whatever the explanation, the experience was sobering.

Nearly at the college now - look, here's the entrance.

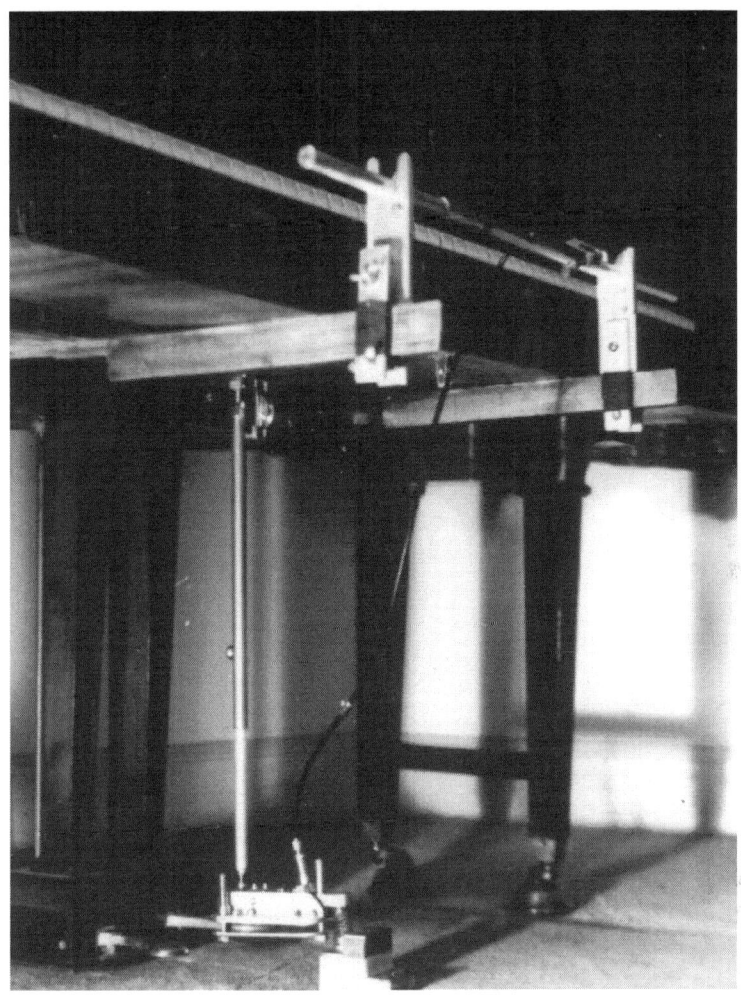

The pedal gadget invented by Percy Prole

Julie using the gadget invented by Geoffrey

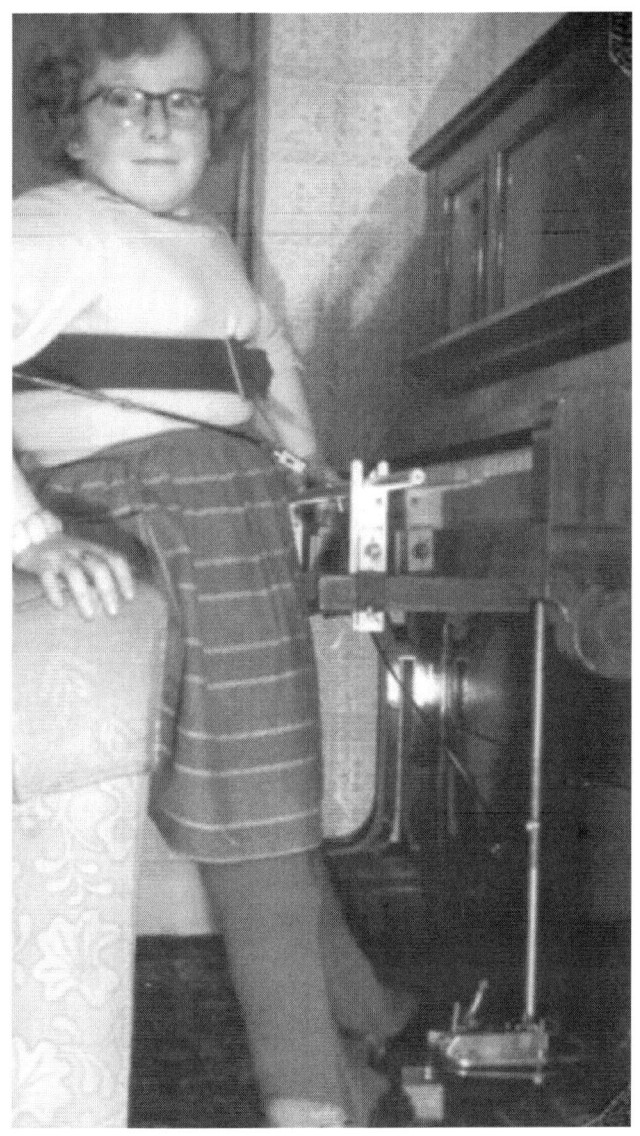

Jayne, with Percy's gadget

Yvonne, at a school concert – Photograph from the Birmingham Post

The recorder band

Evelyn and Janet, Grade 6 recorders – well ahead of the others

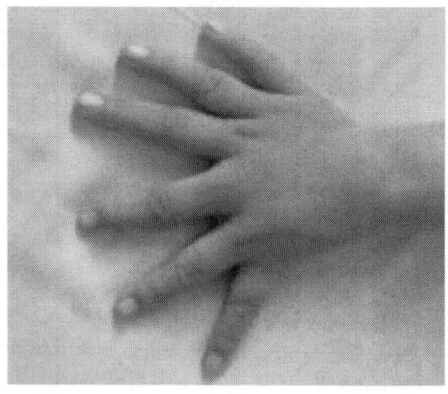

A hand similar to Robert's

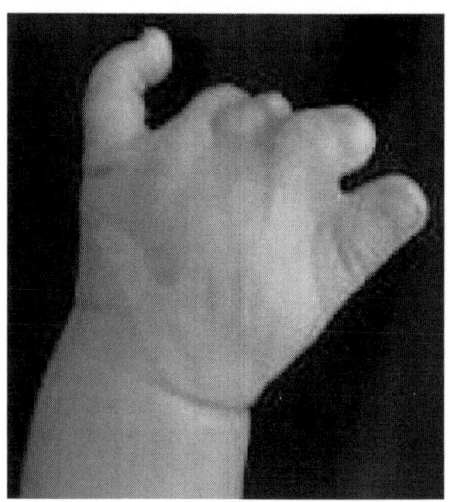

A hand similar to Gerald's

Chapter 9

The Cul-de-sac

We arrived at the Elim College, parked our minibus on the drive and then went into the front hall, not without considerable apprehension, and there we waited for the unknown to happen.

A hectic two years awaited us. Our time in the college was so full of other activities that there hardly seemed to be sufficient time to study for sixty exams in the six terms. Nonetheless Mary passed them all. My score was only fifty-nine. I tried to make my score fifty-eight by deliberately attempting to fail one of the exams - but unfortunately I failed to fail! So fifty-nine it had to be.

We were kept busy with preaching engagements, open-air meetings, plus daily prayer meetings at which the students spoke. But Monday mornings were different. This is when we used our alternative skills. Mary made curtains or whatever was needed at the time, and I made bookshelves, mainly for the girls' bedrooms. That's where I met panda after panda, the cuddles of the time. I had lovely chats with them all - that's with the pandas, not the girls. Mind you, the pandas told me lots of secrets! Sad to say, there were no Biggie Bow-wows to be seen!

However, in my second year, along came a young lady from Norway called Olaug. She was a gifted carpenter, and on her first Monday morning, the beginnings of a new pulpit appeared, and only a few weeks later there it was, complete in all its glory - a work of great craftsmanship. So much for my own woodworking skills! She had already built her own house in Norway, so what was a mere pulpit to her? She ate raw fish and uncooked onions when we were all eating chocolates and sweets, and she prayed and fasted because of what she believed was the low spiritual state of the students.

College life was certainly varied. A group of us spent Saturday nights in Soho - we travelled there by minibus and remained there until three o'clock in the morning, speaking to prostitutes. I don't think they liked our intrusions. Some students had a talent for witnessing to these girls, but I felt it wasn't quite in my line. Some of the shops had transformed themselves for the night into something quite macabre - it felt like a visit to hell. Once we got caught up in a bottle fight between rival gangs, with smashed bottles everywhere. I certainly learned a lot about life through this Soho experience.

But I was only at the very beginning. My time at the college was soon to develop into a gigantic learning experience, none of which came from books or lectures. I learnt that future ministers sometimes cheat in their exams, and that they are not immune from dubious business transactions. Even putting the mileometer back a few thousand miles to be within the warranty seemed acceptable. Perhaps it's no wonder that Olaug fasted. And then I remembered my own list of sins - but mine, of course, were excusable.

The Elim denomination possessed its very own Director of Music by the name of Douglas Gray. Part of his work was to give a weekly lecture to the students on music and hymnology, and to train the two college choirs. However, the Dean called me into his office and asked me to take on the lectures and also the choir training. What a privilege!

The choir work in particular was very challenging, as was making arrangements of various hymns and songs - just the sort of thing I enjoyed. The choirs were always in demand, especially the male voice choir. There was one other choir which Douglas Gray trained on college premises - that was the London Crusader Choir, a choir made up of members of Elim churches within a reasonable distance of the college. Douglas Gray did not give me the honour of taking this choir, which was his pride and joy!

It wasn't long before our piano playing was much in use. Hence I made more and more arrangements for piano duets, which we played far and wide, sometimes for large conventions including one at the Royal Albert Hall. No wonder the Dean allowed us to bring our piano to the college - and our minibus too, for that matter.

On one occasion Mary and I were the Guest Artistes at a concert given by the London Crusader Choir in Barking Town Hall. We had prepared several new duets and were looking forward to an enjoyable evening of music. I drove our minibus to Barking, taking ten choir members with us.

Unfortunately a big problem arose when we discovered that the piano wasn't as good as it looked - many of the keys jammed when played, and only replayed if we lifted them. So we had no option but to refuse to play. What a mess! The powers that be were very cross with us, telling us we were making too much of the problem. But we still refused to play. The Town Hall was packed. In fact every seat was taken, and as we could no longer sit on the platform, there was nothing we could do but depart, and wait a couple of hours in order to give our passengers a lift home. So instead of sitting on the stage under the spotlight, we wandered around the streets of Barking eating fish and chips from a newspaper.

Not long after this, we played duets at another meeting, where Pastor George Canty painted a picture on an easel in the pulpit, and the person who had brought most friends won the picture. We had no idea that this pulpit gimmick was going to take place, much less that our duets were to be merely background music while he painted. But worse was to come. As we sat down to play, the lights were turned off and a spotlight was directed on to the canvas. The music sheets were now in darkness! Eventually our eyes adjusted and we managed to see the music with the smallest amount of reflected light. We 'stuttered' our way through five minutes of agony. And then, to cap it all, there was the pastor's prayer - a prayer with a difference. He went through a long list of items for which to thank the Lord, including green lamp posts, red pillar-boxes, and so on. Adjectives abounded. What an evening to remember! George just loved being different.

We played piano duets in two prisons - Maidstone Prison and Wormwood Scrubs. The latter was very interesting because that's where we played on a piano which had belonged to Ivor Novello. Years earlier, during wartime petrol rationing, Novello had been arrested for forging petrol coupons for his beloved Rolls Royce. He tried to bribe the arresting officer to keep quiet, but without success - hence he was sent to prison. This attempted bribe, together with his homosexuality is believed to have cost him his chance of a knighthood.

However, Ivor Novello was allowed to bring his piano to the prison, where he continued composing. When eventually he was released, he left his piano as a 'thank you' for the VIP treatment he'd received! Yes, Mary and I had the privilege of playing duets on his lovely grand piano, and we too were given VIP treatment in the form of afternoon tea, prepared by the prisoners - with yummy cakes.

We seemed to be forever busy, and hardly knew what was going on in the outside world, but we were certainly brought up with a start when Mary's dad died suddenly at the age of sixty-three. It was a big shock for us both. Barring a car accident or something, one parent usually dies before another, but dare I confess that we thought it would have been easier for us if God had reversed the order! Soon after this, Mary's Mum made a new will, leaving everything to Mary as her only child, but only upon my death. In her nineties, however, she softened in her attitude towards me, and changed her will to include me.

Only a matter of weeks into my college course I was asked to become the assistant minister of the Elim Church in Croydon. I was taken aback to be given this privilege as a mere student. I was in fact the only student to wear two hats. As for the minister himself, he was large in stature and in personality, and was 'high up' in the denomination. He was also very demanding, and I had to mind my P's and Q's. He was the Beryl Dallen of Elim, and it was an excellent learning opportunity to be under his wings.

My P's and Q's slipped badly one cold winter morning when I was leading the service, and the VERY top man of the denomination was preaching. The services in Elim are quite free, and there is scope for popping in extras here and there spontaneously, or 'as the Spirit leads'. Sometimes the question, "At what point are we in the service?" can't easily be answered.

I thought the Big Man had preached; well, he'd certainly done a lot of talking, so after the next hymn I said the benediction, and to this day I can see folk standing up, putting on their scarves and coats. But then the Big Man whispered to me that he had NOT preached, so I had to undo the benediction and watch the scarves and coats being taken off again. It was quite a comical scene!

It was said by the other students that this one mistake would be the end of me in the denomination. They warned me that "you'll never get a decent church now!" I feared they might be right.

Among my other preaching engagements was the occasion when I was asked to take a Sunday service at the Swedish Church in London. I was surprised at the form of the service, which was a variation of the usual hymn-prayer-hymn-reading-hymn-sermon-hymn sort of thing. We sat at large tables and ate a big dinner. Every now and then there was a break for a hymn, prayer, or whatever. Was there any significance in following my sermon by the sweet course?

Somehow, somewhere amongst all these multifarious activities, I was supposed to find time to read over the notes from the day's lectures, and generally to prepare for the exams, but I have to admit that I did very little work, and I must say I felt no guilt whatsoever. In fact, I think my score of fifty-nine out of sixty was quite reasonable, under the circumstances!

I was the only student who hadn't attended Sunday School during childhood (except once with Derek), but because I had done a lot of work with children, Mary and I were asked from time to time to take children's missions. Some of my talks were entirely in verse, which I'd written during the week, something along 'Hilaire Belloc' lines. Our two piano accordions came in useful once again. It was yet another time-consuming but rewarding addition to our busy life.

This brings me to the reason for attempting to fail an exam. We had a series of lectures on Youth Work, taken by a man who required us to learn numerous charts from memory. In fact, constructing charts seemed to be much more important than thinking from first principles, and exploring new ways of approaching young people. It was my naughty plan to take the exam with total disregard for what we were supposed to learn. Then, having failed, I would complain to the Dean. Because of my experience in teaching and in taking children's meetings, I dared to think that I was possibly a suitable person to commit this crime, and could it be that through this there would be a change of lecturer? I could but hope. I was looking forward to failing, but alas, I passed - but I did receive an adverse comment about my disregarding all the lectures. Mary lost five marks merely by omitting to draw a box around one of her charts, but otherwise she was a good girl.

In my second year, although I was still a student, I was appointed as the minister of an Elim Church in Essex, and that necessitated travelling from Clapham to the church and back again several times a week. It was a hectic lorry-ridden journey via Dockland, a journey interrupted by no fewer that sixty-six sets of traffic lights!

The previous minister, Neville West, was very well known as a preacher, and was also greatly in demand as a pianist. He left the church in Essex in order to work in America as an evangelist. In addition to his work as a preacher, he was an internationally known artist, one of his paintings taking pride of place in the White House. Her Majesty Queen Elizabeth has given him her own personal commendation.

On the wall behind the church pulpit was a large mural painted by Neville, and consequently every time I preached, the congregation had a reminder of my popular and highly gifted predecessor behind me. This didn't exactly make things easy in my first few weeks there, as I had to work hard to earn every inch of respect. What a man to follow!

It can be quite difficult controlling a service where freedom is the order of the day. Sometimes a decision has to be made in an instant. One morning, when I was on the point of beginning my sermon, a man from the congregation walked up to the pulpit and said, "The Lord has told ME to preach this morning!" I replied by telling him that the Lord had NOT told him to preach. This situation had the potential to cause some trouble, but the man seemed to accept my words, and he sat down. I wonder what would have happened if he had opposed me. Mind you, if the Lord really had given him this instruction, surely it was his duty to obey God and oppose me!

The time between the conclusion of an Elim service and the moment of leaving the pulpit is the time when anything can happen. Someone might speak aloud in tongues (1 Corinthians, chapter 14), and that would often escalate into many folk speaking in tongues and interpreting, or simply raising their hands in spiritual excitement. Some might give a word of prophecy whilst others might shout out 'Praise the Lord' and other similar exclamations. The atmosphere could easily become charged with emotion, and as I felt uncertain about these outbursts, I would often say the benediction, and then with utmost speed depart from the pulpit, thus avoiding the situation.

The members of the church were very helpful towards me and most appreciative of my preaching - despite my speedy departure from the pulpit - and it was a joy to be their pastor.

One Sunday an elderly lady and her daughter invited us to their home for dinner and tea - an occasion to be remembered! They were excited that the pastor and his wife were in their home and were keen to show us round the house, which had recently been redecorated. They explained to us that the Lord had chosen which paint and wallpaper to use in each room. Oh dear, what were we to say? To ourselves, we thought that the Lord must have poor artistic taste, as the clashes were beyond belief! I wonder by what means the Lord told them? Was it in a dream? And the Lord said 'Crown wallpaper, reference number M324/5'? Was it a message in tongues with its interpretation? They were lovely ladies and we felt happy to leave them with their belief about divine guidance for their decor. Why disturb contentment?

Elim Churches are not autonomous as there is an overruling Presbytery, which sometimes makes decisions outside the powers of the local church. So the time came for the annual East London Revival Rally. This was an occasion when the church leaders had no say in the choice of preacher.

From the start, I was far from happy with the evangelist's preaching, and much disturbed by his over-persuasive invitation for folk to come forward for healing. He asked me to join him in laying hands on the sick and needy. At first no one responded until he declared that the Lord had told him that there was a woman in the midst suffering from arthritis (a safe guess!) but alas, TWO women came to the front. Perhaps the Lord can't count, as well as having poor artistic taste! The arrival of the two women seemed to relax the congregation and many others came forward. We both laid hands on Woman No.1, the preacher shouting out his emotional demands in prayer. The poor woman must have felt to be torn in two, because I was trying to hold her up, whilst he was seemingly trying to push her down, even placing his hands on her shoulders and pushing harder.

'Falling down in the Spirit' seems to happen on occasions, but being pushed down is another matter. I have often witnessed this pushing and decry it. However, after I'd caused his initial failure, our evangelist pushed no more!

I believed God had the power to heal, but I was never happy with organised healing sessions, and certainly not with excesses. Unfortunately, one man's 'excess' is another man's 'normal' and who has the authoritative answer? When I denied the man the opportunity to preach, when I walked speedily from the pulpit after a service, and when I fought against the evangelist's pushing, was I in reality opposing God's will? I think not, but again, who is the one who can adjudicate?

My attitude of caution sometimes worried me, but I found some encouragement in a book called *Concerning Spiritual Gifts*, written by Donald Gee. There I read of this man's conviction that the great majority of so-called charismatic manifestations do not originate from God. That would be a 'nothing' statement if it were not for the fact that Donald Gee was one of the leading lights of the Pentecostal Movement, who after years of holding tarrying meeting in a farmhouse, eventually founded the Assemblies of God movement (known as AOG), so maybe my caution was in order after all.

Back at the college, days of fasting were arranged from time to time. The fact that the kitchen was closed was no problem for Olaug, but Mary and I went to the nearby Majestic Restaurant for a proper meal. Little by little we were able to greet others as they joined us, giving them a cheery, "Here comes another rebel!" We all believed that fasting should not be by decree, but by desire, as was the case with Olaug. Lots of students rebelled, not merely with dinner, but also with doctrine. These rebels became known as the Calvin Club, all the members having uncertainties about some of the Elim tenets. Our year was a bad intake for Elim, as many of the students left the denomination at the end of the course. As members of the Calvin Club, we often dared to deviate from Elim expectations, but nevertheless we were a very serious-minded group of rebels, and yet...

... yes, I must mention the toilet roll saga! During one of the most boring lectures, Norman, a most artistic member of the Calvin Club, relieved the tension by drawing cartoons on toilet paper. Before long the unwinding toilet roll stretched from desk to desk, and from row to row. We tried to conceal our laughter as we looked at one cartoon after another. And the lecturer? He seemed totally oblivious of our capers! And the artist? Norman was our hero! And he's still busy painting pictures -

not cartoons any more, but steam trains, vintage cars, agricultural machinery and the like, which he exhibits widely.

Sometimes the Dean went away for the weekend, and that's when things began to happen! One evening, come bedtime, there were no beds to be found! A group of lads had removed every one of the beds and taken them into the Dean's vacant rooms. I think this terrible sin was committed while all the other students were at some meeting or other. As far as sins go, I suppose it was no worse than the carpet-moving sin which Brenda and I had committed, but on a vastly bigger scale.

As well as accommodating students, the college also served as a guesthouse, but the Dean was not too good at organising this, a fact that only revealed itself when he was away for the weekend. By now I was Head Student, in which position I had to deal with any problem that came along. The doorbell rang. It was midnight, and it was also midwinter. Donning my dressing gown I answered the door, only to find a young couple on the doorstep, having just arrived from America, looking very tired. They had pre-booked two single bedrooms for the night, but there was no mention of this in the Dean's bookings list. However, I managed to find two vacant rooms and then asked the couple whether they would like some food.

Mary and I cooked a breakfast-sort-of-meal for them, and then I took the first tray to one of the bedrooms. I knocked on the door.

"Come in!" It was a lady's voice, and so I opened the door very cautiously, but when I was told once more to come in, I entered boldly. And there was this young lady standing up in her scanty underwear! I hoped the other fellow wouldn't arrive in the middle of the scenario. Had the lady forgotten that food was on its way? Anyway, I put the tray down on her bedside table, and turned to leave, but she wouldn't let me escape from her bedroom until she'd told me the very long story about their horrendous journey. And then I left her, feeling rather bemused, and imagining her shivering in her underwear, and eating cold food.

A second occasion was also a midnight crisis, when another tired couple arrived at the door. They had booked a double room, but this time no room was available. We immediately changed our bedding, gave them our own room for the night, and after much searching we somehow managed to find the key to the Dean's caravan, and that's where we slept - without permission.

There was the occasion when a team of us took an evening service at the 'Shop Church'. This was an ordinary shop, which was transformed into a church-sort-of-thing on Sunday evenings. Twelve of us went there in our minibus, each of us taking some part in the service. I was to lead, and Woody, as we called him, was to preach. Eventually we found the 'church', and from the start we knew we were up against it! There were no hymnbooks, no hymn sheets, and no OHP - but we still had a go at singing a few choruses, with the accompaniment of the worst piano in the world.

Early on in the service the elderly secretary 'preached' the notices, during which he explained to all and sundry that if only they believed in Christ, their finances would improve miraculously.

"Just look at these students," he shouted, "they never have any money problems, and it's all because the Lord has provided for them in abundance." Our feelings of unease were growing.

Most of the folk there were elderly, and dare I say that some were rather odd-looking. One man appeared to be dressed as a Morris Dancer - apparently he was wearing his 'glory' clothes. They were hoping that many young people would come that evening in response to the distribution of hundreds of leaflets. But nobody came - well, not until Woody had just begun to preach, and the door burst open. About ten teenage boys marched in, looking quite menacing. Woody immediately abandoned his sermon, and began all over again.

"There was this 'ere chap called Frank..." Thus began a simple talk on the Prodigal Son. Unfortunately, after about five minutes the lads departed, leaving our unfortunate preacher looking rather foolish. They returned later and then left again. Poor Woody!

After the service was over, a large bundle of ten-pound notes was given to us, for the use of the college, and so off we went. But having travelled only a couple of yards someone ran after us, banged on the minibus window, and asked us to return - they'd found a man outside the shop who was drunk, dragged him into the shop and asked whether he'd like to be baptised in the Spirit. The man nodded, and so we were called in to lay hands on him, and pray. We got out of the minibus, assessed the situation, and then got back in again and drove off at speed.

Soon the two-year course would end, and I had to preach before a few learned judges. I was to preach at the Elim Church in Portsmouth, with a few bigwigs there, and what a fiasco it turned out to be! It transpired that several people were to be received into membership that morning, so in the midst of all the freedom of an Elim service came the formality of repeating various promises. The occasion required the pastor of the church to preach a special sermon on the responsibilities of membership.

Time was passing, and I was getting rather concerned. I wondered, 'When will it be my turn?' Perhaps I wasn't going to have a turn after all.

Eventually the 'Master of Ceremonies' said, "Oh, I'd almost forgotten, we haven't heard Geoffrey preach yet!" He then explained to the congregation that as it was by now rather late, there would be a vote. "Hands up," he said, "all who would like Geoffrey to preach!"

Whether or not they really wanted me to preach, I can only guess, but hands shot up everywhere, and so I preached. I decided that my sermon would have to be greatly abridged. Now Methodist sermons take twenty minutes, Elim sermons take thirty to forty minutes, or maybe more, but mine was well under ten minutes. What did my adjudicators think? Were they at all sympathetic with me in what had become a difficult situation? Certainly not! They just reprimanded me for omitting many important points, and not covering the topic adequately. As for my lack of emphasis on believing in Christ NOW, they certainly didn't like that at all.

Unfortunately, this event was soon followed by my end-of-course interview with the powers that be, concerning my future, and my suitability as an Elim pastor. It was not an easy interview, especially with Portsmouth in mind. Soon I was faced with a big question.

"As you find it difficult to preach the Gospel, are you be prepared to use your music to aid your ministry?"

I answered in the negative, and thought they were all potty!

Despite my answer, a few days later the governing body asked me to remain at the church in Essex, but now as the permanent minister. That was exciting news! If using the words 'good' and 'desired' are allowed, I have to say that the church was a very good one, and it was a church much to be desired by any pastor! However, just around the corner, a few problems were about to arise. Are you surprised?

The first problem concerned accommodation. My pay was to have been £4 per week, which even by 1964 standards was rather low. No house was provided, and no expenses. We thought of buying a second-hand caravan, but despite visiting several caravan parks in the area there was no possibility of being accepted unless we bought a brand new caravan. We appeared to be facing a big obstacle, but we believed that God would find a way, if it were His will. But it seemed strange to receive so little remuneration for such responsible work, especially when I had just been the organist for a three-week Elim campaign in Birmingham Town Hall, and received a cheque for quite a large amount. Better to be an organist than a pastor! I wonder what the evangelist himself received.

Meanwhile I discovered that my paid ministry had to begin by my signing a statement of faith. I had no idea I had to make such detailed promises, and that my preaching was restricted to specified and narrow viewpoints.

Evangelicals believe in a literal Second Coming of Christ, but there are several different interpretations of this teaching, and I was expected to give my signature to a view contrary to my belief. That was a massive blow for me. The Elim set-up allowed many 'freedoms': for example, I was free to leave the pulpit in haste, or never to have an 'appeal'; I was free to preach

112

on any Bible text I chose, as long as I preached on that text in accordance with the Elim pattern - I must only preach what is called the premillennial view on Christ's return. My conscience just wouldn't let me accept this restriction. All at once the accommodation problem seemed trivial.

One further complication arose. A week's visit of a certain evangelist had been planned by the Church, long before I arrived on the scene, and the date was now almost upon us. One of the high-ups at Elim Headquarters had warned me that the man in question was totally unsuitable, as he was known to visit vulnerable older women in the Churches where he conducted rallies and persuade them into parting with large sums of money for his own benefit. Having given me this alarming news, he pleaded with me to intervene and to ask the church leaders to consider cancelling the rally. If necessary he would help me in this difficult matter with a supporting letter.

Quite apart from financial and doctrinal matters, I was little by little building up a picture of a muddled situation, with far too many disappointments and contradictions. Moreover, I was still hesitant about present-day speaking in tongues and prophecy. Was it right to be the minister of an Elim church when I was cautious about these things? My various lines of thought seemed to be converging once again, but this time to some unknown point on the horizon, and certainly away from Elim. It was a confusing situation, to put it mildly.

I looked back to my days of teaching the disabled children in Birmingham - and apart from the accusations which came my way, it was a perfect situation, and I felt to belong to those children. But now? As Ritu Ghatourey once said, "Life is like a grammar lesson - you find the past perfect, and the present tense!"

Yes, tense and bewildering! Despite all my 'studying', and despite believing that the Lord had led me into Elim in the first place, I had more or less decided that I should leave the Elim movement. So had I come to the end of the road? I asked for an interview with the much-respected Dr Lloyd-Jones, the minister of Westminster Chapel, to seek his advice. He saw me very briefly, and after I had pointed out my problems and told him that I was thinking of leaving Elim, he simply said, "Don't do that!" and no reasons were given. I suppose I was hoping he'd give me some encouragement to leave, but I just had to learn to make my own decisions, and to blame myself if they turned out to be the wrong ones.

I arranged to have a meeting with the church leaders, or elders as they are called, and brought two matters to their attention. Firstly I mentioned the unsuitability of the evangelist, but unfortunately he turned out to be a close friend of one of the elders. That was a bit of a setback for me, and my request to cancel the rally did not go down well. Maybe they wouldn't want me to be their pastor after all. When the meeting had concluded, I phoned Mr High-Up, who was now unwilling to support me with his promised letter.

But I'm jumping the gun. I brought my second matter to the elders, telling them with much sadness in my heart that I could not accept the permanent position as their pastor, and that I would be leaving the Elim movement. There was stony silence for a while. Things had gone so well while I'd been the temporary pastor, and a good relationship had developed. So I was not the only one who felt sad that night.

I was asked to leave the meeting while they discussed the matter among themselves. Whilst I was on my own the words of Dr Lloyd-Jones kept ringing in my ears. "Don't, don't, don't!" Had I done the right thing? But when I eventually returned, the mood of the meeting had greatly changed, and despite having blotted my copybook twenty minutes earlier, I was now told that maybe there was no need for me to sign any declaration of faith, as the elders were willing to consider the possibility that the Church itself would leave the denomination and become independent, and therefore I could remain as pastor.

If the whole church had agreed to the elders' proposal, then it would have been an offer almost too good to refuse, but I asked the elders to take the matter no further, because I thought it was asking too much of the church; after all, the church had been flying the Elim flag for years. And so I left the meeting, tearful - all because of a piece of paper! But for that piece of paper I might well have remained as their minister and somehow or other solved the accommodation problem.

Here is a denomination which exhibits such freedom in one sense, and yet bound me tightly with dogmatic promises. Unfortunately, dogma never listens, and however hard you try, 'you can't teach an old dogma new tricks' (Dorothy Parker). So I left Elim, feeling lonely, sad and bewildered. It seemed that the Lord had pushed me into Elim in the first place. So why has He now pushing me out? There seemed to be no answer. Was this perhaps the biggest muddle I'd ever experienced?

Quite recently I explained to a friend how my life had been one of going down cul-de-sacs and coming back again, and that the Elim cul-de-sac had utterly confused me, and almost thrown me into despair. He told me to forget all about cul-de-sacs, and view my life as a journey across stepping-stones. His comment was a great comfort to me. After all, I believe he is right, because nothing has been wasted, and much has been learned.

Someone called 'The Silent Owl' once wrote, 'The difference between a stumbling block and a stepping stone is whether you are cursing your bruised knee or admiring the view.' Well, I certainly wasn't cursing, but where was the view? There seemed to be nothing in sight.

"So whatever am I going to do now?" I asked myself, with tears in my eyes. I certainly understood what the poet Wendy Cope meant:

You don't know what to do. You cry.
You're running out of things to try.

Chapter 10

No Man's Land

Having made a sudden and agonised departure from the Elim Church, I just had to try something. For a start, an income had to be found, and so I tried to find a teaching job - what else could I do? I applied for several teaching posts around the country, almost at random; but finding a post during school holidays was hardly the ideal time as there was nothing much left. However, I was accepted at a secondary school in Cheltenham, teaching religious studies. Soon I was also teaching music at a girls' school in Cirencester, and general subjects at a Junior School in Gloucester. What a mixture - I felt I was merely an educational bran tub, with children dipping in at random, and taking out anything they could find!

At the time of leaving Elim we possessed very little money, but to our relief we had just enough for the deposit on a new bungalow in Winchcombe, a few miles from Cheltenham. That's where we lived for the next fifteen months, but career-wise and spiritually these months were spent in No Man's Land. I hoped that this period in my life would merely be a parenthesis, but at any rate the uncertainties and bewilderments of the previous two years were behind me, and to some extent the air seemed to be cleared. Friedrich von Schiller once said, "Disappointments are to the soul what the thunderstorm is to the air." This was a truth confirmed by my own experience.

I had a shock on our first day at our new abode, when a policeman arrived at the door in order to arrest me. It seems that our car had been involved in a serious accident in Clapham, and I had not stopped! Yes, it is true, we'd just left Clapham (where the Elim College was situated), and admittedly the registration matched ours, but our vehicle had no damage - that's because I hadn't been involved in any accident. Nonetheless I had to produce documents there and then, but where were they? Eventually my innocence was accepted, and that was the end of the saga, though it was rather frightening while it lasted.

We found the local evangelical church, with its adjoining manse. What would the minister be like? We decided to find out, so we rang the doorbell and waited in some suspense. Within seconds we were in the minister's sitting room, and within days I was 'in use'. That's all because of Val, a young lady who happened to be visiting the minister at the time. She'd pointed to me and said, "You've got piano fingers - we could do with you!" I think she must have meant 'organ fingers', because very soon I was playing the organ on Sundays. Mrs Walton (otherwise known as Tubby Walton) had been the organist for years, but she was pleased I'd come. Well, I think she was.

The organ had only one keyboard, or manual; however, it was a most unusual instrument, to say the least. The whole keyboard could be lifted and moved to the left or the right, making transposition a doddle! Some hymns seem to be written in unsuitable keys, making them hard for a congregation to sing, and here at Winchcombe was a quick solution - at the flick of a finger I could change the key.

We became members of the church and before I had time to catch my breath I was asked to start a weekly children's meeting. Mary joined me in this venture, and soon the numbers attending had become large enough to divide the meeting into Juniors and Seniors. It was a wonderful experience.

One of the teenage girls visited us quite frequently. *Amy* was a girl who lived across the road from us, the eldest of many children in the family. She was lovely, but she was also lonely. She was also fearful of others, as I was in my younger days; because of this I would never have dreamt of asking her to do anything in public, but one day I heard myself doing just that. Yes, I heard myself asking her to close one of the meetings in prayer. Immediately I felt devastated at what I'd done, but she prayed without a hint of hesitation - I was gob-smacked, and then I recalled the occasion when I was made to speak about gambling, and all the time it was the Lord who was prompting Revvy, and enabling me. Was the Lord now prompting me, and enabling *Amy*? I don't know, but that's how it seemed.

Soon after starting the children's meetings, I was taken aback to be asked to take a week-long Children's Crusade at the Anglican Church in nearby Cheltenham. I was also asked to take services at other Anglican Churches, where I was given the option of wearing robes or NOT wearing them - and guess what? I chose the latter. Robes and clerical collars were not in my line! And before long I was asked to preach at the church where we were members, and also at other churches in the area.

As you can see, life became as busy as the life we'd left behind us. But although busy, the countryside was peaceful and beautiful, and it seemed to be a symbol of the calm which we felt after the storm of Elim. We enjoyed the peace, in ignorance of the fact that we wouldn't have to wait long for the storm clouds to gather.

Val became a good friend. We admired her greatly, and stood back in astonishment at her hunger for Christian books, many of which seemed heavy-going to me - but our Val would just plough through them all with seeming ease. She was a nurse who lived with her parents in a small terraced cottage. But she had a hard time at home, mainly because her mother liked her booze too much. Val would pop round to see us from time to time with an unusual request:

"Do you think I could borrow your floor?" At first we didn't know that this translated into, "I'm utterly exhausted, I'm at the end of my tether, so do you think I could have a little sleep?" Oh dear, instead of offering her the floor, or a bed, we offered her tea and biscuits, plus conversation. But eventually the penny dropped and we became more helpful.

Mr and Mrs Weller attended the church and we came to know them well. What a godly old couple they were! Mr Weller was a retired missionary with the China Inland Mission. Unfortunately, Mrs Weller was suffering from the beginnings of dementia. One day we were invited for tea, which we felt to be quite an honour. When we arrived, the table was already set, so we were able to sit and chat before teatime. Eventually Mrs W went into the kitchen to boil the kettle. She then returned and announced that tea was ready and invited us to the table. We sat down as requested. She then asked her husband to say grace.

"But where is the food?" he enquired. It seemed there wasn't any. So Mary and I went to the local shops, and returned with food for tea. It was all rather embarrassing for them, but we still thought very highly of them.

Soon we met Peter at the midweek church meeting. He was a single man whose home was in Wales, where he lived with his mother. He worked in Winchcombe, going home at weekends to see his mum and to attend his own church. He became a good friend, and so when his accommodation failed, he lived with us during the week. A friend indeed, but also an inveterate talker, which meant lots of late nights!

During our time in Winchcombe, and just in case life there was not going to be a mere parenthesis after all, I applied for the headship of the New Barns School which was soon to open in nearby Toddington, under the auspices of the Quakers. It was a school for severely disturbed children.

An entire staff had to be recruited, from headmaster to cleaners and gardeners.

Val applied to be the nurse at the school. She would have done her work with skill, and always gone 'the second mile'. But no wonder she wasn't granted an interview, considering the CV she'd submitted. Val wouldn't dream of exaggerating her skills in any CV, but I don't think that, in her utter honesty, there was any need for her to run herself down, and also to explain that she was 'partially sighted', simply because she wore glasses!

My own interview seemed interminable. It was explained to me that this was a school where lawless boys and girls made their own rules, and where the principal instrument in their reformation was not punishment, but affection. I was offered the post of Headmaster there and then, and was also given a book called *The Barns Experiment* which described a similar school in Scotland, which had by now been closed down. Before formally accepting the headship, I read this alarming book, as though with a microscope, and then declined their kind offer!

This new school was soon to experience a quick turnover of staff, so maybe Val and I wouldn't have lasted long anyway. Staff cars were damaged, local residents complained about vandalism in their gardens - so things didn't bode well. But having read the book, none of this surprised me.

Sometime later, eight members of staff fell foul of the law by shutting children in a windowless room known as the 'snug' as a form of punishment. Several teachers were convicted of sexual abuse, and one of them was imprisoned. The Chairman of the Governors had a history of importing child pornography from Holland, and was a founder member of the notorious Paedophile Information Exchange, which campaigned for the age of consent to be reduced to four! These revelations led to the abrupt closure of the school. So much for the theory of reformation by affection! Thankfully I was spared from falling into this pit.

Despite my application for the Headship, I wasn't enjoying teaching as much as previously, and felt somewhat unsettled. Time went by and eventually I spotted an advertisement for a post in Scotland. It was with an evangelical organisation called The Caravan Mission to Village Children. This made me sit up and take a bit of notice. They were seeking someone with experience in children's work to live in a touring caravan and travel throughout Scotland, visiting outlying areas to 'bring the Gospel' to groups of children. I applied for the post, and was granted an interview on a date several weeks ahead.

However, during those intervening weeks everything that could happen seemed to happen! One of these things was my dramatic excommunication from the church in Winchcombe. This is when storm clouds gathered and lightning struck. Was it another roadblock, caused this time by an avalanche?

I had already preached in the church many times and led an expanding children's work, but the time came when I preached my notorious sermon. During the service I had no idea that there was any problem, but it appears that the minister had taken notes during my preaching, and had found no fewer than twenty divisive points. Unknown to me, he had asked members of the congregation for their opinion of my sermon, but unfortunately for the minister, they claimed to have been helped. Nonetheless the minister excommunicated me unilaterally. I was forbidden to enter the church or the manse, the children's meeting was closed down immediately, and of course the organ was now out of bounds. Needless to say, I was completely taken aback and at a total loss to know what was going on.

A few days later, the elders came to our home, without the minister, to discuss the situation. Mr Weller (the husband of the no-food-for-tea lady) was one of these elders, and one who we regarded as very wise. He arrived at the house last, and tears came to our eyes as he entered the room. The tears were because, despite our feelings of helplessness, we all felt to be in the presence of someone who was in touch with God and would know what to do. The outcome of the meeting was a decision by the elders that I should stay, come what may. Mary and I just wanted to leave, to run away or something, but the elders were firm in their resolve that I should stay.

The minister was told the decision of the elders, to which he responded, "Either Geoffrey goes, or I go!"

The elders told him, "Geoffrey will stay!" The outcome was that the minister resigned, though he didn't depart immediately, and so I still had to keep away.

My sudden excommunication together with the dramatic consequences consumed our thoughts and emotions for months. It seemed to tear our souls apart. Words can't describe how we felt. I wish this paragraph could be much longer - pages longer. How can a brief description like this indicate our anguish? Sleep eluded us, and we could think of nothing else. What a good thing that Mary stuck by me throughout this difficult period. Yes, it was another of those dreaded rise-and-fall experiences!

But look, do I see a new pathway ahead? Is the Lord showing me a new opening? Maybe He is: I'd been asked to preach at a Baptist church near Presteigne in Radnorshire, where there was no minister. There were, in fact, two churches - the main church at Ackhill and a smaller church at Bleddfa. Peter was a member at Ackhill and had suggested to the elders that they invite me to preach. In the next few weeks I went there three times and preached a total of eight sermons. I also gave a talk to all the folk in the Sunday School, and used my piano accordion as an aid to the singing. It was becoming clear that the elders were interested in my becoming the pastor. However, on my way back from the third visit I had a car accident, the car rolling over a few times, and coming to rest upside-down, with my piano accordion thrown across the road. The car was a write-off, and I found myself in hospital with a head injury. The following morning I had my first visitor - a policeman! It seems that I had driven without due care and attention, and my sin was duly punished.

This accident was at a critical time, because the following week I was supposed to be flying to Scotland for my interview, so of course I had to cancel the interview and the door was closed to my possible caravan work.

Also, on the following Sunday I was booked to preach at a church in Sheffield, and so that engagement was also cancelled, and what a good thing too! It seems that there were posters all over Sheffield which read 'Come and hear Geoff Smales, the Talking Piano!' What an escape! I had not been asked to bring my duettist wife with me, and I'd never been asked to play, only to preach, so what a disaster the whole event would have been!

As a result of my discovery about this 'Talking Piano' poster, I bundled together all the duets which I'd written, and simply threw into the bin. This was not done in anger, but simply because I didn't want to play them any more - after all, my mission in life wasn't musical, but spiritual, and evangelical.

Years later my hundreds of sermon notes suffered the same fate - into the bin they went, much to the disbelief of fellow ministers. Speaking only for myself, I preferred to think out every sermon afresh, and not to rely on previous thought. Hence destroying my notes was a big help to me. Maybe I regretted the destruction of my music, but I've never had a moment's regret about the loss of my sermon notes.

Things continued to develop regarding the two churches in Wales, and within weeks of my excommunication, I was invited to become the pastor of the two Welsh churches. The vote of the members was unanimous, which seemed to be a confirmation that I should accept the offer. What irony. If only my own minister had waited a while, his resignation could have been avoided. Some of the members wondered why I couldn't have remained at the church, not as a member only, but now as their own minister. But under the dramatic circumstances of the previous few weeks, it is a position I could never have accepted.

No Man's Land would soon become a memory, and I was about to begin what I believed to be the most important job in the world.

But hold on, it was not going to happen all at once. Firstly, I had to resign from my teaching work, giving a term's notice, and then there was a bungalow to sell. But the sale was simplicity itself - no estate agent was needed, as Val's sister offered us a reasonable price, which we accepted.

Eventually the day came. It was snowing, and I can visualise the removal men taking the grand piano out through the front door and facing a blizzard. But who cares about a blizzard? In our hearts the sun was shining and I was eager to begin. I was unaware that the unanimous vote to call me as Pastor was not as straightforward as I'd hoped, and that a silver lining might be shining so brightly that the dark cloud it encircles isn't even noticed; but so far all was well.

So off I went into the future - in fact, off we BOTH went, feeling excited, but also somewhat apprehensive. Looking over our shoulders as we left, we could see the past disappearing into the distance. No Man's Land was now well and truly behind us.

The past has gone,
It's far away,
We must move on
To another day.

Forget the falls,
And all the pain;
The future calls -
To new terrain.

Let's rise and go,
There's hope ahead,
If gales should blow,
There's naught to dread.

Begone to fear!
Begone to doubt!
Our God is near -
He'll hear our shout.

There is no promise that the road ahead will be easy - gales might blow, the unexpected might happen, but I have a God who will care for me.

'Be strong and courageous. Do not fear or be in dread... the Lord your God goes with you. He will not leave you or forsake you.' (Deuteronomy, chapter 31)

Chapter 11

The Most Important Job?

Making a start

It was still snowing as the grand piano was taken into the manse at Ackhill. The floors of the house were quite wet when the removal men left, but none of this mattered, as the prospect of serving the Lord in this new area was exciting. Living amidst such idyllic surroundings was a bonus. The Council's leaflets advertising the area claimed that 'if you have any hope of getting to heaven, then come to Radnorshire to get acclimatised!'

It's 1966, and by now I'm thirty-six and on an income of £12 per week, with no expenses paid. There was no telephone in the manse, but we paid for Post Office Telephones (the BT of the time) to come to our rescue, and then we felt complete. We had no complaints about the financial situation. After all, it was far better than the situation in the church in Essex, with an income of £4 per week, with no accommodation. What more could we want?

Ackhill Chapel was in a highly rural area, and in order for us to be on the phone, we needed several new telegraph poles. And when one of the members of the church moved to a new cottage, twenty-two extra telegraph poles were erected, just for her - and at no extra cost! But despite the very low population, the church was well known and well attended.

The church was packed for the Induction and Ordination Service, with Eric Hayden and Courtenay Harris delivering two good addresses about the responsibilities of the members of the church, and of the minister. These talks had posh titles - The Charge to the Church, and The Charge to the Minister. So now I'm installed, with all due formality and dignity!

During my first week in this new and exciting situation, we invited the elders of both churches to come to a buffet, along with their wives. The appointed hour arrived and we waited for the doorbell to ring. One by one the folk from the Ackhill church arrived, but it soon became clear that no one was intending to come from the Bleddfa church. They hadn't let us know - they simply didn't turn up. I must say that this snub put a damper on the evening and gave me cause for concern. Many questions arose in my mind.

I hadn't long to wait for some answers. On the next Sunday afternoon, when I took my first service at Bleddfa as their ordained minister, the secretary greeted me at the door, not with "Welcome to Bleddfa!" but with "We dunna want you here, y'know!" Not a very encouraging start to my ministry, to say the least.

Eventually I found out that it was indeed true that I'd had a unanimous call, but it applied only to the Ackhill church. The members at Bleddfa, with the exception of one elderly man and his wife, had all voted against me. It seemed that the two churches were not quite on the same lines. So the negative vote wasn't against me as such, but against the Ackhill church. That accounted for the buffet fiasco. No way were the elders at Bleddfa going to socialise with the elders at Ackhill! Oh dear, what a mess. Had I been given the full picture months earlier, I would not have accepted the call. But here I am, so come along Mr Smales, just get on with it!

The Ackhill church wasn't without problems, but they were relatively insignificant, and only related to the notice board and the clock.

The notice board had to be amended to include the name of the new minister, but I didn't want the title 'reverend' to be included, and that caused a bit of a stir! I had no problem whatsoever with other ministers using the appellation, but as the literal meaning is 'worthy of reverence' I didn't want the title for myself. On the other hand I admit that the title has little significance these days, and its use is nothing more than a custom.

"But you ARE reverend," exclaimed Peter's mother. All I wanted was a plain 'Mr' on the notice board, but had to settle for the compromise 'Pastor'. Oh dear, 'Rev', clerical collars and the like are not in my line.

Titles and stuff
Are nothing but fluff.
Just let me retain
The label of 'plain'.

A few days later a letter arrived from one of the members, and to my surprise it was addressed to 'Plain Mr Smales' - so someone had a sense of humour!

But the church also had to do without my maths and music qualifications on the notice board. Maybe they wanted to show me off, but I saw no relevance in my academic qualifications to preaching the gospel. What a nuisance this new pastor was!

Oh yes, there was the 'clock' problem. Almost all the members were farmers, and someone explained to me at the outset that as farmers have an unpredictable life, they couldn't be expected always to come to church on time. I was told I might have to delay the start of the services by up to ten minutes. Did I comply? No, it all seemed so unfair to those who had arrived on time. Unfortunately, I was accused of starting early, so I made a decision there and then to start the services late on purpose. I used to check with my watch before every service, and I began exactly one minute late. Eventually the farmers began coming on time - well, more or less. But I continued with my 'starting late' system.

I've had severe problems with my narrow throat all my life, and experienced many embarrassing choking attacks in public places. Unfortunately I had a choking attack just a few weeks after arriving at Ackhill, and whilst taking the communion service of all things. This was certainly not the best way to impress the congregation. I tried to ask Jack to take over, whilst I was still making frightening noises, fighting to breathe - but all I got was a repeated, "What y'say?" It was chaos!

After the teething problems with the notice board, the clock, and my badly timed choking attack, all went well at Ackhill. The church was in the Baptist Union, known as the BU, but I was not a personal member of the Union, and therefore I had no pension rights or guaranteed stipend, but that didn't matter at all. What was important to me was having the freedom to preach without Big Brother Mr Elim looking over my shoulder and insisting that my preaching was according to some set doctrinal pattern, and there were no rules about the Second Coming.

Mercifully, after my initial shock, peace reigned at Bleddfa for many years, though the business organisation was somewhat ragged: no fewer than three men claimed to be the secretary, and so I decided to solve this riddle by asking to have a look at the minutes of the church meetings. However, they were unable to produce the minutes - maybe there weren't any. Eventually the problem was solved by the death of two of the contenders, leaving me with the 'dunna want you here' fellow.

Incidentally, the name Bleddfa is thought to be derived from the word *Bleddfaich*, which is Welsh for 'wolf's lair'. In due course I was to discover that the name was prophetic, as far as I was concerned.

Despite my wandering spiritual journey over many years, I was now convinced that I was called to preach, and to declare that Christ is the only way to salvation. No wonder there was an urgency in my task, and no wonder I believed I had the most important job in the world. Was this arrogance?

Preaching was paramount: 'How then shall they call on him in whom they have not believed? And how shall they believe in Him of whom they have not heard? And how shall they hear without a preacher?' (Romans 10).

In my preaching I didn't take random helicopter landings on isolated verses of the Bible, but often took series of sermons, taking several weeks, say, on the Sermon on the Mount, or even longer on the book of Revelation or Ezekiel. Yes, it all required much study, but the continuity of the preaching was much appreciated by the members of Ackhill Church. However, I took a very different approach in my preaching at Bleddfa, where I thought that random helicopter landings were more suitable.

But one hot summer's morning in July, I took a helicopter landing when preaching at Ackhill - I had a break from my series and preached a one-off sermon on the life of Christ, from His birth to His resurrection. And so on this one-off occasion, why not begin the service with a Christmas carol? I did of course explain my plan to the congregation, and we began with 'Hark, the herald-angels sing'. But alas, there were some latecomers! They came in looking quite bewildered, wondering whether they were experiencing some sort of time warp.

I had a bit of a problem knowing how to conduct myself when visiting. I know that the postman brings letters - that's expected of him. I know that the milkman brings milk, or did so at the time. But why should the pastor bring prayers? I just couldn't get myself to become a deliveryman and to have a spiritual appendage to every visit.

"Let's have a reading and a word of prayer, shall we?" No, I just couldn't do it. Speaking only for myself, I felt that fulfilling these expectations was artificial - something superimposed by some unwritten law, and was the opposite of freedom. But I prayed and read on SOME of my visits, when I thought it was appropriate, and so I wasn't totally heathen after all! But to this day I also feel uneasy about the reverse situation, when a 'religious' person visits us and conversation flows freely, interspersed with a bit of humour here and there, but suddenly there is a change of mood and we discover that the visit has an automatic appendage, after which there's nothing more to say. Something seems wrong somehow.

By now, I hadn't any doubt about the authority of the Bible - it was the basis of all my preaching, and in any discussion about beliefs, I would always refer to the Bible. However, when I visited folk who had personal problems, I found that I spoke more from my heart than from a book. True, I sometimes quoted a comforting promise from the Bible, but by and large I sought to use my reasoning and my feelings of concern. Is that really wrong? I often remember my very first experience of listening to someone whose life had been emotionally overturned, and I recall that all those years ago I didn't quote anything to *Annette* - I just 'felt', and then said what I felt.

In lighter vein I had to learn how to visit à la Radnorshire.

"Would you like a cup of tea, Pastor?"

"Oh, yes please, that would be nice."

But when the table was laid and every imaginable food item appeared, I discovered that 'a cup of tea' was a full-scale meal. I had to get to grips with the jargon of the area, and now I had a new reply: "No thank you, but I'd be glad of a cup of tea IN THE HAND."

Visiting often meant driving along deeply rutted farm tracks. Our three-wheel Reliant van didn't cope too well with these tracks, the front wheel often slipping off the central mound and falling into one of the ruts - not the best sort of vehicle for visiting Radnorshire farms. Charlie's farm had six gates which were always kept shut, and a bit of simple arithmetic will prove that I had to get out of and into the car no fewer than twenty-five times per visit. Work it out!

Let's meet some of the folk at the Church. At every service, there she was, our Bunty, the soon-to-retire Scottish midwife. She always sat at the front and looked at me intently throughout my preaching, following my every word.

"I like your doctrine," she would say with her lovely accent, meaning that she agreed with me and thought I was absolutely on the right track - that's HER track! However, now and then I diverged from her track and I'd be told "You were in error tonight, Pastor!"

Bunty often popped into the manse for a cup of tea and chat, but was never happy with my brew. "It's not strong enough," was her repeated criticism. So on one of her visits, I added some gravy browning - and this was the best cuppa I'd ever made! But unfortunately she sussed out my sin, because of a brown smear on the side of the cup! You know, deceit needs better planning than that.

Then there was Tom. He lived in a reportedly filthy caravan, though I have never been inside, as he would always see me coming when I visited him, and meet me at the gate. He didn't seem to know much about washing himself, though he did have an annual bath in the river Lugg. Once he emerged from the river, wet and naked, only to find a policeman standing at his side. He was arrested.

I started a weekly informal meeting in the manse, and Tom came. After a few weeks the meetings had to be abandoned. Close proximity was not desirable. But Tom supported me to the hilt; he used to embrace me tightly and say "I'll never forsake you, Pastor!"

Tom was also very helpful. One Sunday the snow had blocked many roads and I thought there would be a congregation of only two - the Pastor and his wife. However, about ten other folk arrived, including Tom. It seemed wise to shorten the service, and I explained that there would be no collection, but that any contributions could be placed in a box at the back of the church, when leaving - but it seems that Tom wasn't listening. Suddenly he stood up, and came to the front. Whatever's Tom doing now? He then picked up the collection plate on the communion table and went from pew to pew. But everybody obeyed me, and so he returned to the front, with an empty collection plate. Poor Tom!

Miss Passey was the Sunday organist and the Lady of the Manor, a lady of real class! Tom was very fond of her.

"I loves yer, Miss Passey, I loves yer!" he would say. One winter's evening the midweek meeting was under way, but our always-on-time Miss Passey hadn't arrived. Then I heard a car door closing, and the outer door of the little unlit porch opening. Was it Miss Passey? Maybe she was waiting in the porch until I'd finished my prayer. Only seconds later I heard a bike being leaned against the corrugated iron wall. Was it Tom? There was an air of suspense in the meeting. For a while, all seemed calm, but suddenly there was a frantic scream! The inner door burst open and a shocked Miss Passey ran in. We were all shaking, trying to conceal our laughter. It seems that in total darkness, Tom had taken his opportunity. So much for the prayer!

Miss Passey had a militant side to her, and she had been known to frighten Tom away from her front door by pointing a gun at him. But good old Miss Passey also had a generous side, and she turned up at our back door every Saturday evening, with the gift of a Sunday joint.

Members of the church held various views on what may or may not be done on a Sunday. Kinsey, for example, donned his best suit for church, but this was the only day in the week when shaving was forbidden. So the only time he ever looked smart was the time when he also looked rather prickly. Farmer Joe made his cattle into members of the Lord's Day Observance Society by not feeding them. Bunty would buy petrol with her American Express card, but not with cash. Some folk were willing to go into a shop on a Sunday as long as no money was spent, but apparently going into a café was different, as they allowed themselves to go in - and actually buy a meal. I think that many evangelicals get tied up in knots with rules they have invented, and attributed to God. There is a verse of a hymn, written in 1850 by William Faber, which sums up my feelings:

But we make His love too narrow
By false limits of our own;
And we magnify His strictness
With a zeal He will not own.

A man from another church ran a Christian Guest House, and employed girls to help - each one receiving his 'attention'. One of these girls came to see me near to despair. She was under intolerable pressure from her boss, and I knew that some action had to be taken urgently. I went to talk to the man, along with Mary and our troubled girl, but discussion was far from easy as the man was severely deaf. *Angela* resigned, and left immediately without her final wages. I had a deep respect for her, and felt she had suffered greatly. Pain hurts, whatever the cause!

A young man in the church was in serious debt. His only way out of greater trouble was when his creditors allowed ME to collect money from him on a monthly basis, and then it was my job to distribute it. Sadly, sometimes he had no money for me!

Both these young people came through the dark tunnel of despair, and out into the daylight. Beginnings don't determine endings!

What can I say about *Brian?* Well, he had extreme views, to say the least. But these extreme views were his passionately held beliefs. One night, getting on for midnight, the phone rang. It was Peter, asking me to go round at once, as some trouble had arisen. *Brian* had visited Peter, and after a while his mum had prepared some supper - ham sandwiches. *Brian* claimed that the Bible forbids us to eat the flesh of a pig (Leviticus, chapter 11) and when offered these sarnies he threw them on the floor and went raving mad. First of all Peter sent for the doctor who tried to give *Brian* an injection, but *Brian* refused, and so the doctor departed, leaving some tablets for him, which of course he also refused to take.

Enter the pastor. Imagine the scene - I held a glass of water in one hand and some tablets in the other, and pleaded with *Brian*. In response to my plea he became angrier. Suddenly he produced a knife and threatened me, putting the point of the knife to my throat. His eyes were staring. His hand was trembling. The atmosphere was incredibly tense. We stood in that position seemingly for eternity. At the end of 'eternity' I spoke.

"*Brian*, in the name of the Lord I command you to take these tablets!"

He immediately dropped his knife on the floor, and shouted out dramatically, "In the name of the Lord I take these tablets!" Suddenly, *Brian* was calm, long before the tablets could have taken any effect. The drama was over, and I went home.

The doorbell rang very late one evening. There he stood - a bedraggled-looking lad clutching his bicycle. He seemed confused, but asked for a bed for the night. We invited him into the manse, gave him a cuppa and a sandwich (was it ham?) and then tried to find some details about him. We got to know very little, but we agreed that he could stay for the night and that we'd have a further chat in the morning. Suddenly he began to tremble, and told me he was frightened of me.

"You're going to murder me, aren't you?" he screamed. But if anything, I thought I had more reason to fear that he might murder me. He shook visibly, and then ran into my study, locking the door behind him, and despite all my pleadings there he remained for the night, bedless! Unfortunately, the phone was in the study and so there was no easy way to contact anybody, but I did manage to get in touch with the Police, though I can't remember how, and enquired whether anybody had been reported missing. I got no help - just "find out where he lives and buy him a railway ticket home!" Shouldn't the Police have done much more?

The following morning our frightened boy emerged, quite calmly. It seems he had cashed in all his savings and bought a bike for over £1,000 - quite a lot in the 1960s. He'd then run away from his home in Birmingham. Eventually he gave me the telephone number of his parents, who I rang. How relieved they were! We then obeyed the Police and bought him a ticket for his train journey home. Not many days later we received a letter from an appreciative mum and dad, plus a cheque for the rail fare. So one night I have a knife at my throat, and only a few nights later I'm thought to be a potential murderer. What an exciting life!

Sometimes Mary's mother would visit us. At first she would come to the services and suffer the preaching of the man who took her daughter away from Methodism. But my preaching would often be punctuated with her loud comments.

"Oh no, no, no, Geoffrey. No, no!" In her later visits she attended the Methodist Church, thus avoiding me.

Bunty reprimanded her. "The Methodist Church?" she said. "They don't believe the Bible there!" Mum rose to her full height and let her have it, and I think rightly so. Wow, I'm sticking up for Mary's mum!

Once we had a visiting preacher who was told quite firmly by Mum that "we don't believe in baptism here, you know!" The poor preacher must have been a bit confused, visiting a Baptist church only to be told that we didn't believe in baptism.

I had never baptised anybody before coming to Ackhill. It would have been helpful if we'd been given a few tips during our two years at the Elim

College, but we were all left to find out the hard way. Most Baptist churches have a baptistry in the building, usually revealed by removing part of the floor, but at Ackhill we used the nearby River Lugg, where naked Tom was arrested. The upshot is that I practised on Mary, and 'did' her over and over again until I'd got the hang of it.

One year, Bunty's son Ian was one of the folk being baptised. There we were at the riverside, singing Ian's favourite hymn, but soon a problem arose - one man must have thought the singing wasn't going too well, and so he sang louder and louder, completely overpowering us all. Unfortunately he had a different tune in mind, and we had no option but to follow him, and change the tune half way through the verse. The man had won the battle, but it didn't make a good start to the service!

Ian had prayed about his forthcoming baptism: "Lord, if I get baptised, please give me a girlfriend." Not a perfect prayer perhaps, but the Lord doesn't restrict himself to answering only the 'best' prayers! Wendy Cope believes He answers all sorts of prayers, which she explains quite light-heartedly:

When I went out shopping,
I said a little prayer:
'Jesus, help me park my car
For You are everywhere.'

Jesus in His goodness and grace,
Jesus found me a parking space
In a very convenient place.
Sound the horn and praise Him!

The poem goes on to explain about the 'parking space in the sky', but as for the present time, Ian emerged from the water and found himself standing next to Barbara - and that was his wife to be!

Jesus in His goodness and grace,
Jesus found Ian a girl to embrace,
And very soon a wedding took place.
Ring the bells and praise Him!
(With apologies to Wendy Cope)

Barbara was one of the girls who had attended our Christian Fellowship for Disabled Children in Birmingham, though she herself was not disabled - and she just happened to be staying with us at the Manse that weekend. The day after the baptism, a church member with an unexpected sense of humour sent me a letter addressed to Mr G Smales at the Ro-Manse! He'd seen the couple holding hands.

Within a few weeks of our arrival in Radnorshire, a more sobering letter arrived, out of the blue, with some bad financial news. It was from the solicitors who had dealt with the sale of our bungalow in Winchcombe, saying that they had made a serious mistake in their calculations, and that we owed them £1,000. A previous letter had shown that the transaction had been closed satisfactorily. We were at a total loss to understand their explanation.

Fortunately, Peter's mother worked for a firm of solicitors, and she said she would get it all sorted out for us. Sorted out indeed! Her learned boss affirmed that we had no option but to pay the money. Maybe I'd better admit that I had a naughty thought about solicitors standing together against the ignorant, but maybe my thought was wide of the mark! The practical problem was that we couldn't afford to pay this unexpected bill. But somehow or other we got through, but to this day, it still remains a big unknown as to why we had to pay anything at all.

It soon became obvious that I needed to augment my income. We lived alongside Offa's Dyke Path, so perhaps we should have set up a roadside café, and offered tea and homemade cakes to the ramblers, and thus quadrupled our income! But we didn't pursue that idea. Over the years, I had a considerable variety of income boosters. In the autumn, I was a driver for a firm of fruit growers, delivering apples to homes in South Wales, a job I did for a couple of years. This took two days each week during the month of September.

Another time I did the accounts for a Residential Home, thus discovering that the manager was buying fillet steak and other costly foods for his own use, and calling it 'expenses'. Another time I taught singing one day a week at an Infants' School - we even put on a few concerts. Another year I taught Religious Studies at Leominster Grammar School, just one day a week, but I'm ashamed to say that I once caused a girl to faint by my over-graphic description of some event. I heard a sudden thud, and there she was, on the floor. I also had a few piano pupils from among the members, and even some from the church at Bleddfa.

My strangest job lasted for only two days - two Mondays to be precise - after which I resigned. It was a teaching post at a school in Shropshire - a private boarding school for boys and girls who had been in trouble. Upon arrival, I was told to teach general subjects in the morning and to organise the building of the swimming pool in the afternoon – "And here are the ignition keys for the tractor." Rather frightening, I thought. From that moment onwards, I never saw another member of staff, and so I couldn't refer to anyone to ask what exactly I should be doing regarding the swimming pool. I taught the whole school at once, just over twenty boys, and one girl! The atmosphere was weird and unsettling.

Come the afternoon, it was the boys who showed me the tractor with its large trailer and told me that we were to fill the trailer with slabs, and line the base of the pool. OK, the slabs are now in the trailer, so how do I drive this wretched thing? Where's the brake? Does it have an accelerator? Well, somehow or other, I managed to get the thing going, with a few boys in the trailer showing me the way. Oh dear, they showed me a 'short cut', and down into an overgrown ditch we went! Was it just a mistake on their part, or…? Somehow I got out of the ditch, and I endured to the end of the day, repeating the whole saga the following Monday, except for the 'ditch' bit. Where were all the members of the teaching staff? Something was not quite right here, and my letter of resignation was written the next day.

A year later there was an article in the local newspaper about the sudden closure of the school. Recently I have tried to get some confirmation of the facts as far as I know them, but I've always met with a strange silence, as though the school never existed. I wrote letters to people who must have known what happened, but never had a reply.

These various jobs helped me to cope financially, but soon things took a turn for the worse when, for reasons yet to be explained, my pay was reduced from £12 to £5 per week.

Little by little I learnt that my unanimous call to Ackhill was not quite as spiritual as I'd thought, as some members seemed to have voted for me as a musician, rather than as a pastor. And soon I was writing 'musicals'.

Despite the rural location of the church, we had a large Sunday School, with an adult class. So we had a big cast available our Sunday School Anniversaries, which were held on Boxing Day. I soon found myself producing what might well be called 'spiritual musicals' - *Pilgrim's Progress*, *King of Kings*, and so on. I always drew a picture in black and white to illustrate the story - a huge picture covering the whole of the back of the stage - quite a task! These events were highly successful, and those members whose main idea was to employ a musician were kept happy. Yes, I admit that I enjoyed preparing these works and training the cast - so maybe I could aspire to be a film producer and director next time round.

Writing these musicals prompted me to think about church music generally. Is it right to get all the youngsters in the Sunday School to sing words such as

133

"O Jesus, I have promised to serve Thee to the end," or, "My Jesus, I love Thee, I know Thou art mine"? I thought not. There seemed to be a lack of hymns which are merely factual, rather than describing a personal experience. Hence I produced a hymnbook for young people with that aim in mind. It was a collection of a hundred hymns which I called 'Hymns of the Word'. I remember that I sold the words copy for 10p and the music copy for 20p. It seemed to fulfil a need, and many Christian Youth Clubs used the book, and also quite a few day schools. Some of the hymns I'd written have been broadcast - sung by a choir, but my attempts to get the hymnbook published were met with zero success.

I never thought much of the Hymn Festivals, which were held annually in nearby Knighton. Churches got together, hired a large hall, and then had a jolly good sing of favourite hymns. Anyway, my attitude was noted, and one of the members who had voted for me as a musician now declared that "Smales won't stop Wales from singing!"

My preaching was well received at Ackhill, but as most churches in the area were non-evangelical I became less popular with other ministers, one of them actually throwing me out of his house because I'd opened my Bible.

He shouted, "Don't quote that book at me!" and then, having spoken, he acted quite forcibly. I'd merely opened my Bible to give him a couple of letters which were hiding between the pages. I was totally innocent!

However, amidst all the outside criticism, one cheering compliment kept cropping up: "He takes a good funeral!" To be precise, the wording was "'BUT he takes a good funeral."

One funeral was memorable. Mrs Rees, a former member of the church, had died, and had donated her body for research. Eventually there was a cremation service, followed by a memorial service at Ackhill, which included scattering her ashes over the family grave. Mary and I tidied the Rees grave and took our coffee table into the church for displaying the urn. The service proceeded smoothly. The folk left the church afterwards and went across the lane into the graveyard (adjacent to our kitchen), but to my dismay they went to a different grave. It seems we had prepared some other 'Rees' grave. Not a good start as the correct one was also overgrown.

Worse was to come. Having prayed, and read an appropriate portion of scripture, I tried to open the urn and scatter the ashes, but I couldn't remove the lid. I tried and tried, and I tried yet again. The silence was unbearable. Eventually I had to go into the manse, returning with a screwdriver to prize off the stubborn lid. It was still difficult, but at last I was successful, though it wasn't very dignified!

There is even more to relate - I had a long black coat which I wore for funerals, but unfortunately, when I scattered the ashes, an unexpected gust of wind threw the ashes back at me, all over my coat and into my eyes! What a transformation from black to white in an instant! I must say I was glad when I was tucked up in bed that night, though I wondered who it was who'd planned to send that gust of wind in my direction at just the wrong moment.

Then there was the problem with those wretched flies which buzzed around noisily during the services - in very large numbers. They dwelt mainly in the apex of the roof, but frequently made unwelcome excursions to visit members of the congregation.

We decided that enough was enough and we had an exciting time fumigating the place with Lindane pellets. After one midweek meeting about twenty of us took our places at strategic points around the church, each armed with a pellet and a box of matches. After a count of 1 - 2 - 3 we lit our pellets and ran for it, escaping the fumes at lightning speed.

We returned nearly two weeks later, only to discover a completely black interior, with dead flies everywhere! The floor was black and crunchy with millions of corpses. A black pulpit, a black organ, black pews - it was a horrible sight, but at least our troubles were all over. But I did recall Albert Schweitzer's stress on the need for 'reverence for life, from elephants to blades of grass', and I wondered.

Two Elim ministers came to stay with us for a few days, with their wives. They knew that my views on the second coming didn't match theirs, and early in their stay they brought up the subject in conversation, giving rise to a long and difficult eschatological debate! I think they were trying to put me right.

Meanwhile the two wives hadn't a clue what was going on, and sat there looking bewildered. Initially I admit that I regarded them as ignorant - but maybe Mary's mother had a point when she'd shouted out "Just leave me alone with my simple faith." After all, is there really anything wrong with a simple faith which bypasses all controversy?

Sometimes I wonder whether men tend to be more aware of doctrinal matters than women. If so there are many exceptions - Mary was well versed in doctrinal matters, as you might have guessed from her bedtime sermon a few years earlier. As for Bunty, she had all her doctrines tightly packed in neat bundles, and she would never dream of repacking any of them; she was someone who KNEW, and Bunty's Biblical Bundles were sacrosanct!

I think that there is much to be said for a less complicated faith, and maybe these two Elim wives, in their so-called ignorance, were the ones who knew best.

A vicar's wife was once asked about her views on Christ's second coming. She looked somewhat confused, but turning to her husband she asked, "What DO we believe, dear?" Well, so the story goes.

Family matters

Early on in our Ackhill days, and twelve years into our marriage, Mary and I came to the conclusion that we should try to adopt a baby. We began making applications, but soon we bumped into a brick wall. We'd wondered whether our poor financial situation might prove to be an insurmountable wall, but no, that seemed to present no problems at all. The wall turned out to be my own health history. The fact that I was well at the time and had been well for several years was of no consequence. Hence we had a long list of refusals, which was all very discouraging.

Eventually we had an affirmative answer from Dr Barnado's Homes - we could adopt a baby boy, a black baby boy! We were thrown into confusion. Was this the child the Lord had chosen for us? After all, we'd prayed about it, hadn't we? Was this boy the answer to our prayers? We asked ourselves whether we had any aversion to a black child in our family. "Certainly not," was our answer. But after much hard thinking we declined the offer for the simple reason that, as far as we know, he would have been the only black person in the county.

We kept on making applications, and yet another offer came our way - a disabled baby girl. Again, more confusion! I had taught disabled children for seven years and felt such an affinity with them, so was the Lord telling us that my teaching at the Wilson Stuart School was but a preparation, and now it was 'for real'? There was a further aspect, which seemed rather strange, in that the girl's father (a racing driver) lived a few miles away. The girl would have needed much hospital treatment, and as the nearest hospital was in Hereford, over thirty miles away, we thought the whole idea was impractical. The proximity of the father also seemed a bit of an unknown. And so we declined. Did we do right?

These two refusals on our part were among the hardest decisions we have ever made, but we felt we just had to keep on and on making further applications, but seemingly getting nowhere.

Although I was a Baptist minister, I had no idea that there was a Baptist Adoption Society. When we discovered its existence, we wondered whether a Baptist organisation would look upon me more favourably. So we applied, and all at once things began to happen! We had a visit from the 'inspectors', and soon we received a letter to say we could collect our baby boy the following week. What wonderful news!

Yes, it was wonderful news, but not all that straightforward, because we had also received a letter from the Cardiff Children's Committee the previous day to say we could collect our baby boy the following week! We had been led to believe that we'd been rejected by Cardiff, and no one had ever been to interview us. So this was a very surprising and very perplexing turn of events.

What were we to do? Which baby will be our son? A decision, which stands for a lifetime, had to be made in a moment. All our adoption decisions were difficult and poignant, but this, our third big decision, seemed beyond our reasoning powers. In the end we used the 'first come, first served' principle, and so Cardiff it was! The Baptist Society was extremely helpful and we received a further letter to say we could adopt a baby girl in due course.

January 1967 is when it all began - yes, that's when we first met Andrew, aged six weeks. That day in Cardiff was very exciting and emotional; there he was in his cot, fast asleep - he looked beautiful. I very gently touched his hand with my finger, and immediately there was a big explosion! Wow, Andrew erupted into frantic yelling, and so it went on for years!

Within twenty-four hours we knew that life wasn't going to be easy. His screaming through much of each night was very hard to cope with, and our concern grew. Soon a pattern emerged - he would sleep for about half an hour and then the nightly explosions would begin. His yelling was intense and frightening. When friends came and stayed the night, they too were frightened by the experience. It seemed that Andrew needed me rather than Mary, so there was no taking it in turns, though Mary got up with me every time. I would try to hold him and rock him as I walked about through the night hours, and I continued until he became calm again. This explosion happened several times every night, and each time it would be about half an hour before peace descended.

As Andrew grew older and could toddle, these nightly explosions were accompanied by his attempts to run violently into a wall, and restraining him was very demanding on my heart. Eventually Andrew became afraid of going to bed, because he too couldn't face the experience.

Our own doctor didn't seem to believe that there was really any problem, and refused to investigate. This is where Bunty came to our rescue, and arranged for the doctor for whom she worked to contact us - unprofessionally. He referred us to a consultant who conducted a full EEG examination, and declared that Andrew was probably a genius, and was unquestionably hyperactive. It was discovered at a later date that his IQ was over 150, but at the time his intelligence didn't really interest us, as we were far more interested in taming the beast!

For years we 'fed' Andrew on the drug largactyl, which took the edge off his 'hyper' problem, without removing it.

Despite all this, Andrew was a wonderful boy, with a big winsome personality, obviously very clever, full of smiles and full of fun. Miss Passey had her own views.

"What an ugly baby!" she told us when she first saw him, but we thought, 'What a rude woman!'

Andrew liked teasing us. He always wanted me. "Daddy, Daddy!" he would shout.

But we pleaded with him, "Andrew, please say Mummy!"

His lips would then prepare for the 'm' sound, and he'd hold that position, keeping us in suspense, and then, with a twinkle in his eye, he would change his lip position and say a cheeky "Daddy, Daddy!" He knew he was teasing, all right. Listen to this conversation from our very early days with Andrew:

"Come on, let Mummy cut your meat for you."

"Annoo do it," he grunted in a gruff and resolute voice, and the name 'Annoo' has stuck, and that's what we often call him to this day.

As a toddler, Annoo's reading skills were way beyond expectation, though there were some occasional amusing lapses. He'd noticed a sign outside a restaurant, at which point he read the words aloud: "Come and try our lovely girls!" I'll leave you to translate back to the true wording.

June 1968 brings us to another big day in our lives when we went to The Haven, in Yateley, near Reading, to fetch our baby daughter who we called Margaret. She was the girl the Baptist Adoption Society had promised for us.

After fifteen months with Andrew, we wonder how we dare have an addition to the family, especially when we had been warned that there was a history of epilepsy in the mother's family. But we went ahead all the same.

Margaret was also six weeks old when we adopted her, and this time round there were no explosions - just smiles, and more smiles! In fact, she turned out to be the perfect baby (sorry, Annoo!) who slept through all our little boy's explosions and never caused any trouble - that is, when she was a baby and a little girl! She was a 'Mummy, Mummy' girl, which must have been some relief for Mary.

We managed to get Andrew to sleep by playing a record of 'Scotland the Brave' on the bagpipes. We kept our old-fashioned turntable on the landing floor, and returned every few minutes to place the stylus at the beginning again. Andrew soon learnt to climb out of his cot, whereas Margaret just lay in her cot, smiling and gurgling until we arrived - always content.

By the time Margaret came into our lives, we discovered that three other Baptist ministers in the area had adopted a boy and a girl, who were roughly the same age as our children. Uncanny!

At first Margaret showed no signs of epilepsy, though there were occasions when she slept for very long periods, which seemed a bit strange. Once we left her in the cot at 6.00 p.m. but soon afterwards Andrew's problems began, and seemed more extreme than usual. We were completely exhausted by the next morning, and as we'd heard no sound from Margaret's room, we actually forgot about her (sorry, Margaret) and didn't go in to see her until noon the next day, only to discover our lovely baby, quite unperturbed, gurgling and smiling at us.

When Margaret was a toddler, she became a chatterbox par excellence - she loved words, but would sometimes amuse us with word-variations. Every time I did some DIY she enjoyed naming my tools one by one, and if I tried to get something level, she would say, "Daddy, I think you need to fetch your devil-spirit!"

Margaret loved me to tell her stories. I didn't read them to her, but thought up various plots as I went along, but every now and then one of my stories would be added to her 'favourites' list. "Daddy, Daddy, will you tell me the story of Freda and the yellow curtains!" I've forgotten the storyline by now, despite the frequent narrations, but maybe Margaret could enlighten me.

Unlike Andrew, Margaret was never more than a little bit naughty, and at such times all I had to do was give her a stern look, and she would immediately dissolve into tears of repentance! Margaret's worst crime was when she refused to say 'thank you' to a waitress when she was about four - we were horrified. But that was a mere nothing compared with Andrew's crimes!

When she was about three, Margaret suddenly became seriously ill, and couldn't walk. The doctor came almost immediately and she was rushed into Hereford Hospital, where she stayed for several days. It was a very worrying time, but thanks to a massive injection of antihistamine, she just as suddenly improved. We discovered that she'd eaten some holly berries, and given herself giant urticaria.

One day, Andrew fell and cut his head very badly. The following year on the same date, Margaret did likewise, and we could even see part of her skull. Yet another year later, and on the same date, Andrew fell and cut his head, and had to be taken to hospital for repairs to his forehead. When the same date came in the fourth year, we watched our children on a non-stop basis. All was well! Were we just a little bit superstitious?

As already hinted, Andrew could be very very naughty at times. Once, when the church and the manse were being repainted, he plunged his hands in a tin of black gloss paint and then rubbed his hands in his hair and all over his clothes. We washed his hair in turps. Another time he kicked his Sunday School teacher in the tummy. He apologised to her about thirty years later.

She said, "That's all right, Andrew!"

Despite Andrew's problems and Margaret's background of epilepsy, we had no regrets whatsoever about the adoptions, and the children's early childhood at Ackhill was a happy time for us all. Perhaps now and again, when Andrew was at the height of his nocturnal screaming, we recalled that moment when we'd had those two letters, each offering us a baby boy, and we were tempted to ask, 'What if?' But then we'd simply dismiss the thought. Mind you, sometimes Mary made a naughty comment when we went into some store which offered BABY CHANGING FACILITIES.

"Mmm, that's an idea," she would say.

I often thought up little rhymes with matching tunes. The words were usually about the children's teddies and other cuddly friends, or about members of the family. Andrew can still sing, "Andrew's little piggy is a nice little pig, a nice little pig, a nice little pig, etc." Yes, we enjoyed singing these songs, especially when going on a car journey.

One day, on our way to see Mary's parents, we had an especially happy time singing a silly song which I'd 'composed' for the occasion. We sang it over and over again until our breath began to fail. What fun! We just had to sing it for Granny immediately upon arrival. But alas, our grins were wiped off our faces, with a severe rebuff. So what was our song?

Granny's had too much to eat,
Her tummy's all a rumble-o.
And now she's fast asleep
In her lovely little bungalow.

And her angry response? "Granny NEVER has too much to eat!" And that was the end of the fun!

Crisis Time

The Church at Bleddfa had a Sunday School of three children, complete with Mr Hardwick, the elderly Sunday School Superintendent. He and his wife were the only members who had voted for me in the first place, and as far as I know, they were the only evangelicals in the church. But not to be outdone by Ackhill, the Bleddfa church must needs have its own Sunday School Anniversary. And so, in the absence of children, a secular singing party was invited each year, rendering about thirty songs. This replaced the Sunday service and it became an evening concert.

After several years of my ministry, I went to see Mr Hardwick, who readily agreed with me that replacing the Sunday Service by a secular concert was not God-honouring, and that ditching the Sunday sermon is

140

not the sort of thing that evangelicals do.

He said, "Next time it will be a 'more spiritual' event."

Poor Mr Hardwick, I think he hardly dare put the new idea into practice, so without reference to me he once again booked a singing party, and I only found out by looking at posters around the area.

It was the evening of the Bleddfa event, and I made my big decision, which was to go to the concert myself! So after the Ackhill service was over, Mary and I went to the Bleddfa church, while Bunty stayed at the manse looking after the children. We arrived in some trepidation, climbed up the long steep path and joined the concert party, which was now in full swing. The place was crowded, not an empty seat to be seen - with lots of Ackhill members in the audience. Despite Ackhill's poor relationship with Bleddfa, it seems that many Ackhill-ites couldn't resist the fun of a concert. As I entered the church there were audible gasps, and folk were whispering, "It's the pastor! It's the pastor!"

I walked straight into the pulpit, whereupon the chairman asked me if I would like to say 'a few words'. I nodded. I preached very calmly; Mary timed me and confirmed that I spoke for no more than three minutes. I well remember my text. 'Go your way by the footsteps of the flock.' (Song of Solomon, chapter 1.) It was a highly poignant three minutes.

The following morning Mr 'Dunna' arrived at the Manse with a letter from the elders giving me three months' notice. However, my notice would be cancelled if I wrote a letter of apology to each member of the singing party. But as I had no regrets, I couldn't do that, and hence my dismissal stood.

I suppose, in a sense, the Bleddfa folk were quite pleased with me, because I'd given them just the opportunity they'd always wanted. I'd walked straight into the wolf's lair, and so fulfilled the meaning of the word *Bleddfaich*.

At the beginning of my ministry, I had failed to get the elders of both churches together for an informal buffet. But at last I'd succeeded, even if it was only to discuss me.

The manse was adjacent to the old church, now used for Sunday School and other meetings. Mary attended the midweek Bible Studies, and a wire was left in place permanently from the manse to the old church building, so that a baby alarm could be used. Of course, there was always the possibility that the baby alarm could be reversed, and we would then be able to hear, in the comfort of the manse, what was going on at the meeting. It was quite a temptation on this 'Discuss Smales' evening. But surely we'd never do such a thing! Would we?

We heard every word. One man said, "He lost his temper and shouted!"

But if Bleddfa won't have me, then Ackhill won't have Bleddfa! And soon Ackhill's connection with Bleddfa was severed - what an unexpected turn of events! So that's that - in three months' time I will be the pastor of just one church.

I expected that my weekly pay would be reduced because of this severance, but it seems that the smaller church which 'dunna want me' contributed the greater part of my pay, which was rather puzzling as far as a proportion sum goes. Anyway, whatever the mathematics of the thing, my income was suddenly reduced from £12 to £5 a week.

As our finances were not looking too healthy, I withdrew my Teacher's Pension payments, not without some financial penalty, thus giving us some ready cash. Mary and I agreed that we should sell her engagement ring! Surprisingly we received very little for this, but we both believed that we had acted correctly. However, years later Mam bought Mary a replacement ring, which looked just the same, but there were no diamonds this time round! No diamonds, and also no financial miracles such as we experienced when we'd bought the minibus all those years ago. This time round, when we needed money, there were ways and means of earning some.

In 1971 there was a serious crisis in the Baptist Union, which caused over a hundred ministers, along with their churches, to resign from the Union. For each minister this meant a loss of the guaranteed stipend and all pension rights, and so resigning was financially costly. The crisis was caused when Michael Taylor addressed the Annual Assembly on the theme 'How much of a man was Jesus?'

If Joe Bloggs had given the same talk, it would have all been forgotten. But Taylor was the Principal of the Northern Baptist College, and as such his words were noted carefully.

"It could not be claimed," he said, "that Christ is the Son of God; we have to stop short of saying unequivocally that He is God." Michael Taylor's speech raised a storm of protest in the BU. Even the MP Cyril Black stepped in to denounce Taylor's words. Paul Beasley Murray, who was soon to become the Principal of Spurgeon's College, wanted the Baptist Union to disassociate itself from Michael Taylor.

But it is easy to forget that Taylor himself was going through a time of trial by being denounced by so many. He thought about things, and then he told us what he'd thought - what trouble it caused!

Graham Greene wrote, 'Heresy is only another name for freedom of thought,' but perhaps the Assembly Meeting was not the best place to express such freedom. I was certainly distressed by Taylor's statement, but told myself that this is the view of only one man, however important that man might be, but when each minister received a letter from the Union telling us that we must tolerate such views, that seemed a more serious matter. Many ministers at that infamous Assembly urged the Union to remove Taylor from Office, but instead, the Union just sent out these 'tolerance' letters.

Ackhill was an evangelical church, so it seemed to me that the church would readily agree to come out of the Union, and become independent. I personally was not a member of the Union, and so if the church were to secede from the Union I would be no worse off financially, as my income was completely independent of the BU.

To my dismay the Church refused. That was a terrible blow to me. It put me in a difficult position, as I believed that, under the circumstances, it would be wrong for me to remain as the minister. Maybe I'm more broadminded now, but I just had to act as I believed at the time. It was all so worrying and painful.

My preaching had been well received through the years, but my pleading on the matter of leaving the Union turned out to be unwelcome, and it was summarily dismissed. It was to be the end of the road. Incidentally, two ministers later, the church finally severed its connection with the Union.

Towards the close of my Ackhill days I was invited to preach 'with a view' at a well-known evangelical church in Kent, and one which was NOT in any union. This was encouraging, to say the least.

I had a struggle in preparing my first sermon for this church. I'd decided to preach on a certain verse, but 'something' was pulling me in another

143

direction, urging me to preach from another verse. I fought against this, and it was late on the Saturday evening when I conceded defeat, and prepared a new sermon, which included quoting some verses from a little-known hymn. Come the Sunday morning, I obediently preached this new sermon.

At the end of the service, the secretary made a beeline for me, accompanied by a young man in tears. The secretary told me that this man had called round to see him the previous evening in a worried state, and he'd told the lad on the Saturday exactly what I had said, point by point, on the Sunday. He'd even quoted that hymn which I'd found in an out-dated hymnbook! The young man was completely dumbfounded, but he was, of course, doubly helped. Surely it was the Lord Himself who had 'organised' all this, and I felt humbled and very thankful.

I preached six sermons over three Sundays, but I soon discovered that there was a division among the elders on the interpretation of baptism - does one baptise a baby, or wait until there is personal belief? I felt I couldn't cope with this division, and so in reality, I'd come to yet another 'no entry' sign.

Looking back, I must have preached well over a thousand sermons at Ackhill. I'd been involved with the problems of many of the members, and gained a real sense of belonging. Occasionally I heard the teasing comment, "Well, he's English, isn't he?" That's when I hadn't quite conformed. But apart from that, all had gone well for seven years. However, early in 1973, I resigned as the minister. There was no other option.

But despite all the setbacks, this was the end of a very happy and fulfilling period of my life.

Good-bye, Ackhill, good-bye.

Ackhill Chapel - the old building. Still used for Sunday School and other meetings. Notice the porch where Miss Passey was trapped

Ackhill Chapel – the new building

Ackhill Chapel - the baptistery. This is the River Lugg, just down the lane from the church

*The view from the bedroom. Part of the garden and graveyard, with the hills beyond —
a preview of heaven, according to the Council leaflets advertising the area*

Here we are at Ackhill with our bundle of boy!

Our two little innocents – still at Ackhill

Chapter 12

Ladies of Wealth

Across the border, back into England!

I was accepted to teach piano at a rather posh boarding school for girls in Shropshire, beginning in March 1973. Mary's mum was over the moon, and couldn't wait to view *Murfield School* for herself. Wow, all at once I was in favour. I was a good boy at last, because I'd raised my social standards to Mum's level!

When I applied for this post, we were still living at Ackhill. I was invited for interview, upon which Mary sprang into action with her usual infallible directions, even describing the scenery around the school! She told me to look out for a house called *Oldfields*, and the entrance to *Murfield School* was next to it - simple! Knowing the direction to some place or other is nothing to Mary. No wonder her friends these days call her Sat Nav! I got there as directed, and she was right, the house really was called *Oldfields*. True, we'd journeyed along this particular road previously, but how could Mary remember so much detail?

My interview was quite a revelation to me. The Principal was an elderly and highly bejewelled lady. I felt I was in a palace, and here was the queen.

"You've been selected from thirty-five candidates," she told me, but it was untrue. She also told me that the school would pay part of my mortgage until we 'got on our feet', but the offer was never mentioned again. I'd only been at the school a short time when this grand lady committed suicide on school premises.

Having managed to save £1,000, it proved to be sufficient for the deposit on a 100-year old semi in Shropshire, which we bought for £6,000. So far, all was well and good - but then, on our first day there, and within minutes of arriving, a policeman knocked at the door. In a severe voice he said, "I have a warrant for your arrest!"

Not again, surely! In a flash my memory piled up other first-day experiences - my first day at Bleddfa with its 'We dunna want you here, y'know', my first day in Winchcombe with an attempt to arrest me after a serious car accident, and now this! Shouldn't the copper have checked my identity first, instead of frightening me? However, I soon proved that I wasn't the previous owner of the house. It was in fact our vendor who was in trouble.

The house was quite cheap because of its poor condition, but the mortgage was subject to our agreeing to a roof repair. That was a big problem as we'd used up most of our money by now. However, out of the blue, Dad told us he was going to give us £1,000 to help with all the expenses. What wonderful news! So we went ahead and arranged for the builders to do the work. Unfortunately we didn't get the money after all, as Dad suffered a stroke and couldn't drive, and so he gave us his car instead of the money. Ah well. Our own car was nearing the end of its life, anyway, but we were hoping it would survive a little longer. We sold it for a mere £25, and that was that! Unfortunately, the builders were already on the roof, beavering away, and we knew that paying them was not going to be all that easy.

Worse was to come. Within the first week of living in our new home, the plug sockets failed to work one by one. We soon discovered that most of the wiring was live, and that the whole system was lethal! We had some plastering done in the kitchen, but the poor plasterer had an electric shock when the damp plaster touched the wall. We visited the surveyor to complain about his report on the state of the house, asking how he could possibly have said that the wiring was up to standard. Our innocent surveyor then pointed out the actual wording in the report, which said that 'the wiring throughout the house APPEARS to be satisfactory.' So why bother having a report? Of course that meant finding money to have the whole house rewired urgently! It was a disastrous start to our new venture.

At the end of my first month's teaching, everybody got paid - well, everybody except me! It was something to do with the school's system of calculating staff salaries, based on what part of the year a new member of staff was appointed. I never understood the reason, but just had to put up with it.

Somehow or other we got through, but we did feel to be on a different level from most of the girls at the school, some of whom were princesses. However, not all these 'ladies' were wealthy. Some parents were not well off, but made huge sacrifices to get their daughters into the school. But some were so wealthy that other girls thought it 'stank'. When parents lowered their helicopters into the car park, most of the girls were disgusted. But, generally speaking, they were just normal girls, with normal problems, and normal naughtiness, except for just now and then!

In my first few weeks of teaching, I observed a 'now and then' which left me gasping. I was in the grounds of the school when I saw lots of the smaller girls carrying buckets of water.

"Whatever are you doing?"

"We're going to pour water over *Mrs Richards*!"

Now *Mrs R* was a German lady who had married a Yorkshireman, and every now and then we would hear "Ee bah gum, that were fair champion" slipping through her lips, with a German accent. She was a housemistress and a violin teacher, and had earned herself the nickname 'The Gestapo'. Soon *Mrs R* emerged from her accommodation, and it happened just as they'd said. Water everywhere! Then, like ants at work, these little girls surrounded her and somehow managed to lift up her jumper, almost managing to remove it. And there was this rather buxom and drenched lady, with her head wrapped in her jumper, and looking resplendent in her bra! I was transfixed, and did nothing at all. Unfortunately Bob, from the Maths Department, was passing at the time, and one bucket of water misfired and doused him. He was none too pleased, as he had to go home to change his suit!

Poor *Mrs R!* She was having problems with her son concerning debt, and she had sacrificed a lot to help him financially, eventually selling her Steinway grand piano to give him some more money. Little by little, she was losing her grip on life, and beginning to do strange things. On two occasions, she wakened the younger girls (for whom she was housemistress) in the middle of the night, taking them on to the playing field in their pyjamas, where she entertained them, playing her violin. The Head decided that she could stay no longer, and terminated her employment. Almost immediately there was a response from her psychiatrist: "Her suicide will be on your shoulders!" But of course, it was impossible to keep her in the school. She left, and on her third attempt she died. What a sad story.

One morning the Head announced the hymn for assembly, but we never sang it. Why not? Because some girls must have found a jar of jam, and spread its contents all over the keys of the lovely Bechstein grand piano. Not a good idea. No, I had not accidentally accepted a teaching post at St Trinian's, I'm simply relating the rare behavioural exceptions in a happy and well-disciplined school.

As for me, there I was in the music block, just enjoying myself giving piano lessons all day long. Each teaching room had a composer's name on the door: Alberti, Berlioz, Corelli, Dvořák, etc., and I was happy in my little Dvořák room. Unfortunately, I went to *Murfield School* at a time when the pupil intake was lower than ideal, and the school was facing financial problems. Within a few months there were redundancies. Pablo, one of the Latin teachers, had to go. Some gardening staff were laid off. And I was warned that as I was the last to be appointed, my future there was far from secure. Pablo had been there for many years, so why he had to go, and for the time being I could stay, I don't know.

Things didn't look good. However, not long after this warning, the Head of Maths died suddenly. So I offered my services in the Maths Department, and was accepted. Yes, while there is death, there is hope! He died early in July, when I'd been at the school for just over a year, and in the following September I was to teach piano, plus several maths classes, including Second Year Sixth Further Maths.

By now my maths was very rusty, and I'd given away all my maths books years ago. The fact that the crisis arose in July was a godsend to me, because I was in no position to teach A-level maths at a moment's notice. I visualised Dad on holiday, sitting on a deckchair on the beach with his briefcase at his side, papers on his knee, and oblivious of his surroundings. Well, my summer holiday was a copy of the beach experience, especially my two weeks sitting on a deck chair on a campsite. I got some maths books from the library, and that was my holiday 'food' - a diet of equations and theorems!

Sixth form maths had not been popular, and there were only two girls taking A-level in the second year. So I taught Further Maths to Marina (the only girl in the school who was engaged) and to twenty-year-old Majesty (an eastern girl who we called our Princess). True, I did get in a muddle now and then, but I learnt to teach my way through muddles without losing too much face. I soon gained in confidence, and I have to admit that I had a whale of a time. Maths is so lovely, and teaching it is even lovelier.

Sad to say, my teaching of maths didn't get off to a good start when half my class walked out on me! During one of the lessons, Princess Majesty, who was a day girl, suddenly rushed out of the room, leaving me with a class of one. She told the school secretary that she was ill, upon which the secretary hired a taxi to take her back to her 'digs'. She was absent from school for two weeks. It appears that she was seriously upset because I had not been pleased with her work - hence her dramatic exit! Majesty and I shared the same doctor, who told me quite unprofessionally that he'd had to put her on librium, all because of me! Eventually our princess called round at our house to apologise, explaining that being told off by her maths teacher when she was working so hard to please him, was just too much! This made me feel a bit frightened, wondering what other troubles I might cause in the future.

A few months later, a new Head arrived on the scene by the name of *John*. I must say he put the school back on its feet. Soon the numbers in the school increased, and new buildings appeared on the campus. *John* was an excellent businessman, and his building fund appeals were always successful. But I was taken aback when he asked me to become Head of the Maths Department. Wow, I could hardly believe it, but I accepted, and my job was now secure.

So my piano teaching ceased immediately, and it was round about this time that Mary began teaching piano at the school several days a week.

What a good thing I'd stopped teaching piano, as I'd just committed two serious crimes with my pupils. Janice had just had her last lesson before her piano exam, so I gave her an encouraging V for Victory sign, à la Winston Churchill, but I will never forget the girl's look of horror. I felt rather confused, and it didn't dawn on me for several days that in my ignorance I might have given her an alternative sign! Maybe Janice didn't know Churchill's V-sign anyway, but whatever the explanation, I decided that least said, soonest mended.

Secondly, I'd entered Louise for her Grade 6 piano exam, but forgotten to teach her one of the pieces and half the scales! It doesn't seem possible that I should make such a terrible mistake, but that's exactly what I did. I was teased by other members of staff, who claimed that I'd been kicked out of the Music Department in disgrace. But I also heard the confessions of several sympathetic teachers, admitting their own past educational misdeeds. Of course, the girl failed her exam and was in floods of tears. All I could do was to say I was sorry and buy her a box of chocolates. The Examining Board allowed her to retake the exam three weeks later, at the school's expense. But it was now holiday time and I'm glad Louise didn't live in Japan! She lived on the Wirral, and I was able to visit her several times in the next three weeks, and managed to repair the damage. She gained a merit, and I was forgiven.

A little while after becoming Head of Maths, *John* asked all the Heads of Departments for a five-year plan. I must be an awkward customer, because although all the other heads got busy producing pages of ideas, I felt I couldn't do this. My five-year plan was fully laid out in one sentence, as all I said was that "day by day, I would do my best, and as a need arose, I would deal with it." Perhaps I was a bit naughty.

Yes, I have an aversion to five-year plans. What a lot of waffle and wasted time! Better to get on with the job. That's what I think, anyway. Maybe there are times when such plans are needed, but why make a plan for its own sake? *John* never commented on my so-called plan, which I thought was a pity. But maths became a very popular A-level subject, and so my day-by-day plan must have worked, as soon there were well over thirty girls in the Sixth Form taking either Maths or Further Maths.

Preparing girls for Oxbridge entry in maths was very challenging. Once I spent weeks trying to answer just one question, borrowing books from the library to help me. Eventually light dawned, and the answer 'just came'. This prompted a comment from one of the girls.

"Sir, if you're stuck, what are our chances?"

I wonder why I allowed the title 'Sir'. What about my previous comment that titles and stuff are nothing but fluff? Maybe my logic was inconsistent, but I thought 'Rev' and 'Sir' were in very different categories, so 'Sir' it was.

A new teacher was appointed by the name of Dr *Wendy Dale*. She was a keen evangelical who, like me, was unhappy with titles and stuff, but she went much further, and insisted that the girls called her Auntie *Wendy*! As for requiring the girls to stand when she entered the room, the answer was a definite NO. Her lessons were chaotic! Soon she realised that teaching was not for her, and now she is high up in the Diplomatic Service. Good luck, *Wendy*!

I've always been averse to formalities and stuff, nevertheless I insisted that the girls always stood as I entered the classroom, and I never pushed this formality aside. However, once we got going with a lesson we had lots of fun and lots of teasing, as well as doing lots of hard work.

There was one A-level girl who yawned again and again. She got many teasing rebukes from me. On one occasion I said, "What you need is a cup of very strong coffee!" At that precise moment, there was a knock at the door, and Anne the Cook entered, carrying a tray on which was a cup of very strong coffee, plus a plate of chocolate biscuits! It had all been very carefully planned. Anne and I had set our watches to be in perfect agreement. I hadn't asked for chocolate biscuits though, but maybe Anne felt sorry for the girl. I admit that I liked playing tricks on the girls - it all added to my own enjoyment, and it was, I think, to the girls' benefit.

Some of the fun was accidental. I'd given the class an exercise to do, which I'd printed out the night before, intending to go from table to table to give some help. But there was an interruption; *John* arrived on the scene and asked to see me in the corridor. Suddenly, there was a mighty roar of laughter from the classroom. I returned later with a "Well?" and that set them going again. They couldn't tell me for laughing, so they showed me instead. I'd omitted the letter 't' in one of the words, and written 'In a breeding experiment with 120 rabbis, 30 of which were lop-eared, and ...' I wonder what lop-eared rabbis look like.

My inveterate teasing has gone wrong many a time, but maybe my worst blunder was when the Head Girl thought I was threatening to remove her clothes! She became red-faced, and looked totally confused. Unfortunately the poor girl didn't know that the word 'unfrock' referred to her

APPOINTMENT as Head Girl rather than to her APPAREL! I had teasingly threatened to unfrock her, after some infinitesimally small misdemeanour. I gave her an English lesson there and then, and thankfully, she saw the funny side of my unwise teasing remark.

My next sin was to walk out of a maths lesson when some formula had not been learned. I had gone round the class, asking each girl in turn, but in vain. The atmosphere was tense. I left the room in silence. The next two lessons didn't happen. The parents were paying a lot of money for me to teach their little dears their mathematical skills, so I'd definitely acted wrongly. However, on my third occasion of not turning up, two of the girls came to see me in a most contrite matter.

"Sir, we're all very, very sorry - will you please come and teach us again?" I yielded to their pleading request. Yes, I was naughty, but it worked wonders!

I used to devise lots of mnemonics to help my maths pupils, just as I did for myself during my own schooldays. Can you decide how the following mnemonic can help? It's for GCSE pupils. Have a go! And here's a clue - the opening word 'sign' is homophonic:

Sign on hospital:
'Can anyone help to operate? Anytime!'

I had a wonderful mnemonic for my A-level pupils: the phrase 'Papa lost in subtropics' solved problem after problem in calculus. Aren't you curious?

Here's a well-known motto: 'If at first you don't succeed, try, try again', but that won't always work in A-level maths. THIS motto works though: 'If at first you don't succeed, try another method!' That's what 'Papa' is all about - it's a mnemonic which gives a list of methods, and is an aid to lateral thinking.

Let's move forward. The A-level exam was the following morning. But during the evening, one of the candidates came to show me a very strange question from a past paper. I was initially a bit uncertain myself, but having solved the thing I had a hunch that I should call the class together. That's exactly what I did, explaining to everyone how to tackle this strange problem. Can you guess what they told me excitedly as they emerged from the exam? That's right, last night's question was on the paper, word for word and number for number! I recalled looking up the word 'skater' before my French exam all those years ago, and reading *The History of Coal Mining in Russia* before my actuarial exam. It was uncanny.

But quite apart from these 'intuitions' which I had from time to time, the girls obtained very good grades, and found A-level maths nearly as exciting as I did. An exam in solving puzzles? Marvellous!

Once I was standing by a Thai princess who was stuck with her calculus. I gave her a few hints, upon which her writing accelerated; suddenly, with arms outstretched, she shouted out a royal "da-DAH!" in triumph, nearly knocking off my glasses! I felt proud to be her maths teacher. You don't 'da-dah' unless you're enjoying yourself!

Skip this paragraph if you don't want to read words relating to maths! Now Mary was certainly no mathematician, and thought I was crazy. "Imaginary numbers? How ridiculous," she would say, "you might as well believe in fairies!" But she picked up all sorts of phrases and could bluff her way through many a mini mathematical conversation. She would refer to Maclaurin's theorem, integration by parts, and the complex cube roots of unity. She would explain that a complex number could be expressed as $z = $ cis q, all in total ignorance. One day, Mary was in my office waiting for me, but there was a delay because I was helping Girl No. 1 with her A-level maths. In comes Girl No. 2 wanting help.

"Oh, just ask my wife, will you?" which she did. Mary 'studied' the question.

"Why not try integration by substitution?" The girl's face lit up - Mary was right! Believe it or not, this same scenario happened once more, a few months later, with Mary giving the correct advice with a different question!

It seemed that I was rising in status at *Murfield*, but I was taken aback when I was offered further promotion as Director of Studies. All at once I had my own office and secretary - all very nice! I continued to teach maths, but only in the Sixth Form, giving me more time for other duties. Suddenly I became a point of reference for staff, girls and parents. Things became more hectic, but my work was even more rewarding.

Sometimes I had to make difficult decisions. The Sixth Formers had a timetabled discussion once a week, on matters spiritual. It was taken by the new chaplain, who was a keen evangelical. From the start I was doubtful about his approach - he tried his best to be 'one of them', but it just didn't work. And when he introduced one of the discussions with "Do you kiss on your first date?" I began to receive complaints, and eventually I made my first decision in my new position - the lessons would be optional in future. Maybe, once more, I was naïve, as I never expected that no one would ever attend again. Oops! I felt a bit frightened by this, and regretted my overreaction.

Mike was certainly a top-notch Economics teacher, and girls often chose his subject as one of their A-levels. However, he always appeared to be quite strict at the start of the course, showing the class who was boss.

"Use your brains," he used to shout, "and think laterally. JUST THINK

LATERALLY!" In other words, think à la Papa! But he would relax after a few weeks of proving the point. One September, just one week into the term, Girl No. 1 came to see me asking me if she could she drop Economics. Then Girl No. 2 came, Girl No. 3, and so it went on. Within two weeks lots more girls had been to see me - some of them in tears. Yes, I did allow girls to drop subjects sometimes, but certainly not after only a couple of weeks. But I was soon to have a surprise - two of the girls came to see me with a present, beautifully wrapped. It was a box of tissues with a card signed by every girl, and by *Mike* himself. It read, 'For drying the tears of all the girls!'

Because of this box of tissues, I thought that *Mike* must have a good a sense of humour, so I decided to ruin his next lesson. I barged into his room, armed with my piano accordion, and a pile of papers on which I'd printed words to fit to a well-known tune:

Oh dear, what can the matter be?
Sir says we've got to think lat'rally.
We say it's two years of agony.
How can we bear it so long?

He promised to teach us and make us so clever.
But as for his lessons, they go on for ever,
And we're just about at the end of our tether!
So how can we bear it so long?

... plus more verses. Papers distributed, we all sang. The girls were delighted when their teacher joined in the fun and laughed, and they all lived happily ever afterwards! And hurrah, they all gained good grades two years later, thanks to *Mike's* excellent teaching!

This wasn't the only time I'd barged into a lesson with my piano accordion. My musical intrusions always seemed to work out well. In fact, I think that every school should have a member of staff with an accordion at the ready, and then use it to ease tensions when necessary!

One year, the Deputy Head Girl kept coming to see me. It seems that the Head Girl and the prefects didn't want her around. She reminded me of myself many years previously - fearful of her peers and not knowing how to cope. I felt an affinity with her, and was glad I had a box of tissues at the ready! My work as 'counsellor' was just as important as other aspects of my work. Maybe more important?

Katie came to see me frequently. She was immensely clever, and rather large. She was also very unpopular and unhappy, hence the need for the tissues once again. The school had monthly assessments, with each girl being given a grade for every subject. These grades were then analysed, and afterwards *John* and I interviewed the good girls and the bad girls, for praise and rebuke. *Katie* was always among the bad girls. She deliberately did badly, in order, in some inverted way, to gain favour with her peers. Mary taught *Katie* piano, and our large *Katie* played well and showed musical feeling - she also used lots of bodily movement, and soon earned herself the nickname 'The Gyrating Hippopotamus'. Poor girl!

Eventually *Katie* entered the Sixth Form, insisting on taking A-levels in all her weaker subjects, as a challenge! She ended up at Oxford.

Jane was a bishop's daughter, a girl who lacked confidence - and certainly there was no dash and daring about her. One day *Mr Swift* sent her to see me during one of his lessons, and I sensed there was trouble.

"Well, what have you done?"

She looked downwards and muttered something, which I asked her to repeat clearly. With head still bowed, she said just one word, very rapidly, "I-let-off-a-stink-bomb-Sir!"

A bishop's daughter letting off a stink bomb - how about that? I didn't react, and so she became more fluent. "You see Sir, the lessons are very boring, and so I thought I'd liven things up." In a way I felt quite proud of her; after all, she wasn't altogether wrong about *Mr Swift*. I admit that my reprimand was mild, but I was so pleased that there was some life in the girl after all. Being sympathetic towards a girl when I'm supposed to be disciplining her is a bit difficult.

I enjoyed having fun in my office, and the 'Magnus' fun is worth recounting. One September, a Sixth Former returned to school from Belfast, bringing me a very large present. It was a photograph of Magnus Magnusson in his brown suit - a life-sized cardboard cutout! Imagine her boarding the plane with Magnus! I wonder why she gave him to me.

I sat at my desk with my back to the window, facing the door at the other end of the room. Magnus stood at my side, and I waited! Soon there was a knock at the door.

"Come in," I shouted, whereupon one of the teachers entered.

Marion looked totally confused and left immediately with the words "Oh, I'm so sorry to disturb you!" I imagined her walking along the corridor and thinking 'That looked just like Magnus Magnusson talking to Geoffrey; surely not!'

That was the first of several quick exits from my office. Magnus remained at my side for a couple of weeks, and I loved every minute of his company! *John* never came into my office during those two weeks, which might have been a good thing!

Soon after this saga, I went into a nearby supermarket and noticed that they were having a clear-out of advertising material. And lo and behold, among various bits of rubbish was a life-sized cardboard cut-out of a beautiful girl in a bikini.

'Wow, you look lovely' I thought, 'I could do with you in my office - you could replace old Magnus!' Perhaps I could find a member of the supermarket staff and ask if I'd be allowed to 'help' them by removing some of their so-called rubbish. Dare I ask? Whatever should I do? I pondered for a while, and then I ...

Quite often, the girls gave me cause for amusement. Wealthy Louise once asked "Don't you mind being poor, Sir?"

And how about this for a conversation stopper? "*Jenny*, you look a bit grumpy; whatever's the matter?" And her reply?

"You'd look a bit grumpy Sir, if you had a period like mine!"

It was this same *Jenny* who knocked at the staffroom door and asked to see Dr *Smith*, who obediently went to the door.

"Sir, is it true that you're having an affair with Dr *Jennifer Jones*?"

"Yes, it is. Now off you go!"

How dare she ask such a personal question! At least Dr *Smith* didn't lie, but wouldn't 'off you go' have been sufficient?

I went to see Daphne, the Head of Art, during one of her Sixth Form lessons. How was I to know that she was using her slide projector at the time? And how was I to know that a painting of a nude woman was projected on to the screen? I quickly looked away, but the effect on the girls caused by my unexpected entry was electric - they gasped and didn't know what to do with themselves in their embarrassment. Meanwhile, I found the whole thing quite entertaining.

Whilst teaching one lesson, I had a continuing sense that someone was standing outside the classroom door. I kept on teaching whilst walking nearer to the door, lowering my voice as I approached (oh what deception!). And then, with dramatic suddenness I opened the door, upon which a startled Angharad fell into the classroom at speed, coming to rest almost at the other side of the room. She had been leaning on the door, listening in. But why?

"It's so that I knew when it was a convenient time to knock, Sir." Mmm!

Morning assembly could be interesting. I 'did' it once a week, and sometimes twice. *John* would say, "I've left the prayer book open at the correct page, just make sure you use it!' He knew I wouldn't. "Do you make up your prayers as you go along, Sir?"

The day came for the Confirmation Service at the nearby Parish Church, which was to take place that evening. *John* had arranged for the girls who were to be confirmed to be at the front of the hall during morning assembly. And of course these special girls needed special prayers, and so the prayer book was open at the ready.

My own attitude to confirmation made me a bit tense, and maybe that's why I was about to have yet another 'green bottle' experience, just like the one I had as a boy, when the whole audience laughed at my downfall. The staff were present, men included, and old Smales blurted out, "And tonight at the service, no one, I repeat NO ONE must wear trousers!" There was uproar! I meant, of course, that the girls must wear skirts.

On another occasion three Sixth Formers were caught sunbathing, completely naked. *John* was intending to 'expose' (!) them at assembly the next morning. Unfortunately he forgot. He forgot? Am I allowed to doubt that? The following morning he was away (most opportune) and of course the task fell to me. No, I did not forget, but I did find an excuse for shelving the matter as I'd heard that there were two other guilty girls, but I couldn't discover who they were. Now would it be fair to chastise only three of them and let the other two get off scot-free?

But it was *John* who personally dealt with the rape incident. I'm glad I didn't have the task of phoning the girl's parents and relating such news. The Sixth Formers had their own ground floor accommodation with individual bedrooms. It was the rule that windows must be closed at night in case of intruders, especially as we were aware at the time that a rapist was 'visiting' girls' boarding schools. It was a hot summer's night, and *Jennifer's* window was wide open. He threatened her with a knife, and then raped her. A few weeks later he was seen leaving a girl's bedroom at Bedstone College in Shropshire - there was a chase across fields, and he was caught. So that was his final attack.

The teaching standard in the school was high, with minor exceptions. The 'stink bomb' teacher was most conscientious and worked hard to help the girls, but he just didn't have the knack, and I felt sad that a stink bomb seemed necessary. The teachers in the Maths Department were all top notch. Bob's lessons were full of fun, and the girls really enjoyed his teaching and made excellent progress.

It was a joy to go into the staff room, and find that much of the conversation centred around the welfare of the girls. And members of staff were very helpful towards me personally, and we always had a good relationship, despite occasional blips.

Once I had a 'little word' with one of the teachers, and although I thought I'd approached her in what I hoped was a gentle manner, she reacted very emotionally. Later that day she collapsed on to the floor whilst invigilating an exam. One of the girls fled from the exam room, knocked frantically on my door, and asked me to come quickly. I completed the invigilation myself, while the teacher recovered in the staff room. I felt certain that my little word was the cause of the problem. Oh dear, was it another 'Princess Majesty' crisis?

I can't leave the subject of teachers without mentioning *Jim*. He was Head of English, and took his Sixth Form class to see a play. During the interval, they went to the bar, where all the girls managed to get a drink, although some of them were underage, but *Jim* was refused because of his youthful appearance.

"Never mind, Sir, we'll get a drink for you!" Soon after this event *Jim* grew a fluffy beard. Poor fellow!

Pat was a wonderful secretary. I used a cassette tape recorder to dictate my letters to her, but I tended to include some light-hearted comments, just for Pat's ears. There were occasions when she popped into my room, holding a letter she had already typed, and pointing to one of the paragraphs she would say, "Do you think we should say this, or shall we soften it a little?" And she was always right. Thank you Pat!

One of the teachers asked me to lend her a recording of a certain sermon. She took it to her midweek church meeting, and after a hymn-reading-prayer sort of thing, it was played. Alas I'd given her the wrong recording - it was my dictated letters to Pat, complete with silly comments. I'll say no more!

Each time a parent-staff meeting took place, I had a long queue of parents waiting to see me. Mine was always the longest queue by far, simply because I dealt with ALL the pupils in the school, and the girls persisted in telling their parents to be sure to see me. Each dad had a name-tag pinned to his lapel and each mum had a tag pinned elsewhere. But quite frequently only Mummy came to see me, and I was forever staring at bosoms - merely for identification purposes, of course!

Daughter Margaret spent three years at *Murfield* as a daygirl - two years in the lower classes, and then a further year in the Sixth Form (half fees for staff daughters). It didn't really work out in the Sixth Form as she had a growing concern for folk who were needy rather that wealthy.

It was Parents' Weekend, with people everywhere, and a couple of helicopters in the car park! I was in my office in academic dress, with the staff procession almost ready to begin. That's the very moment when a member of staff came to see me in some panic.

"We've got to do something quickly," he said, "your daughter has brought two strange-looking boys with her, and also a big black dog, and she says you'd given her permission to bring them!" Oh dear, of course I hadn't.

There was very little time left for me to deal with the matter. However, I asked the boys to come and see me, plus black dog, and decided to let them stay, despite their inappropriate appearance. They were no trouble. If I had declined, what would have happened? Oh blessed pragmatism!

The timetable was my responsibility - it took me all the summer holidays to construct, with each girl having a separate and distinct programme. Come every September I almost dreaded the first week, waiting for a knock at my door, and wondering whether I'd made any serious mistakes. Maybe a teacher would appear,

"I'm supposed to be teaching French, but there's a geography lesson going on in my room!"

A girl by the name of *M Johnson* came to see me. "Sir, I'm down for ballet during my maths lesson!" Oops, another bloomer! Oh dear, there were TWO girls by the name of *M Johnson* - hence my mistake. So I had to give *M for Megan* a maths lesson on a one-to-one basis once a week for the whole year! Her sister was *M for Moira*. Oh parents, why can't you choose less confusing names?

M for Moira's dad *Donald* came to see me quite often, with requests for 'impossibles' for *Moira*. Once he asked me to arrange for her to take thirteen O-levels in the same year. I had to say 'No'.

His face was a picture:
'You say NO to me?
I say what happens,
And you just agree!

I know my own daughter,
I know what is best,
I've made my decision -
Now sort out the rest!'

Oh dear, there was tension -
Many a frown, many a glower,
As we battled it out
For over an hour!

But at the end of an hour,
He said, 'Well, just at a pinch
I suppose I could yield
Perhaps half of an inch!'

... well, something like that! Discussion with *Donald* was never easy - nevertheless we became good friends, despite our different views about education, and also about God for that matter.

When *Moira* went to university she had a Lesbian partner. This caused Dad intense anguish, and long after I left *Murfield*, he would phone me in a state of despair and summons me to come to have a chat. 'Whatever have I done to deserve this?' he would ask. But I digress.

Life at *Murfield* was enjoyable, though extremely hectic. On a few occasions I dared to take a day off 'sick' in order to catch up with my work. But I was taken aback when three Sixth Formers came to see me, telling me that they didn't want to interfere, but as I seemed to be so busy, were there any little jobs they could do to help me? Wow, that was something! But I had to turn down their offer.

One September, the whole staff came to my rescue. I had been at school for the first week of the autumn term, and I'd checked that the timetable was working correctly. But then a couple of members of staff went to see *John*, on behalf of all the others, and requested that I should be given a week's holiday immediately.

It had been an unbelievably hectic summer holiday, what with the timetabling day after day, and often late into the night, going to school to dictate letters, and so on. So off I went for a week's holiday whilst all the others worked hard! I even climbed Snowdon - by train, and sent the staff a postcard!

Nearly every time I went to see *John* in his office, the visit was cut short by the use of his 'magic words', causing me to leave with haste. He had a phenomenal ability at cutting short any interview.

The day came when *John* was ill. Soon he was in hospital, having a brain tumour removed. Mary and I travelled quite a distance in order to visit him, but no sooner had we arrived at his bedside than he uttered his magic words once more - and off we went!

John was away from school for many months, during which time I took over many of his responsibilities. He returned, and apart from wearing a cap, he was back to normal. There was a hushed atmosphere of deep respect when he first took assembly with no cap, and no hair.

This miscellany of my day-by-day experiences which I've recounted is but a sample. My involvement with parents, girls and staff had grown over my seventeen years at the school, but towards the end of this period, things began to go a little bit pear-shaped.

The fact that people tended to see me so often seemed to me to be perfectly understandable. After all, I was the one who dealt with the nitty-gritty of the place. Nevertheless I don't think it was all that easy for *John*, and some tension began to develop between us. And before long there was something much more than tension - it was the day the axe fell.

That day, the Head and I, plus two other members of staff, were to interview candidates for the vacant position of Head of Religious Studies. It was the custom for two Sixth Formers to take 'prospectives' round the school and generally to put them in the picture. So far so good.

The candidates came into the interview room one by one, and after a few hours we came to the last candidate. Towards the end of the interview, *John* asked whether the fellow had any questions. There was an immediate reply.

"Yes, just one," he said, "who's Mr Smales?" I could feel the tension rising and almost reaching breaking point. I pointed to myself, whilst *John* asked a severe and clipped "Why do you want to know that?"

The man's answer was my death knell. "Because I asked the girls who they preferred to take assembly, and they said it was Mr Smales…" There was stunned silence. But eventually the fellow continued, "because the girls said that Mr Smales doesn't talk down to them!' Well, that made things even worse.

I felt to be in a very awkward situation, to say the least, and I instantly remembered how Father Christmas had dragged me down at a previous school. This man's one comment was lethal. His few words caused my downfall. Not surprisingly, his words also caused his own downfall.

The following day I asked Pat to bring me my letters to sign. She looked worried, and said "There's a bit of a problem!" It seems that *John* had asked to read my letters! Soon *John* came to see me in my office and tore them up in front of me, because they were 'totally unsuitable'.

From this point onwards all my letters were intercepted by the Head, and ALL were rejected. My authority had suddenly gone. My fall at the Wilson Stuart School was slow, but this was immediate. I had come face to face with another roadblock, and I felt I had no option but to resign.

However, despite the tension and the disagreement, I looked to *John* with much respect - after all, he had supported me to the full for many years. He'd also done so much for the school, and *Murfield* was without doubt a much better school as a result of his headship.

But things can change, sometimes with startling suddenness, and soon after I left *Murfield, John's* reign at the school came to an abrupt and dramatic end. Who would have expected that?

I loved my work and I missed it greatly. But my biggest wrench was leaving the Lower Sixth maths group half way through their course. The girls gave me a lovely card, made by Bella, with a personal 'thank you' message from each of them. I found this gesture very touching, and it softened my fall. Mind you, Bella's imagination seemed to have run riot, as I never found retirement to be as she depicted on her card.

A rise, and then a fall? Just pause and look around for a moment - it happens to nations, it happens to governments, it happens to businesses, it happens to churches, it happens to pastors of churches, it happens to marriages. It just happened to happen to me - once more! But life must go on.

A rise? That's fine,
It makes me proud.
A fall? It hurts,
I cry aloud.

But that is life,
With ups and downs,
With joy and strife,
With chains or crowns.

So up I get,
Whatever will,
And let me climb
Another hill.

Yes, there is hope,
Pursue the quest.
It's not the end -
It's just a rest.

As I stand up again and pursue the quest, I must remember that I'm not alone, that the Lord is with me. 'His rod and His staff they comfort me.' (Psalm 23)

The card from the First Year Sixth on my retirement. The artist is Bella

Mary and Julia

Richard the Pianist. One of Geoffrey's pupils

Richard the Violinist with Mary and Julia. This was at an outdoor music event in period dress, in support of keeping the local hospital open

Chapter 13

3,002 Sermons

Life had been hectic at *Murfield* for the last seventeen years, but concurrent with all this was my other hectic life - the non-*Murfield* bit. But come to think of it, maybe it was a bit more than a bit!

When we first came to Shropshire, Andrew was six, and Margaret was four. They both settled well, though they always regarded Ackhill as home.

Soon after our arrival at our new house, Andrew went missing. We were extremely worried and searched up and down our road, and adjoining roads, but in vain. Shall we contact the Police? Whilst asking ourselves this question, a little boy appeared in the distance. Yes, it was Andrew, clutching a huge toy panda, and as the boy drew nearer, we saw he was wearing an equally huge smile. It seems he'd walked into the town, crossed the busy main road on his own, and walked into the Parish Church where a jumble sale was in progress. He'd bought himself a raffle ticket, and won first prize! Annoo-do-it had done it again, all on his own. He was in high spirits. An hour later Annoo and Panda were tucked up in bed. So were we cross with him?

Unfortunately, within days of starting teaching at *Murfield School*, Margaret developed scarlet fever, which caused the doctor to insist that Dad and Daughter should not go to school. And so I had a two-week absence from *Murfield* - not a good start to my new teaching career!

After Ackhill, I'd hoped that before long I'd be called to be a minister of another church, maybe one that was independent. Although there were a few invitations to preach at churches without a pastor, they were all at some distance, and because of my school involvements, it was difficult to fit in these visits. This barrier was very puzzling to me - what about my 'calling'?

Mary and I began attending an evangelical church in Shropshire, and in a matter of weeks, it seemed that the Lord was dealing with my 'call' in an unexpected way. Suddenly it all began to happen. I preached at the church, and afterwards everyone was full of praise. It was extreme praise, it was quite unreal, and I was completely dumbfounded. But this one sermon set off a whole series of events which soon led me into troubled waters.

Now, during my life many accusations have been made against me, but I have also received praise from time to time. But this particular sermon gave me my ultimate acclaim. I was then invited to the manse, where I met the minister and the elders.

"You're the Bible teacher we've been praying should come!" And because of my 'amazing' sermon I was asked to start a mid-week Bible Study in our home. That was an opportunity I could not miss, and so I agreed. Then there was a time of prayer, with the elders asking the Lord to prosper this new work. And off I went in a daze.

Quite a few people came to the first house meeting, which was encouraging. And after a few weeks, some of the physiotherapy students from the local Orthopaedic Hospital began attending, bringing others with them. Among the others was *Jean the Extrovert,* and also *Danny the Unpredictable* who suffered from cerebral palsy, and whose speech was extremely difficult to understand. He was yet to feature in our lives to a great extent.

As the numbers attending grew, we had a problem with seating. However, we happened to pass a nearby school where stacking chairs had been dumped in a corner of the car park, awaiting the skip. I made an enquiry, and these chairs were readily given to us. So now we had ample seating capacity, and easy storage.

So far in my life I have preached sermons galore without any hitch - well, apart from two of them, which I've previously mentioned. The first hitch was at Winchcombe, causing my excommunication, and the second was at Bleddfa, lasting for three minutes, and was the sermon that caused me to be sacked. But sadly, I was soon to preach another sermon, and one which had devastating results.

It all happened when I next preached at the church. I well remember my text - it was 'for many are called' (Matthew, chapter 22). The reaction was beyond belief. This time my sermon was regarded by many as highly controversial. It was said by some that my preaching was contrary to the teaching of the Bible. It was clear that I was in deep trouble. The chasm of contrast between the reactions to my two sermons seemed absurd.

It was all the more baffling, because I had said nothing knowingly outside normal evangelical belief. Admittedly, the text goes on to say, 'but few are chosen', and those words do give rise to different interpretations, but I deliberately omitted that part of the verse from my sermon, in order to steer clear of controversy. A good intention, but it failed!

In my Ackhill days, a serious problem had arisen when someone preached a sermon at the Baptist Annual Assembly, a sermon which was regarded by many as heretical, causing me to resign from Ackhill. Maybe Michael Taylor had preached 10,000 sermons - far more than I'd ever preached, but only caused trouble with one. He was the highly respected Principal of the Northern Baptist College, but he was vilified because of this one sermon.

Imagine Taylor looking around afterwards, and seeing all the turmoil he'd caused! He must have gazed in astonishment and dismay when more than a hundred ministers resigned because of his words. But at least I think he could see why all the trouble had arisen, whereas I had not the slightest idea why my sermon had caused trouble, or why so many folk were against me.

Whilst living in Shropshire I must have preached about 3,000 sermons - well, 3,000 plus 2. The first plus was my wonderful sermon, my famous sermon - and the second plus was my notorious sermon, one which caused havoc, bringing about widespread suspicion of me.

Anyway, the house meetings had started, and those folk who were attending asked me to continue, and so I did. After all, we had received no instructions from the church to close the meetings, and we felt that in reality it was the Lord who had instigated the meetings in the first place, and so who were we to stop them? After several months it was agreed among ourselves that I should start a Sunday afternoon meeting, in addition to the midweek meeting. An afternoon was chosen purposely so that everyone who came to our Sunday meeting was free to go the church services at other times, but no one ever did.

For years, accusations kept coming. Folk were warned not to visit us. Some said I was a false prophet. It was spread around that I forbade the women who came to the meeting to go to the hairdressers! Why anybody should think this is difficult to understand, and I felt utterly bewildered, for the fiftieth time in my life!

My notoriety spread far and wide! I'd spotted a notice in the local newspaper - an open invitation to a meeting in the Anglican Church on the subject of creation, so I thought I'd attend, only to be met at the door by Father Edge who said, "We don't want you here" (familiar words), and he forbade me to enter. He gave me no explanation - merely a command to depart. So that became bewilderment No. 51!

Now and again, one of the church elders came to our meeting - a kind of spy, I thought. It was reported back that I'd said nothing wrong, but that my sermons were way above the heads of the young people. If that's the case, why did so many young people come? And if I'd said nothing wrong why did the accusations continue?

Mind you, accusations were not unknown to me. In an earlier chapter, writing about my Head Teacher's serious allegation, I said that "her accusation was often repeated, but I ignored it, and things just went on as normal. It was like hearing an ugly discord from time to time, a nasty buzz in my ears, and then it was quiet again." Well, my preaching just went on as normal, and I preached in many other churches in the area, all without mishap! I put the nasty buzz in a soundproof room, and just got on with life.

From the title 'the Bible teacher we've been praying should come', to the title 'false prophet' was a big and baffling fall - it hurt!

But I have also experienced some amusing lesser falls in my life: I always moved around in the pulpit when I preached, and once I fell down the pulpit stairs in the middle of the sermon, making a total fool of myself once again. It was a jolly big fall too - that's because the pulpit was more like a high tower! Falling down at the wrong time is well known to me; that fifth green bottle still seems to haunt me!

We were having a camping holiday in Powys, and come the Sunday morning, I was booked to preach in the big church in Newtown. Bathroom facilities were minimal on the camping site and maybe that why I'd put my toothbrush in my breast pocket - where else could I put it? After the service I was asked to preach on another date, so I took out my 'pen' to make a note of the date, but it was my toothbrush! It had been sticking out of my pocket during the service, brush upwards!

Back to the house meetings, most of the folk who came were keen evangelicals, and were very helpful and supportive. Even some of the girls from *Murfield* came to the meetings - until the Head put his foot down! Amongst the others was Bunty from Ackhill, who had by now retired and come to live in near us. One day I explained in a sermon that I was not the possessor of absolute truth, and that despite all my studying, there must be times when I get things wrong. Bunty had a strong word with me afterwards.

"When have you been wrong?" she asked, "because if you'd been wrong, I'd have told you!" Strangely enough, she had 'told me' at Ackhill several times.

Bunty's strong beliefs had become universal truths by which everybody else was judged. Bunty was a kind and helpful lady, one who endeavoured to live according to Biblical teaching. She was not an arrogant person, even though she was always right! It's good to meet someone with strong beliefs, but I am saddened when their absolute certainty becomes a point of reference by which all others are judged.

Sam was renowned for his dogmatic Biblical views, and once after I'd preached at his church, and while puffing away on his pipe, he said to me "I have to admit that I can't actually find any error in your sermon!" It seemed to me to be a reluctant admission.

I've already mentioned *Jean the Extrovert*, with her beautiful jet-black hair. She was in her thirties when she first came to the meetings. Not an intellectual, to put it mildly, though she was a very nice person. After the meeting we always had a cuppa, and she used to entertain our children, drawing pictures for them with great expertise. Her English gave us cause to smile.

"I slept like a rocket," she would say, "he shut up like a clock," "I bought some semi-skilled milk," or, "my sister's exhaustion pipe fell off," and so on.

Jean was a cleaner at the local Hospital, and her cleaning was always of the highest standard. One day, a surgeon saw her in the corridor, and took the opportunity to give her a word of encouragement - the conversation left the poor man somewhat bemused. Here's the gist of it:

"Your cleaning is just perfect, Jean."
"Oh no, I haven't done it."
"Who did it then? Was it the Queen?"
"Oh no, the Lord - He's done it!"

She was forever telling us all how the Lord helped her in her life.

But *Jean* was quite an enigma. Once she didn't come to the Sunday afternoon meeting, but remained outside. We saw her through the window swinging round a lamp post!

Now, how we came to have a very nice tramp coming to many of the meetings I can't remember. At first *Maurice* was living rough, but then the local vicar allowed him, along with two others, to sleep in his garage. This hospitality went on for many months, but the day came when *Maurice* decided (for reasons which perhaps no psychiatrist can explain) to set fire to the garage, thus losing his accommodation. He tried to get into trouble with the Police, hoping to sleep in a cell. He did this by getting himself drunk, then going to the Police Station, just across the road from where we lived, and behaving threateningly. His attempt failed. So he crossed the road and knocked at our door. There he was on the doorstep, drunk, abusive, and asking for a bed. I refused.

Mary was in the bath at the time, but she overheard *Maurice*'s shouting, got dressed at speed, and ran over to the Police Station via the back door. A policeman came across straight away, upon which *Maurice* pointed to me and yelled, "He calls himself a Christian, but he won't help me!" The policeman then took him by car, depositing him at his sister's house.

Before the end of the week *Maurice* had got himself into the headlines of the local newspaper by jumping to his death from Pontcysyllte Viaduct, near Llangollen. This isn't the only time in my life that I've questioned myself after a suicide. What if...?

'If' is a very big word. If I went my own way, if I did my own thing, if I kept clear of folk with problems, if I shrugged my shoulders more often, if I hid myself under the duvet, if, if, if ... then I myself would have fewer problems, confrontations and accusations. If it isn't *Maurice*, then it's *Danny*. And if it isn't *Danny*, then it's someone else. But these people are all needy people, and needy people need people!

Mind you, these days, as I write this book in my eighties, I seem to have fewer 'people' problems to face. Is that good or bad?

Anyway, what can I say about *Danny*? When he first came to the meetings he was eighteen, and he was obviously a troubled boy. His parents had abandoned him when he was born, and he was brought up in various institutions, during which time both his parents were killed in a car crash. *Danny* was a student at a residential college for young disabled teenagers with learning difficulties.

He became friendly with the young ladies who came to the meeting, all of whom were physiotherapy students. These girls lived in a large mansion divided into flats, with *Jean* living in a caravan in the grounds. Our *Danny* was much helped by visiting them, but he wouldn't leave! We sometimes had a phone call from the girls, late at night, asking us to remove *Danny* and return him to the college! He was without doubt a difficult boy, quite unpredictable, and there were always lurking fears in our minds - what will he do next, and how safe are we in his presence?

Meet Annie - she was one of the students who came to the meetings. One Sunday, Annie and I went to pick up *Danny* from the college, but he was nowhere to be found. We walked down corridor after corridor, opening doors and peeping in.

"Let's try this door," she said. There was no sign on the door to indicate that this was the Gents, but there were a few boys inside, doing what boys have to do - so it must have been the Gents! One boy was facing us with the cubicle door wide open. Annie took the initiative, walked straight into the Gents, and asked "Does anyone know where we can find *Danny?*" Meanwhile Annie never even noticed what the boys were doing, and had no awareness that she'd visited the Gents. Neither did the loud guffaws that issued from the Gents just after we'd left make any impression on her.

Danny always listened to my preaching intently, and though his speech was very difficult to understand, he would often quote what I'd said.

But a problem arose. The college had arranged for *Danny* to have his summer holiday at a residential home for the elderly! *Danny* was none too pleased about this, and nor was I. It seemed to me that I should step in and try to help in some way. Now we knew of a place in South Wales by the name of Ty Brasil, which gave missionaries and other folk in need, a free holiday. It wasn't specifically for young people, but for all ages. As it happened, I knew the owner (he had preached at Ackhill), so I phoned him, and he agreed to take *Danny* for two weeks, but it was conditional on his good behaviour.

The next step was to see the Principal of the college, who told me in no uncertain terms to buzz off. Yes, it is true, I was interfering, but I thought rightly so. I took the matter further and contacted a solicitor who told me there was no legal reason why I should not proceed, and so I did. The Principal lost the battle, and the arrangements went ahead. Various folk gave me money, and we were able to send a gift to Ty Brasil. And so the day came when Mary and I took *Danny* to South Wales and left him there. They treated him well, even buying the lad some new clothes. Nevertheless, three days later I received a phone call to say *Danny* could stay no longer as he'd been causing some trouble with the girls in the kitchen. So we brought him back. I was cross, and admit that the journey was a silent one!

I daren't let *Danny* stay at our house for the night, for our children's safety. So I had to dare to return him to the college. But first he came home for a meal, after which he did a runner. This was frightening - how safe was he? The Police helped in the search, but in the end I found him, as I had the advantage of knowing a few of his haunts. To cut a long story short, I got him back to the college, knowing that my plan had turned into failure, and feeling I could hardly face the Principal, who was now the final victor.

Soon after this event I learned that *Danny* had been attacking me by means of voodoo, as he was angry with me about his failed holiday. He'd used the pink pins of death - but here I am today, unhurt!

Well, things got back to normal, and *Danny* continued coming to the meetings, still listening intently. That went on without a hitch for the next few weeks. But then one Sunday afternoon we were all standing, singing a hymn, when he suddenly went into a storm of madness. He threw his hymnbook on the floor and shouted abuse. Every word could be clearly heard. When he talked to our cat every word could be heard, likewise when he was angry. I told everyone to sit down, and he and I stood for a very, very long time. He shouted. He threatened. "I'm a communist, and we'll come and get you!"

I fixed my eyes on him for ages. What tension! But suddenly his strength left him, and he sat down and whispered meekly "You can carry on with the meeting now."

Carry on with the meeting? Not easily done under the circumstances. I remember that we didn't sing again. I shelved my sermon, turned to Psalm 91, and just made a few brief comments about it. And that was that.

I reported *Danny's* behaviour to the Principal, knowing full well that I was an unwelcome visitor. He was a big man, and he grabbed hold of me and threw me out of his office, saying he wanted nothing to do with me, and that it was my Christianity which had caused all the trouble, and not *Danny*! A few weeks after this, our troubled *Danny* was expelled from the college, having wrecked a bus shelter!

He went to live in Banbury, and phoned me from time to time. He'd found someone there who was willing to help him, which was a good thing. The phone call would always begin by the fellow in whose house he was, explaining to me what *Danny* was about to tell me, as I would merely gain a rough idea if only *Danny* had spoken. The gist of his comment was often about the preaching he was hearing. "It's rubbish," he used to say. There was no give and take in his views.

As for the students who brought *Danny* along in the first place, they continued to be a great encouragement. We remember two of them in particular - Ann and Jackie. It wasn't long before they came to know Val, and all three of them eventually went to live in Minsterley, and when problems began to accrue in their lives, they became a mutual help to each other. We are pleased that we still see this threesome, and can talk to them so freely. We call them 'The Girls' despite their present age!

Over the years we have known Val so well that Wizzy and I used to call her Wizlet!

But back to the meetings, I could go on and on, describing all the folk who came, and how supportive they were. I took the wedding service for one of the students. Then there was Joyce and Irmgard (two of the older ladies) who asked to be baptised - we used the swimming pool at *Murfield*. *Paul* came week after week, but suddenly stopped attending, because "if I continue, I think I might believe!" So he 'ran away'.

Our children came to the Sunday meetings for many years, but the day came when they chose to go their own way, and we did not try to persuade them otherwise.

It was a joy when *Raymond* began attending, but there's quite a history behind this. Whilst living at Ackhill we visited a swimming pool in Shrewsbury, where I sat watching Mary and the children swimming. There was nothing noteworthy about this visit. However, a couple of years later, having moved to Shropshire, a man greeted me in the town:

'Whoever's this?' I wondered. He seemed to be a complete stranger to me. It seems that he and his wife and children were also in the pool on that particular day, and he had noticed me, and said to his wife, "That man over there is a Christian," and he'd still remembered me - it was uncanny.

We soon discovered that we were both evangelicals, and we visited each other several times in the next few months. But then came a shock when I went to see him the next time: he told me quite politely that he was not going to allow me into the house, because of my erroneous views on the Second Coming. Oh dear, here we go again!

So that was that! We didn't see each other again for well over a year. So I was pleased when he phoned one day, asking me if I would help his daughter with her maths! And believe it or not, soon after that he asked if he'd be 'allowed' to come to our meetings. He proved to be a big help, even preaching a few times, though I admit I was disappointed when he preached his own views on the Second Coming, when my views, of course, were right!

Different views on the second coming do lead to a few problems. Irmgard listened to me week by week, and she also listened to an evangelical programme on Radio Luxemburg. I asked her how she coped with listening to different viewpoints on the second coming. Her answer was an example to us all; listen to her words:

"That's no problem Geoffrey. When the Lord returns, if He says 'Be quick Irmgard, we're off to heaven now,' I'll go; but if He says 'Hold on Irmgard, we've got another thousand years down here,' then I'll stay!" Those two viewpoints are not the only ones taught by those who seek to understand the teaching of the Bible - different views abound!

I invited several others to preach from time to time, including the mathematician Kyriacos, who came along with his wife Brenda. A mathematician as a friend? Wonderful! He was bold in his preaching, and his sermons were much appreciated. He told us of the time when he went to a Pentecostal meeting, at the end of which the evangelist urged folk to come forward for healing. Well, Kyriacos went forward, but he turned down the offer of laying on of hands, as he'd gone to the front merely to ask one simple question: "So why are you wearing glasses?" Maybe this time his boldness wasn't appreciated quite as much! But he had a point, don't you think?

As already mentioned Dad lived for his work, but after he retired, the motive to live all but disappeared. Soon he suffered a series of strokes, after which Mam and Dad just sat on the settee holding hands and staring into space, with hardly a word passing between them. It was a distressing sight. A few years later Dad had a heart attack and died, aged 74. That was the week we were enjoying our camping holiday in Betws-y-Coed, which came to an abrupt end.

Dad left £500 to me, and the remainder to Mam, but it was many years later that Mam told me that when Dad died there was only £500 in his account, all of which came to me, leaving my mother with nothing. Dad had never had to wait before he could afford to buy something, as he had a good salary. But what my mother didn't know until long after he'd died was that ALL his spare money had been spent in buying more and more shares in the Britannic Assurance Company for which he worked. This addictive buying of shares was to further his hope of becoming a director, which never happened anyway. Neither had he taken out any life insurance. Fortunately, Mam received a third of Dad's pension, and continues to receive it forty years after his death! Years later these shares suddenly rocketed to a huge value, and Mam could have sold them for nearly £1,000,000, but she didn't know this. And only a few years later these shares plummeted dramatically and became of little value.

After Dad died, Mam never bothered to make meals. For the next thirty years, she lived on coffee and chocolate biscuits, plus a piece of cooked chicken from the local supermarket once a week. She ate chocolates galore, but no fruit, no vegetables, nothing! Her cooker was never used, and neither were Mary and I allowed to use it when we visited her, in case we got the thing dirty! Her friends pleaded with me to do something about the situation.

"Geoffrey, if your mum gets an infection, she'll have no strength to withstand it." These advisors have long since died, but Mam goes on for ever!

Meanwhile Mam enjoyed her chocolates galore, and even started doing crosswords. Up to the age of ninety-nine she frequently shopped for poorly neighbours, bringing back 'proper' food for others!

Well, let's get back to our own home. Val came to visit us from time to time, along with her mother and thirty-six toilet rolls - yes, always thirty-six! Her mum was a lady of extremes, whether it was alcohol or hygiene. She was hygienic to the point of mania, especially when she sat on the 'throne', consuming roll after roll! She never locked the door, and so the occasion arose when I went in and found her enthroned.

"Come in, Duck, and have a little chat with me!"

On one of Val's visits (after I'd left *Murfield* and begun teaching privately), we had a visit from *Danny*, completely out of the blue. He had travelled from Banbury by taxi, a journey of a hundred miles! I was teaching piano at the time, and Mary was out. So poor old Val had to entertain him, unaided. Fortunately (?) *Danny* soon became irate, which meant that he could now be understood! He was telling Val that she was not interpreting the Bible correctly. What a fellow!

Oh, and then there's the young lady who we knew from our

Birmingham days. She was the friend of one of the young people who used to come to our children's meetings. When we were at Ackhill she often visited us for weekends, and we got on like a house on fire. But sometimes we were wakened in the middle of the night when she had one of her panic attacks. We'd find her lying on the floor, shouting "I'm dying!" She was a young lady who was very concerned about folk with problems and was always wanting to help them. Nothing was ever too much trouble for her.

She also visited us in our house in Shropshire, and on one visit she met *Danny*, and just longed to help him, but unfortunately she always expected me to be the interpreter. *Danny* would say a few words, and then I would give him a reassuring 'yes', which certainly didn't mean that I'd understood him, but she never seemed to believe that I hadn't grasped his meaning, and was forever asking me "What did he say?" I was then forced to own up and reply, "I don't know!" Oh dear, that was no help to *Danny*!

Eventually I took her wedding service at a church in Walsall. It was quite a family affair as Mary was the organist, Margaret one of the bridesmaids, Andrew an usher, with little me at the front!

Soon they had a son. As a toddler, Tim had a Teddy, and Tim invented a rather peculiar name for his cuddly friend. This invented name caused Mum and Dad a great deal of distress. Surely Tim had never heard this word before, so where had it come from? They tried to veer him away from this offensive name, but it was all in vain. Eventually Mum and Dad conceded defeat and told their son that the invented name was OK.

"But Tim, you must learn to say it properly." And so it was that throughout Tim's early childhood, he always addressed his Teddy with precise and deliberate articulation as Boo-Gar!

Out of the blue, someone we knew from years ago contacted us, asking to visit us for a week - but she stayed for two months! We'd met her at the Elim College. It seems that at last "I've found someone who cares," she would say "and I feel at home with you!"

We had a mini crisis at one of our house meetings, whilst this lady was with us. At the end of the meeting, she went into the kitchen and made cups of tea for us all. She left the room, closing the door behind her, but when she eventually returned, she couldn't open the door, and neither could we at our side. Forget the tea, how do we get out of here? We considered various options, including climbing out of the window, but some of the folk were not too nimble, and there was quite a drop anyway. We could force the door open, of course, but that would probably have to be done by our tea lady as the door opened inwards, so we ruled out that option. Ah, perhaps our tea lady could find some tools and hand them to me through the window. At long last I received a hefty screwdriver and prised the door open, with splinters of wood flying all over the place!

Despite her eagerness to help on that evening of captivity, her visit wasn't without problems - she began behaving rather oddly, and causing Andrew and Margaret (who were still quite young) to be fearful of her. Maybe I was very naughty, but one evening I followed her when she left the house, and discovered she was pub crawling. I felt worried, and phoned her minister who told me she had long-standing alcohol problems.

We now understood why she felt at home with us - it was a fresh start for her, with folk who didn't know her background. But in the end I asked her to leave - a decision which I found difficult to make, but one which had to be made for the children's sake. A few years later she emerged from her tunnel, and now she is busy in her church doing work with children. Beginnings don't determine endings!

Oh yes, children! What a time we had with our two rebels as they went through their teens! Fortunately they got on well with each other, despite their vastly different temperaments.

Margaret reminded me recently that I taught her to play chess. Apparently I taught Andrew as well. But I certainly remember teaching Mary, and although I didn't intend to win our first game, I accidentally won after only about six moves. I told her I was very sorry, but she's refused to play with me ever since!

Mary taught Andrew to play the piano, but for two or three weeks only. His understanding of music notation was immediate, and it was quite baffling to us, so much so that we began to wonder whether he'd had a secret teacher beforehand! After his first two or three lessons he declared "I understand music now, so I don't need any more help!" And that was the end of his music career. I think he would have turned out to be a one-sided pianist - he'd have left Mr Bach and his contemporaries to their own devices, and just revelled in emotional, turbulent music - fortissimo, bravura, and all that! But we'll never know. However, surprise, surprise, when he listens to music, he sometimes turns to Mr Bach. He claims that Bach's music is like singing without taking any breaths!

I taught Margaret to play the piano, and she proved to be a most competent and musical pianist, climbing through the grades quite quickly. I felt really proud of her. She was also a good violinist, and even dabbled with the oboe!

Soon, Margaret joined the school orchestra. Off to school she went each Wednesday morning, armed with her violin. She came back late due to the after-school rehearsals, and now and then she would relate the news of some incident during the rehearsal. However, the day came when the orchestra gave a concert, and so Mum and Dad attended. But when the members of the orchestra came in to take their positions, there was no

Margaret to be seen. It turned out that she hadn't been to Wednesday rehearsals for months, and now at last, her sin was discovered! So, I wondered, where's my pride now? Oh, teenagers!

In her mid-teens, Margaret exhibited a few strange mental absences and had some unexplained falls. Our doctor felt certain that some form of epilepsy was the cause, and arranged for her to see a consultant. Unfortunately the consultant was most unsympathetic, and without even examining her, simply declared that we as parents were wasting his time, and that we'd better deal with our daughter in a firmer manner. Our doctor was furious.

Some weeks later, Margaret went to see the doctor because of an abscess on her leg. The doctor unexpectedly phoned us. "I've got good news for you," he said, "your daughter has just had a major epileptic fit whilst in the surgery!" And then he added "so now we know!" In a sense it really was good news, because soon she was in hospital having an EEG and other tests.

Having arrived at the hospital, Mary was worried about Margaret's fear of injections, and became excessively tense because of her concern, and that's possibly why she suddenly passed out in the corridor. Soon Mary was surrounded by nurses, and got far more fuss than Margaret! As for the official patient, Margaret was dealt with sympathetically, and was soon under treatment, though the problem did prevent her from driving for many years.

Andrew and Margaret were good at teasing us. Mary and I like weak tea, so one day our two naughty children offered to make us a cuppa. We thanked them, enjoyed our drink, only to discover many years later that they'd giving us boiling water, plus a little milk and a tiny speck of gravy browning. They probably knew about my own sin when I used this same method to give Bunty some strong tea.

Andrew was a businessman and entrepreneur par excellence. When the children were small, I would go into a shop to buy sweets for them both. Margaret happily accepted them, whereas Andrew would say "Can I have the money instead, please?" Oh Annoo! As a teenager, Andrew manufactured diaries. He made display boxes for them, holding twenty diaries per box, and then sold them to newsagents in the area. And still as a teenager, he persuaded a coach company to use his services, and organised skiing holidays in Scotland and Switzerland. He enjoyed checking out the various hotels, spending several days at each - with nothing to pay!

The stories of teenage Andrew would make a book in its own right. Not least of his exploits was when he climbed to the top of a large gasometer, taking photographs from the top as proof.

Andrew gained good grades with his thirteen O-levels, and then studied maths, computer science and photography for his A-levels. However, one week before the exams were to be taken he went to America, as he'd been accepted to teach photography in a youth camp! We let it all happen without demur! Upon his return, he set up an accommodation agency by the name of National Homesearch. How he dared to include the word 'National' I will never know, but that's Annoo-do-it once again!

Meanwhile Margaret was busy with her boyfriends! Mary and I learnt a lot through all her friendships. We learnt that there is 'good' to be found in the most unlikely people. Most of Margaret's friends were not (dare I say it?) in the upper crust of society. Wayne's mum and dad were often drunk, and his dad was sometimes in prison. His mum died whilst drunk, falling to her death down a flight of concrete steps. So Wayne's background was not the best. He was nowhere academically, but when he came on holiday with us on two occasions, we discovered that he was a caring and intelligent boy, but he was one who had never had a chance. Sad to say, Wayne himself was soon in prison. But for Margaret, we would probably have thought that there would be little to say in praise of all these lads.

When Margaret was nineteen, she gave birth to a beautiful baby girl. Mary and I just had to come to terms with this new situation, which we did. It was a time of considerable emotion for us all, but especially for Margaret who had a big decision to make, but eventually she had her baby adopted - a decision which caused her much heartache in years to come.

I must say that Margaret's relationships were often rather turbulent, but eventually all turned out well, as we shall see in a later chapter.

Andrew and Margaret's friends were in different camps. Margaret always had a leaning towards, and a concern for those in need, whereas Andrew was forever making friends in high places, and persuading millionaires to support him in his enterprises. Not that Andrew was lacking in concern for others, but his general orientation was upwards.

We'll leave all their varied friends at this point, and move on to the time when Mary and I went on a caravan holiday. Within an hour of arriving we had a chat with the couple in the next caravan who told us they'd brought their chip pan with them to prevent their teenage children using it in their absence. We decided there and then that on our return we would buy an electric chip pan.

However, when we returned, we found that Andrew had set the kitchen on fire by means of an unattended chip pan! Oh dear, we were just too late. The kitchen was more or less gutted, and I'd only just finished rebuilding the cupboards and renewing the work surfaces! In addition there was quite a lot of smoke damage in the bathroom and elsewhere.

But the worst aspect of this fire was my allergic reaction to the fumes, making me unable to speak or preach for a couple of months. At the time I hadn't yet resigned from *Murfield*, and now that I was 'off sick', I was very worried about all my A-level students. I made many recordings on cassette tapes, all in a whispered voice, and I also printed booklets which were used at the school during my absence without making too serious a dent in the girls' education. Twice a week the girls taking Further Maths came by taxis and had a whispered lesson in our living room. Anyway, they all passed their exams.

Andrew's next venture was to set up his own company, publishing magazines for children. He produced four magazines every two months - two on maths and two on science. They were used mainly in schools, but copies could be bought at supermarkets.

By now Andrew had his own house, and was living with a young lady, a scientist. Eventually they got engaged, but two days later Jenny left him for a TV personality, earning herself five pages in *Hello* magazine! A year previously, Andrew had suggested to her that she should apply to *Blue Peter* for a science slot in the programme. She did apply, along with her sister, and soon they became known as 'The Science Sisters' on the programme. And that's where Jenny met the Blue Peter vet.

Andrew was utterly devastated and angry, kicking his fridge as an expression of his feelings, and he still has this dented appliance in his kitchen as a reminder of his distress. He took months to recover, but he did recover, though his life was seldom without colourful events.

There was the time when his debit card was eaten up by the cash machine. He went into the bank to try to reclaim it. "Sorry, but we're just closing," he was told. That did not suit our Andrew. Whatever he said to the cashier I don't know, but it was sufficient for her to press the emergency button! Immediately the doors were locked, and all the customers were trapped inside. Soon the Police arrived, but little by little the tension slackened as the Police decided that Andrew was NOT a bank robber after all. The doors were unlocked and all the customers escaped, including Andrew, who emerged from the bank with his debit card, plus the needed cash!

Incidentally, we used to call Andrew (all six foot six of him) our son and hair! I wonder why. Not only was he tall, but very strong too. He gave Mary a great big hug, and crack - he'd broken one of her ribs! Sitting on a dining chair one day, he stretched - the chair back was on the floor! He turns a door key, and snap - the blade is stuck fast in the lock, with the other half remaining in his hand. That's how he once locked me out of my office at *Murfield School!*

Thinking of locked doors reminds me that Margaret wasn't without her own adventures. One Saturday, after having had a bath, she discovered that her bedroom door had slammed shut, but unfortunately the door was fitted with a Yale lock, and Margaret found herself well and truly locked out of her own bedroom. The problem was that all her clothes were behind that locked door! So, draped merely in a towel, she called for the fire brigade, and somehow the men rescued her. They left with a cheery "See you next Saturday, Love!" Their comment was prompted by the fact that Margaret had already called the fire services on the previous Saturday when she'd found that her washing machine was on fire.

It wasn't long before my *Murfield School* crisis arose, which caused me to resign. But if the road ahead is closed, surely there must be an alternative route.

At the time of leaving *Murfield* I was asked to become the minister of a church in Wales. I had preached there many times, and after each service there was always an open invitation to the home of one of the elders. Now this was a very 'Welsh' Welsh church, but I didn't expect that no English at all would be spoken during these after-service visits, and I felt rather like an island. Why did they want an Englishman as their pastor? I decided that our home fellowship was too important to lay aside, and so I declined, and decided to teach privately.

In case not many pupils came my way, I also advertised as a painter and decorator! My first assignment was in the house of a Jamaican lady, who stood by me all day long, saying "Quicker, quicker!" Well, I just about covered my expenses, but no more. That's because the woman diddled me, and as I was certainly no businessman, I put up no fight.

My second and final assignment was to decorate Ann's living room. Ann was one of the students who used to come to the meetings, and I chose to do this work without any remuneration, as a friend. But all in all, it cannot be said that my new venture was much help financially. However, quite unexpectedly I had a large influx of pupils from the local Tertiary College, all of them in trouble with A-level maths. What a wonderful encouragement for me!

When I was at *Murfield*, Mary didn't see much of my maths as it was well out of sight. But now it's maths in our own house - maths for dinner, maths for tea, and maths for supper. Poor Wizzy!

Living with maths, it must be a strain;
Poor Wizzy! So does she complain? (Maybe a bit!)
Cos q, log denominator, integration by parts,
Newton and Leibniz, Maclaurin, Descartes -

Circles and tangents, geometric constructions,
Equations, expansions, and proofs by induction,

A formula here and a formula there,
With Wizzy left gasping in utter despair.

But soon piano pupils began to arrive as well, and so maybe Mary was a bit happier! And it meant that our finances were now safe. I also had some pupils for piano accordion, and some for English.

Rachel's mum came to see me to ask me to teach her daughter A-level Religious Studies. Mum gave me a list of all *Rachel's* academic achievements, including all the A grades in her O-levels. She was aiming to take her degree at Oxford, and so all in all it seemed as though she might be a good 'catch' of a pupil, and so I readily accepted her. *Rachel* and I got on well, and we enjoyed our lessons, especially when we went through Paul's letters to the Corinthians. But having been told of the girl's great ability, I was rather puzzled by her poor essay writing. However, I received volumes and volumes of praise from Mummy. "At last we've found someone who understands our daughter!" I must admit that it sounded a little bit fishy to me.

All went well for several months, until I was asked what grade I expected *Rachel* to obtain. By now I could only hope for a D grade at best, so I explained this to Mummy, and 'BANG, with open jaws a lion sprang' (thank you, Mr Belloc). Mummy was the lion! Soon a letter arrived, attacking me for my inadequate teaching, and for my appalling attitude towards her daughter! Soon Daddy joined in the attack.

It was a difficult situation, as I decided that I was unable to carry on teaching the girl. A tearful *Rachel* came to see me, pleading with me to continue, but as her parents persisted with their invectives, I felt I must decline. Soon afterwards I learned the truth - *Rachel* had in fact very few O-level passes, all with low grades, and maybe she only got a place at the Tertiary College because of Mummy's exaggerations. Not surprisingly, the poor girl didn't manage to gain a single A-level.

My piano pupils were a great encouragement to me, many of them reaching a high standard, and winning trophies at various competitions. Richard was my most advanced pupil - a young boy who played with much sensitivity, Eventually his technique began to amaze me, but even at his advanced stage, he still needed guidance: "Richard, I'm not too happy with the way you play bars 20 to 30." But my comment was met with a twinkle in his eyes as he replied, "Well, come and show me then!"

We used to hire a large hall once a year and put on Pupils' Concerts which we advertised and managed to have a full house each time. The concerts were in aid of a local Children's Hospice. I always played a piano solo on these occasions, but alas, sometimes my pupils put me to shame:

My Mendelssohn I played with ease,
No note was out of place -
A great display of expertise,
Of beauty, charm and grace.

There never was a moment's doubt,
No cause to sweat or fear.
I knew the music inside out.
But then the hour drew near -

The audience came in one by one
And filled the hall with awe.
My expertise had all but gone,
My charm and grace? No more!

Before they came, I played with ease,
But now it's shame and sweat!
I'd caught the 'cannot play' disease,
With fingers limp and wet!

Although I had composed music in the past, I began composing music to suit the particular needs of various pupils, and little by little my output increased, and even now in my eighties I'm still busy composing. Sometimes when I've finished writing a piece, I stand back and wonder 'How did I write that?' It's all very puzzling to me.

Teaching piano gave me a few surprises. What about John? At the time we had a Bechstein grand piano. "I've got a Bekkerstein too," John told me, "and it's just been reconditioned at a cost of £2,000." He was in his early twenties, and passionate about his music. Soon I discovered that his name was actually *David*, but for some peculiar reason I alone was asked to call him John! He also gave me an incorrect address, apart from the postcode. He practised for hours and hours a day, but his playing was insensitive and unbelievably loud. I thought that this troubled young man deserved as much encouragement and help as I could give him, but it didn't surprise me at all when things went wrong and he had a nervous breakdown.

During his absence I received a phone call from a don at Belfast University, asking for some clarification about a reference I was supposed to have written regarding *David Ford's* application to study music there. At first I explained that I didn't know a *David Ford*, but soon the penny dropped - it was John, of course! It seems that I had stated in my reference that he had eight A-levels to his name, all with A grades, and all under my personal tutelage! In addition, he was an accomplished concert pianist, whose compositions deserved widespread acclaim!

I wrote to John indicating my displeasure. The postcode did the trick, and he actually received the letter. To John's horror, it was his mother who saw my letter drop through the letterbox, and noticing the incorrect name and address, she opened it, thus discovering John's secret. That same morning John and his mum came to see me. He'd written to about twenty universities with a very exaggerated reference purportedly written by me. He'd even applied to colleges at Oxford and Cambridge. His poor mum was distraught. Despite John's forgery, I offered to continue to teach him, but he never came again. By the way, there was no Bekkerstein grand piano after all, just an upright of unknown pedigree.

Then there was the lady who had failed her piano diploma under her previous teacher, and came to me for repairs. Lessons were often chaotic - that's because *Carol* brought her baby with her, and when Baby cried, she sometimes handed Baby to me! Not easy, especially when I needed to illustrate at the piano. When Baby became Toddler, lessons were even more chaotic.

What about *Jenny*? I gave her a lift in my car to the bus stop after one of her lessons, but my help nearly went drastically wrong! She was wearing a shoulder bag, and when she closed the car door as we parted company, some of the strap must have been trapped inside the door. I drove off, unaware that we hadn't parted company after all - well, not until someone waved at me frantically. The poor girl had been running at the side of the car at the end of a long lead! Fortunately I stopped just in time.

When *Jenny* left me in order to go to university, Mum failed to pay me for the last four lessons. Perhaps that was my punishment for the car saga! At the same time, an evangelical minister failed to pay me for his daughter's last four lessons. That's when I decided to charge for lessons a month in advance, rather than in arrears. Do you blame me?

Someone by the name of *Mrs Germany* rang to make an appointment to see me, to discuss piano lessons for her daughter. The appointment was made, but she didn't turn up. She phoned a few days later to make a new appointment, but once again she didn't turn up. This time she did NOT ring to make a further appointment. Well, that's not quite true, because she actually rang about eighteen months later, with the same request! Because of her unusual name I remembered her, and explained that I was doubtful about arranging to see her on the third occasion, but she persisted, and a meeting was arranged, and to my surprise she arrived - on time!

Believe it or not, I always have to ask the same question when someone requests piano lessons for a beginner: 'But have you got a piano?' There wasn't one in *Mrs Germany's* home, but eventually she conceded that a piano was needed, and asked me if I would help with choosing one. I agreed, telling her that I make a charge for this, but not for those who become pupils.

We arranged a date to look at a piano some thirty miles away. *Mrs G* arrived at our house two hours late - just at dinnertime. We abandoned dinner, and Mary quickly prepared sandwiches as a picnic for us all at our destination, and off we went in OUR car, as *Mrs G* daren't drive her car so far! And yes, she bought the piano, and a date was set for her daughter's first lesson - but guess what? The daughter never came! After many weeks of not coming, I thought enough is enough, and sent Mum a bill for my services. I was paid ages later, but the cheque was accompanied by a letter telling me that I was the sort of person whose unfair demands cause so much trouble in the world, and had brought her to close to a breakdown! A year later two new pupils arrived - two brothers. How had they heard of me? Through the recommendation of *Mrs Germany*!

How did *Martha* first come to me for piano lessons? Well, she was having a lesson with her previous teacher, and asked "Can I go to the toilet, please?" And she kept on asking.

"Oh *Martha,* just wait until the end of the lesson. "But she couldn't wait, and she didn't wait, but I'll spare you the details! So did the teacher sack her pupil, or did the parents sack the teacher? I don't know, but the following week I was her teacher.

Soon I had sufficient piano pupils for Mary to join me in teaching. We purchased a second piano, which was placed in my study upstairs - and now we could teach simultaneously. Margaret had her own piano in her room, and she also taught a few pupils.

Every year we had two days of auditions, when our pupils came and played for Mary, myself, and an invited musician. Pupils could opt out if they wished, but almost everybody had a go, even the adults. They all received certificates, and some received prizes, but the two we considered best of all were taught at half fees for a year. On one occasion, Julia, our invited musician wasn't well, and so I sent her a recording of the auditions, but decided to play a mischievous trick on her, but it was a trick that backfired on me; I pretended to be a pupil, and played three pieces for her to adjudicate! Well, Julia did not award me a scholarship, not even a prize. In fact she complained about my playing. Did she suspect me, and was she teaching me a lesson? I just don't know. Maybe she'll read this book one day. Oops!

Julia was a gifted cellist who gave concerts in the area, with Mary as her accompanist. Once we hired a hall, and when the day came we all went along in the afternoon to have a rehearsal, and also to check the seating, ready for the evening's concert.

Unfortunately the grand piano was locked and despite all our enquiries, we couldn't get hold of a key! The concert was in a nearby private school, and because of my work at *Murfield* I knew the Head quite well. I went round the school seeking help, and found some rather untidy-looking fellow and made a total fool of myself by assuming he was the Caretaker. Yes, he was in fact the Head! After all, it was now the school holidays and Sir was dressed rather casually, to put it mildly. But even the Caretaker-cum-Head was unable to produce a key for us. However, thanks to the skill of Julia's husband, the lock was defeated by means of a piece of wire. Clunk - and the lid opened! Well, that was the first problem solved.

But then we discovered that there were no toilet rolls in the place, so I fetched a dozen rolls from home and placed them in the Ladies and Gents. After the concert was over, I decided that there was no need for me to leave the toilet rolls as a gift for the school. Well, I THOUGHT everyone had gone home, but alas I bumped into a woman entering the Ladies, just as I was emerging with my tall pile of 'stolen' toilet rolls reaching up to my nose! Oh dear, I suppose I should have given her some toilet paper!

I think every book needs to include some stories about toilet rolls, don't you? Well, there are certainly plenty of them in this book!

On a much more serious note, we had a friend, Richard, who taught violin. He came to see me, asking for my help. Looking back, how I wish I'd detected that he needed much more help than the little I gave him. He was not doing too well financially because insufficient violin pupils were coming his way, so could I give him a few tips on how to teach piano to beginners? But he never put his new plan into action. The next day he fitted a hosepipe to his car exhaust, and you can guess the rest of this sad story!

This was now my sixth experience of knowing folk who had taken their own lives. I thought, 'if only, if only!' - but it was always too late, with one amazing exception. Don would also have been on my list, but for accidentally finding him, and managing to rescue him from the gas oven.

Soon after Richard's distressing death, I had a small accident, which made a big change in my life's direction. All I did was to fall from the top of our loft ladder. How often a split second of misjudgement can cause a lifetime of change! I knew instantly that something was seriously wrong. In the evening I was supposed to be preaching at our midweek meeting, and so that had to be cancelled.

After various scans it was discovered that I'd bruised my brain (cerebral contusion). I lost my memory, and didn't recognise people. I was also incredibly dizzy (a dizzy Wizzy?) and lying down at night was very difficult, as I had to lower myself into bed centimetre by centimetre. My dizziness continued for nearly two years - not very nice!

When things in life go wrong, I have to remind myself that it's not everything that's goes wrong. Adrian Plass has something to say about this: "No burglars came again last night, just as they failed to come the night before; no burglars yet again!" Quite a comfort when you come to think about it. In my teens, I started having problems with my jaw, which frequently became dislocated (or unhooked, using my own terminology), and I had to find medical help urgently. It happened once on New Year's Day, just after Lionel and I had sat down in the cinema. But my jaw problem hasn't recurred for years now - no dislocation happened again last year, just as it failed to happen the year before, and as for this year, no dislocations yet again. Hey, let's be thankful for all the bad things that HAVEN'T happened to us!

But my minor brain injury DID happen to me, and it made a major impact on my life - it meant that our house meetings came to an abrupt end, and sadly all those attending had to make other arrangements. The road ahead was well and truly closed! I was sixty-six, and had preached for the last forty-six years - and for the last thirty-five years I'd preached several times a week, and now nothing at all! It seemed like a catastrophe. It was!

A few months before my accident, I'd had a request to preach once more at the church where my two previous sermons had created such an impact, both positively and negatively.

"We're prepared to give you another chance," I was told. I accepted the offer and prepared my third sermon with ultimate caution. The church was normally packed, but not this time, as many had voted with their feet. So I won't be preaching there again! In fact, I won't be preaching anywhere - not in such a state of dizziness.

Yes, I had to make a sudden change from pulpit to pew, and that was very hard. Mary and I 'tried' several churches, and we soon discovered that we were becoming very critical. The music? The preaching? Oh dear, it seemed that we were not adjusting too easily, and in a sense we felt ashamed of our critical attitude. What a mess! We just didn't know what to do!

But after a whole year of trying, failing, despairing, and almost giving up, we found an evangelical church across the border, in North Wales. At last we felt happy with the preaching - and the folk at the church were so helpful and welcoming. Soon we moved to a bungalow in a village over the border, fairly near to our new church. And now we could more easily take an active part in church life.

Meanwhile, despite my dizziness, I managed to keep on teaching privately. When we left Shropshire, one of my pupils, who was herself a piano teacher, offered me the use of her music room and grand piano, so that I could continue teaching near our old home. However, it was a lovely surprise for me when all my pupils decided to come to our new abode for their lessons, despite the much-increased mileage. Thank you *Rebecca*, all the same. Don't tell her, but I didn't really like her piano. How ungrateful can I be?

Looking back, my life seems to have been made up of change, more change, and yet more change. As the author Faith Baldwin once said, "Time is a dressmaker specialising in alterations." Is my 'dress' finished now? Or will there be some more alterations in the years ahead? But whatever lies ahead, 'the Lord is my helper.' (Hebrews 13)

Ruth

*Ruth, Geoffrey and Mary at one of the concerts held in aid of the Alzheimer's Society
(photographed by Gary Russell, a member of the audience)*

Wizzy and Wizzy. Oops, we're sitting together!

Win and Mary. The Opus Two Duo

At Lake Vyrnwy Hotel on Mam's 101st birthday. From left to right: Margaret, Mam, Dave with Megan, Andrew, Matthew, Mary and Geoffrey

Mam on her 107th and 108th birthdays at Brook House. Photographs by kind permission of the Oswestry Advertiser

Chapter 14

Pianos, People and Puffins

Whenever we move house, we have to think 'piano'! We found a removal firm specialising in moving grand pianos, but when the day came, our Steinway defeated these so-called experts. They said we'd have to wait a couple of days until they got 'expert' advice! But the following day I had a couple of piano pupils coming to our new abode for their last lesson before their Grade 8 exams, so I remonstrated.

Oh dear, moving into our house twenty years earlier was beset with problems - beginning with an attempt to arrest me; but somehow, this moving-out-of-the-house problem seemed worse! I ask you - what can be worse than a pianist having no piano?

Anyway, the removal men sprang into action, contacting Steinway & Sons in London, and within a couple of hours, a chap arrived in his Merc, and explained how to remove the legs and the pedal lyre from the body of the piano - a procedure which is normally a very simple matter. He then drove over to our new abode and helped the men to reassemble the piano. I guess the removal firm must have lost out financially on that transaction!

Well, that was merely the 'getting there'. Almost immediately I was busy, not only with my involvement at the church in North Wales, but also with teaching all my piano pupils, plus some new ones.

One of my new pupils was *Susie*, and little did I know how this young lady was soon to become so prominent in my life, and have such a deepening effect on my attitude to people who are in trouble.

Susie was sixteen when I first taught her, and was living in a local Children's Care Home. She's a girl with a horrendous background of sexual cruelty at the hands of three men in her family, and there were other very serious sexual abuses too, which I can't mention in detail. As a result of all this she turned to drugs and self-harming. In fact, her arms and neck are grossly disfigured, with thousands of scars!

After only a couple of lessons she began to talk to me quite freely - we got on really well. She told me the story of the time she'd slit her throat and been rushed to hospital, and how, a few days later, she'd escaped from the ward and somehow got on to the hospital roof, threatening to jump from the top of this three-storey building. The fire brigade arrived with a mammoth ladder and the men more or less forced her down! She showed me a newspaper cutting about the incident. Relating the story made her look really sad, and it made me feel sad too, especially when I knew that this wasn't the first time she'd slit her throat.

Sometimes *Susie* brought up the subject of God, asking why He had let her suffer so much. Mary and I took her to church twice, but on the first occasion there was an unfortunate incident: after the evening service, and before the tea-and-biscuit time, *Susie* wanted a fag, so I took her outside, and we strolled round the car park while she puffed away, but alas, we were seen! We had the impression that our spectator didn't look too pleased with her, or with me for that matter. It didn't help her to feel wanted.

When *Susie* was living in a secure unit, several years earlier, she witnessed many events which could have put an extra strain on her life. One of the girls disliked a certain male member of staff, and was determined to get him sacked - and she succeeded. I'll leave you to guess how she did it. *Susie* wondered whether she dare report the girl, but never did. Who would have believed her anyway?

At the same secure unit was a Filipino boy - the lad who had stabbed the headmaster Philip Lawrence to death in 1995. *Susie* was quite friendly with him, but had no idea at the time that he had killed someone, but one day she arrived for her lesson in some distress, having just seen a TV documentary about the knife attack. She was horrified and seemed quite frightened.

Mary and I visited *Susie* in Addenbrooke's Hospital in Cambridge, after she'd taken a hundred paracetamol tablets. On another occasion we went to visit her in a secure psychiatric unit, only to find that she'd somehow escaped. We arrived at the very moment she was being forcibly rescued from attempting to jump off a flyover on to the busy A55 below. We saw it all happen.

My involvement with the church grew so much that I thought the time had come to stop teaching. But what about *Susie*? There was no way that I could stop teaching her, and so she became my only pupil. Despite all her problems, she passed two exams with merit.

Eventually *Susie* left the Care Home and was allowed to live in a flat, and that's when she began a lesbian relationship. Maybe she'd learned to hate men, after her appalling experience with the three men in her family. So who is going to be the first to cast a stone at her?

Living in a flat can be quite a problem for a pianist, with neighbours on each side. So Mary and I took *Susie* in search of an electronic piano, which could be played using headphones. The purchase now completed, we all returned to our house for a cuppa. We had a nice relaxed chat, though *Susie* did throw into the conversation the fact that the shop where she worked part-time was a scene of some unfairness. All the girls had been invited to the wedding of one of them - that is, all except *Susie*! The next day she went to work armed with a knife and tried to kill all these girls.

I sometimes wonder how much her mind had been affected by the sudden revelation that her Filipino friend had killed with a knife. Anyway, the fact remains that she soon found herself in Styal Women's Prison on a charge of attempted murder. And, for various reasons this poor girl has been without her freedom ever since. So *Susie* has never played her piano - it's now in our house, on permanent loan!

This 'knife' incident wasn't her first. There was a previous occasion when Mary and I searched the streets of Ruabon, after *Susie* had escaped from a secure psychiatric unit, armed with a knife, with intent to kill a woman who lived there. We didn't find *Susie*, and I'm glad to say that *Susie* didn't find her woman. We wondered whether we'd find our young lady on our doorstep when we returned home, armed with her knife and angry about her failed attempt, but all was well.

Try to answer these questions, if you dare: where would WE be today if we'd had a background like *Susie*'s? Are we certain that we'd have gritted our teeth and come through in triumph? Are we absolutely certain that we ourselves wouldn't be in prison? So is *Susie* a bad girl? I don't think so. I liked her, I miss her very much and I wish it could all have ended very differently.

I was still in touch with *Donald* - the Dad I'd met at *Murfield*, who had confided in me so often about his daughter's sexual orientation. Sad to say his lovely wife *Sheila* died of cancer, and her death played havoc with *Donald's* mind, and this otherwise clear-thinking man began to act irrationally with his financial dealings.

Gambling with international competitions became addictive - as though it had become *Donald's* new career. He gambled in order to win millions, so that he could set up a new charity to help cancer patients. He said to me "I've won the first million, and I'd like you to be the administrator of my charity!"

He frequently showed me letters 'proving' that he'd won the money, and he sent large sums of money to these cheats to cover their so-called expenses. The expected money never arrived, but undeterred, he still believed that an immense fortune was just around the corner. He even offered me his car and the gift of a world cruise for two, in the expectation that he would soon receive 'the cheque'! It wasn't long before *Donald* was without house and virtually without money.

A few years later I took *Donald's* funeral, and I included a poetic caricature of him in my talk, a few verses of which I quoted earlier in the book. It was a bit daring, but it worked. I looked back on our friendship with joy, but not on the last few years, which I viewed with much sadness. True, he'd acted foolishly, but do we therefore call him a fool? Or do we look on him with compassion and a measure of understanding?

It wasn't long before we came to know Ruth. No, she wasn't wielding a knife, neither was she a gambler - well, not as far as I know! She was simply a member of the church, but I knew her largely through music. Ruth had played the piano as a girl, but stopped having lessons after she'd failed Grade 5, but soon after meeting her she asked me to help her to get going again. She had recently gained a first-class honours degree in mathematics, and so glorious maths was something we had in common!

We sat at the piano and began! Soon Ruth gained a posh-sounding music diploma - AMusTCL, based on harmony and other theoretical matters. She began entering music competitions, often bringing back trophies - which she always kept under her bed! So her Grade 5 result had temporarily hidden her true talent. Beginnings don't determine endings.

But Ruth's main work has been teaching mathematics, both privately and at an international school. I believe she is a very good teacher, and so I hope she will pay me handsomely for this advert.

Despite Ruth's mathematical skills, her maths once came completely unstuck - and mine too for that matter! Ruth had recently bought a house, and the previous owner had left a wardrobe in the bedroom. Well, Ruth decided to sell the thing, and so she and I made some calculations about how to get this large item down the narrow stairway and turn the corner at the bottom of the stairs.

We then put our fool-proof removal plan into action. I came down the stairs first, but soon the wardrobe was completely jammed, with Ruth trapped on the other side. It wouldn't budge. In desperation I went home to bring an electric saw, and then set to work cutting the wardrobe into pieces. So much for our mathematics! So much for selling the thing!

Ruth is a keen cyclist and has 'done' Land's End to John O'Groats on her own, bringing in nearly £1,500 for The Alzheimer's Society. She took less than two weeks to complete the ride, despite some trouble with her bike, and heavy rain in the first few days.

By now Wizzy and I only play two-piano duets, because when we used to play on one piano, Mary always complained that 'you stick your elbows out so much that I can hardly play!' Well, that's only Mary's opinion. Ruth has always played duets with me on one piano, without complaining about me - well, not to my face! So what can Wizzy say about that?

For many years Mary was the accompanist for cellist Julia Richards, and now she accompanies violinist Win Conway. Win and Mary call themselves 'The Opus Two Duo' and play at venues over quite a wide area. Win has become a good friend, and she's also a wonderful raconteur, forever entertaining us.

Over ten years ago we began holding piano concerts in our music room, to an audience of up to fourteen folk. Nowadays we give these concerts in aid of The Alzheimer's Society. The three pianists are the two Wizzies plus Ruth - we play solos, duets and trios. I must say that writing 'fun' music for our trio playing is an enjoyable diversion - such things as 'Anything you can play, I can play better', hoping for the forgiveness of Irving Berlin!

We need fourteen chairs, but where on earth do we keep them? Have a look - they're in all sorts of strange places, including two in the wardrobe, and another four hidden under the piano!

Recently a family of four Persians came to a concert, and as Mum spoke no English I decided to hold up a card on which was written 'Welcome' in Persian. Did I succeed? I'll let you judge. Firstly I searched the Internet and came up with what I hoped were the requisite squiggles, though I did suspect that the squiggles seemed to rather numerous. At the beginning of the concert I held up the card with some trepidation. I asked the man of the family to translate into English. There was a roar of laughter when he translated it into 'Welcome to Wikipedia!' Well, I was nearly right.

I was warned of the spiritual dangers of placing too much importance on these concerts. But our concerts really are important to us, but are they too important? Who possesses the ruler which measures excess of musical importance?

Mary and I often accompanied the Sunday services with organ and grand piano (a piano which once belonged to Dame Myra Hess). We also played 'non-church' duets from time to time at other less formal meetings. So maybe our enthusiasm for music is more acceptable when it's within the church.

Mind you, I did wonder whether the Lord was telling me that music wasn't all that important anyway, when I couldn't bend my thumb because of a growth on the knuckle. And was the Lord stressing the point when I chopped half an inch off one of my fingers? In addition I developed Dupuytren's contracture in my hand, and my pianistic future didn't look too hopeful. But the surgeon removed the lump on my thumb, and another surgeon repaired my finger, and amazingly, my contracture hasn't worsened further, otherwise my hands would have become claw-like. And so my enthusiasm remains intact.

Life doesn't seem to have become any less hectic as I've grown older, but after years of having no piano pupils, along came Megan and asked me to teach her! Whatever shall I do? Aren't I far too busy to have a pupil? But in one of my weaker moments I agreed to her request - but Megan is keen and very musical, and she won't accept anything less than a distinction in every exam she takes, and so far her determination has paid off! So hey, I'm really enjoying it. Maybe there's still some life left in me, even in my eighties!

As for Mary, she spends lots of time with the birds these days, even going on 'bird holidays', or off to Skomer to see the puffins. But I wonder what's wrong with seeing blackbirds in our own back garden. Why not stay at home and enjoy our own birds?

All that way to see a puffin?
But I think it's best if I say nuffin'!

Life with Mary can be most frustrating; I have to exercise great patience, especially when we go for a so-called walk:

A walk with Mary? What a flop!
I can hardly say a word.
It's never a walk! It's always a 'STOP!'
Guess what she's seen? A bird.

'Oh look, it's in that rowan tree.
Don't move, don't breathe, don't talk,
Don't cough, don't sneeze!' Oh dearie me,
You can't call that a walk!

Finances take so many knocks,

202

Buying birdseed by the ton.
New books, new 'scopes and new binocs -
More shopping to be done!

Equipment goes through fields, up hills,
No matter what the weight.
She's got to find that great grey shrike
Before it is too late.

Passions rise - there's no defeat,
She's on an urgent mission!
Aching limbs and blistered feet
Won't hamper her ambition.

But I'm at home in luxury,
No aches, no pain, no stress,
No blistered feet, no urgency.
It's bliss, I must confess.

No heavy scopes - I stroll with ease,
No rules, no 'STOP' - I'm free!
I'll cough and sneeze just as I please.
Yes, that's the life for me!

No frenzied search for great grey shrike,
I just sit down and play.
It doesn't cost a penny-piece,
And I'm happy all the day.

So as you see, my mind is sound,
It's Mary who's the nitwit!
I think she'd even look around
To find a pig-tailed tit-wit!

I wonder whether Wizzy will ever forgive me for these cheeky verses. Maybe not! It seems that the seriousness of my poetic efforts during those two years of my boyhood illness has evaporated. It's usually leg-pulling these days. Maybe I'm back to my 'snap crackle pop' days, in more ways than one!

I even wrote one of these 'sillies' for Mary's eightieth birthday, some of the verses of which I've already quoted - all about that promise I'd made all those years ago, to build her a rowing boat if she agreed to marry me. However, my promise was very carefully safeguarded, because I never gave a hint as to WHEN I'd build it! Getting on for sixty years later, there was still no boat, but I did feel guilty, and so at long last I decided on a compromise. I BOUGHT her a rowing boat - but sadly, it was only a model!

Mary and I have had our share of illness and operations in the last few years, but somehow we've kept going. My last operation was a hip replacement after tripping over a cable whilst doing some DIY in Ruth's kitchen. I was on my own at Ruth's, and couldn't get to the phone. But, to my relief, on lifting my hand to the table next to me, I found my mobile phone and dialled 999. The ambulance soon arrived, plus two policemen, and just before breaking down the door, Ruth's neighbour Dave appeared, who was experienced in double glazing; it was Dave who used his skills to rescue me, whilst the police just stood back and watched.

After my operation, and while I was coming round in the recovery room, my surgeon, still in his operating gown, came up to me and introduced himself. "Hello," he said in a quiet voice, "I'm St Peter." His words made me wonder where I was for a moment! But no, this couldn't possibly be heaven, not when I discovered how badly the nurses treated me in my two-week post-operation period:

They came armed with needles
And pierced me at will.
They removed all my food:
'By mouth it is nil!'

There's one thing I wanted -
A hug from my Mum,
When nurses pushed nasties
Right up in my ...!

Then there's Marj who loved biscuits,
And took mine at will.
I called her 'my thief' -
She stole from the ill!

They're a funny old lot
When you view them from bed,
But despite all their quirks,
There's much more to be said ...

When I returned home I sent a 'thank you' card to the nurses to say this 'much more'. Yes, I included the verses about how dreadful they were, together with more verses thanking them for being so caring and encouraging, which they were throughout my stay. Even Marj, my thief, was a wonderful nurse!

Mary has had two cancer operations and subsequent treatment. On top of that she had a spinal fracture, and was in severe pain and unable to do much. However she was determined to overcome her immobility, and by now she is enjoying walking again, and she's back with her birds! She's also accompanying violinist Win again, and joining with Ruth and myself in giving piano concerts.

When Mary fractured her spine, I started having some help with the house cleaning, and hence got to know Mirka from Slovakia quite well, even giving her English lessons from time to time. One day, she asked "Do you think you could buy me some new clothes, please?" Wow, I didn't realize I was such a close friend! It turned out she needed some new dusters or 'cloths'. Perhaps a few more lessons in English would benefit her after all - and all the more so when she tells me that she's taken her children to the cinema to see some cartons, and explains that her Mum and Dad are divided.

Despite her amusing English, Mirka is a wonderful help, and even moves the furniture and arranges the chairs for our concerts. And sometimes she assists with the heavy work when I'm busy with some DIY job. Nothing is too much trouble for her.

So how important is Mirka? Well, she's only a cleaner, isn't she? But what is the deeper meaning of 'important'? Was I really doing the most important job in the world when I was the minister at Ackhill? But to the Lord, is there any difference between us?

This chapter cannot close without having a last peep at our family.

As I write, Mam is still alive at the age of 108. She can't walk, can't hear anything at all, and although she can see, her eyesight is poor, and by now she can't read anything we write. However, she's on no medication whatsoever, so who says that living on coffee and chocolate biscuits is bad for your health? And she's eaten chocolates galore, but they've done her no harm. The carers at Brook House (where she's lived for nearly ten years) look after her exceptionally well, and buy her chocolates from time to time - they certainly know what she likes!

Unfortunately Mam's dementia is beyond belief, and what she says is amusing and distressing, all rolled into one: "I was murdered yesterday; they tied me up with a rope and shot me with a bullet through my head. So I'm dead now - are you dead as well?" She's also quite concerned about a three-legged man who lives upstairs.

Margaret gave Mam a white Teddy Bear to celebrate the millennium, and he's been on her bed ever since. So does she snuggle up to him? No, she punches him in the face these days.

Seeing Mam in this state makes me recall how she used to be, and it confirms my thankfulness to her for all her past love and care. And wasn't it Mam who gave me my lovely Biggie Bow-wow all those years ago? She has no idea that I still like Biggie Bow-wows, Dimmon Demmons and Teddies, and never punch them.

Incidentally, I always embarrass Mary when I make a beeline for the toy department in a large shop, and have a friendly chat with Teddies large and small! Yes, I'm still a little boy!

In the last few paragraphs I wrote about Mam, using the present tense, but that is about to change to the past tense. Soon after the punch-ups with Teddy began, Mam fell out of bed, and it seems that this set off a spiral of decline. She died peacefully in her sleep - one month short of reaching the age of 109. At the time of her death she was the thirty-eighth oldest person in the UK - quite an achievement, one might say! However, her other achievements can't be measured numerically. You can't put a number on her love and her self-effacing nature. Even extravagant adjectives like 'amazing' barely fit the bill. Or putting it another way:

As far as mums go,
There's no one I know
Who's had one like mine -
So patient and kind.

What can I say more?
With chocolates galore,
It must be confessed
That Mam was the best!

Do you remember that at one time Mam would have been quite rich if she'd sold Dad's shares? Well, the shares plummeted dramatically, and Mam would be sad to know that she's hardly left us anything. But 'small' seems 'big' when you love someone.

By contrast, Big Andrew seems 'small' in his awareness, never learning anything by experience! His house was built in 1640 - it has low ceilings with thick wooden beams, strengthened by means of big bolts - but he doesn't seem to know where these bolts are located. He rushes around the house, oblivious of everything, and bang, he's knocked himself unconscious once again!

And do you remember Annoo's little piggy, and his big Panda? Well, big Annoo is still a little boy, when it comes to cuddly toys - he seems to take after me. He bought me a lovely Teddy some years ago, and for our fiftieth wedding anniversary, he gave us Wuffles, who now sits by my printer, on guard.

Unfortunately, at the time of writing this book, Annoo is experiencing a few difficult years. The problems began when he found his natural family, and became particularly close to Nicky (one of his sisters).

Soon after he got to know Nicky, she became ill with cancer, and from that point her health has gone downhill. This has caused Andrew deep distress. Nicky has a husband and two lovely children, and finds coping with life very hard. Andrew spends much of his time helping her, to the detriment of his business, which has suffered greatly, leading him into financial trouble.

Only a matter of weeks after writing the previous paragraph, I've had to insert another paragraph, the one you are now reading. Nicky's health problems suddenly accelerated, and no more treatment could be given. She died just a few weeks after her forty-third birthday. A week prior to Nicky's death, her father (and Andrew's, of course) had died during an operation. What a terrible time for the family!

There were hundreds of people at Nicky's funeral, with Andrew giving a short talk. For Mary and myself, it was a poignant moment when we met his natural mother at the funeral. I said to her "Thank you for giving us a lovely boy, and also a load of trouble." She gave me a knowing smile!

Andrew is devastated by Nicky's death and he feels to be torn apart. But 'sometimes what holds you together and what tears you apart are the same things' (Cherlynn Shakespeare), so come on Annoo-do-it, you really can 'do it' and I believe you really can hold yourself together!

As for Margaret, she is happily married to Dave. What a nice son-in-law we have! The two children, Matthew and Megan, are both super - Matthew is a prize-winning darts player aged sixteen at the time of writing, and younger Megan is learning to be a pianist, amongst many other things!

Margaret is a caring mother, and has been very good in visiting my own mother, even though Mam kept telling her "Your nose is ugly!" However, I can't really say that Margaret's life has been altogether straightforward, but she has put all her troubles behind her, and gets on with her life with a will. Not so long ago she trained a singing group at the local school, and has been active on the Board of Governors. She's even running her own business at the present time. Yes, she's pulled through.

At the time of Nicky's death one of those awkward conversations took place when Margaret explained to a friend that her brother's sister had died:

"Well, aren't you going to the funeral then?"

"No, I don't know her!"

Oh dear, more explaining to be done!

Ruth at the start of her Land's End to John O'Groats ride for The Alzheimer's Society

Ruth's surprise home-coming. Photograph by neighbour Neal Frost

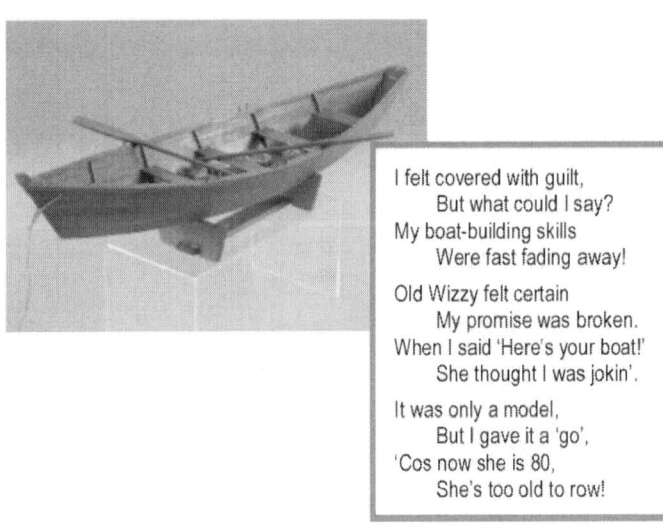

I felt covered with guilt,
　　But what could I say?
My boat-building skills
　　Were fast fading away!

Old Wizzy felt certain
　　My promise was broken.
When I said 'Here's your boat!'
　　She thought I was jokin'.

It was only a model,
　　But I gave it a 'go',
'Cos now she is 80,
　　She's too old to row!

Mary's promised wedding present from Geoffrey, 58 years late!

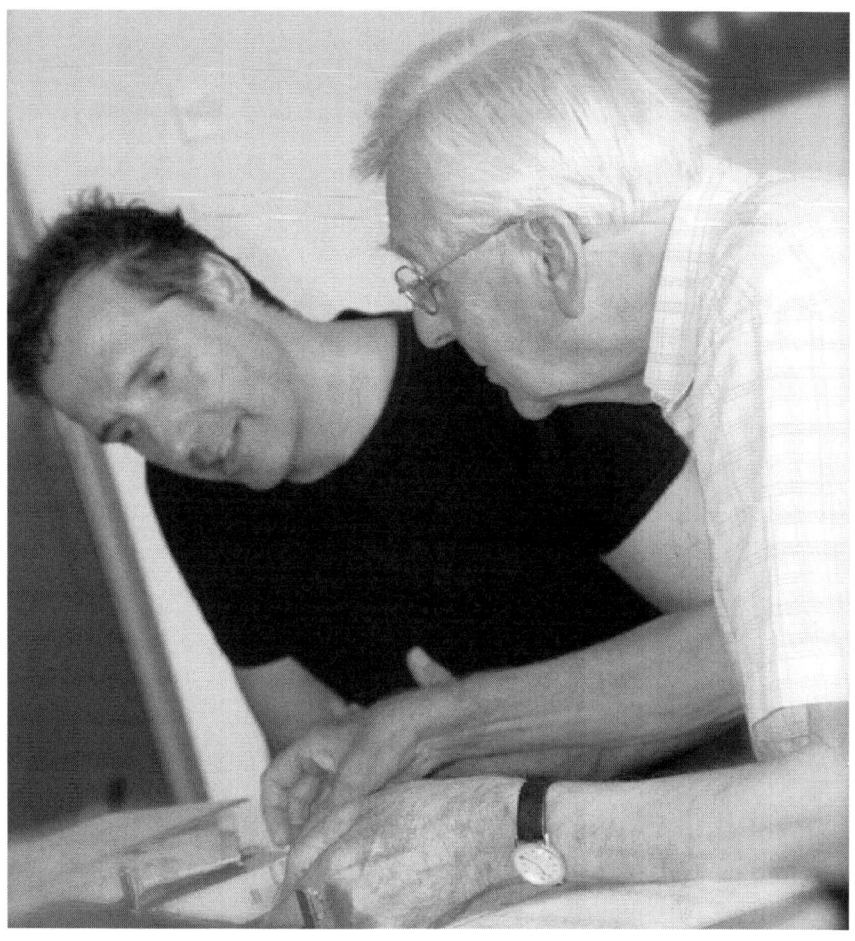

The composer Graham Fitkin with Geoffrey. Graham is examining one of my compositions in order to decide whether I'm suitable to join his Composers' Masterclass

Annoo, Wizzy and Wuffles in order of size!

Margaret and Dave's wedding day in 2005

Megan and Matthew eight years later

Chapter 15

Near the City Boundary

After the previous chapter about life in our village in North Wales, I must not forget the reason why we moved here in the first place, which was to be near our new church.

From the start, we felt at home in the church, and it was good to have fellowship with fellow evangelicals. Before long several hospitable members began inviting us for Sunday lunch and tea. Once when we'd been invited to someone's home for Sunday dinner, it hadn't been made clear whether tea was included! So after dinner we looked out for some clues.

We hadn't long to wait as the little daughter suddenly asked in a squeaky voice, "Mummy, when are Mr and Mrs Smales going home?"

"Oh I don't know, Lowri. Maybe they'll want to stay for tea."

"No, no," I responded, "we'll be going now!"

As I was no longer the minister of a church and no longer leading a house meeting, I wondered how I would cope, and what I would do. But the way just opened out, as little by little I came to know quite a few troubled folk.

One elderly lady phoned me frequently, usually two or three times a day, but sometimes as many as thirty times a day - and it was always something which she deemed to be of utmost urgency! Once she rang at 3 a.m. to tell me she couldn't get to sleep, and then, believe it or not, she

215

rang again half an hour later to apologise for her previous phone call!

The phone rang, but it wasn't our troubled lady this time. I answered, fled into the bedroom, hid my head and handset under the duvet, and had a long muffled conversation with *Alison*! All this was so that the couple who were visiting us couldn't hear me talking in confidence to their own troubled daughter! Oh dear, what complications!

Once again I thought that life would be much simpler if I hid myself under the duvet permanently, but maybe without the phone!

There were times when I deliberately told lies in order to keep a confidence, and I think rightly so. I'm sure there are some circumstances when it is right to do what is seemingly wrong. What about the Bible story of Rahab?

Doris was a lady whose mental state was a little bit wobbly. She bought an orthopaedic bed from a door-to-door salesman, for over £1000. It was my job to undo the transaction, although by now the bed had been delivered. This involved many visits to the home, going with her to the doctor's to ask for a letter describing her mental problems, visiting the Trading Standards Office, contacting one of the directors of the firm, and arguing with him about the pressurised sales methods, and so on. Eventually we undid the sale! But soon there were other emergencies, and suddenly it was 'all go' again.

It was a privilege to know folk with firm evangelical beliefs, but sometimes I was a bit surprised by their comments about others. Their comments and judgments set me thinking once again, questioning, wondering and worrying:

"My next-door neighbour has no regard for the Lord," *Madge* stated as a stark fact! And so in order to avoid seeing her neighbour's washing on the line each Sunday, she had a two-metre fence erected to hide the offensive scene from her eyes. "Sunday is the Lord's day," she declared. Somehow I felt sad.

At the time of the 2004 Indian Ocean tsunami, with its massive loss of life, one lady said "Well, we deserve God's judgment, don't we?" But the colossal wave didn't reach Wales, and we were merely observers via a television screen - it was all too easy to make her pronouncement from the sanctuary of her home. It was still good to visit her, a lady with deep convictions, someone who sought to please God in all she did. But her comment made me feel sad once again, and a little bit worried.

I also visited the two rebels quite often. They weren't generally known by the name 'rebels' - that was just my own name for them. And both of them were MEN. Are you surprised?

After nearly two years, the dizziness resulting from my brain injury began to ease, and I was able to consider taking services again. It seems that both my visiting and my preaching were appreciated, and maybe that had some bearing on my being invited to become an elder of the church. Whatever would that involve? I accepted the position, though with some trepidation, but in the very first week I had visits from three church members who asked me to sort out this and that. What a start! But at any rate I now knew something of what eldership involved!

However, little by little it was becoming clear that just as I'd been sympathetic towards the 'stink bomb' girl at *Murfield School*, I was now the elder who was sympathetic towards the two rebels in the church. Oh dear, that just won't do!

So what is the definition of a rebel, in this context? No, he is not someone armed with a stink bomb, or worse; he is merely someone who persists in making suggestions about possible 'improvements' in the church. I didn't always agree with them, but I still believed that they were simply trying to follow the teaching of the Bible. But the elders were also trying to follow the teaching of the Bible, and to view others with love. Nevertheless I thought that these rebels were viewed rather negatively, and with some irritation, and I felt uneasy about this.

Soon after we'd joined the church, a Luncheon Club was started for retired folk. It was a weekly event, with two teams working in the kitchen on alternate weeks. Mary took part in this venture for a couple of years, and then I replaced her. Alas, the team which I joined became known as 'Geoffrey's team', even though I was the least experienced! There were two other members of 'my' team, one of whom was Ruth. We told ourselves that having two mathematicians in the kitchen was the perfect arrangement - after all, who better to measure the ingredients for the puddings?

Even one of our 'customers' lent a hand. Rhona was a big help and always kept us amused with her lively stories and bits of verse - one verse in particular kept cropping up:

Little Jimmy in his jersey
Fell into the river Mersey.
'Never mind' his uncle said,
'We'll pick him up in Birkenhead.'

Let's leave Birkenhead for now, and visit a few other places around the world - places which I'll describe by means of an allegory:

On my life's journey I've passed signposts to quite a few cities, with many settlers in each. In one city, the folk are certain that there is no God, and are perfectly happy residing in their City of Atheism. However, in other cities, there is no doubt about the existence of God. And depending on which city you visit, the citizens might be Jews, Catholics, or various sorts of Protestants - maybe Presbyterians, Methodists and the rest. In other cities you'll meet Buddhists, Hindus, and so on, or maybe Christadelphians or Jehovah's Witnesses. Wherever you look there are more and more signposts to other cities.

In many of these cities, the settlers are absolutely certain that they've 'got it right'. What a religious muddle! Even the 'Bible' people are divergent - there seem to be muddles everywhere!

But in the context of this book, I will especially mention evangelicals. Of course, I was one of the settlers in the Evangelical City myself, and so I'd also got it right! It's obvious that I was right - after all, my beliefs were based on what the Bible taught, and I had chapter and verse as proof!

However, I was beginning to think that this matter of always being right in all our judgments and beliefs was going a little bit too far. So in what direction was I heading?

There are hundreds of isolated verses in the Bible which are a great comfort to me, such as 'The Lord is my helper, and I will not fear what man shall do unto me' (Hebrews, chapter 13). But I became more and more concerned about collections of Bible verses, sometimes brought together to support a doctrine. And depending on which Bible bits are collected and how they are assembled, different viewpoints emerge. Hence there is the danger of division, even among sincere 'Bible people'. And for that matter isn't it the same method which produces a multiplicity of sects?

The Bible then becomes more like a builders' yard, with avid builders paying a visit, choosing various types of bricks and other building materials - and then off they go and build houses. Each builder then claims that HIS house is the only one fit to inhabit!

Anyway, whatever our 'house', and whatever our beliefs, once we claim we've got it right, certain things follow - our judgments are now from a completely different standpoint, and so is our attitude to other religions and other individuals. It is then all too easy to develop a black-and-white attitude towards others.

Surely it's right for us to judge, but exactly what should we judge? It is right to judge dogs at Crufts, or gardens at Chelsea Flower Show, and it is right to judge Ruth and Megan's piano playing at music competitions. It is even right to judge people's deeds, and sometimes to decide whether they are good deeds or bad deeds.

But judging hearts? Who are we to adjudicate on a man's inner self? "John isn't a true believer, you know!" That just makes me squirm. I keep on hearing similar assessments of others, and so I just have to keep on squirming! "Jim is in a very dangerous position - he's completely off the rails doctrinally." Yes, Jim might well have a different viewpoint on spiritual matters, but isn't his spiritual 'position' something for God to judge?

I wonder whether I'm allowed to be sympathetic towards *Susie*, a girl who has attempted murder? Or towards that woman with a tyrant of a husband, who eventually had an affair with another man? Should I find appropriate Bible verses to show them their sin?

On another level, am I allowed to have atheists as friends, or folk who are gay? And must I judge *Susie* in her lesbian relationship? I can't!

I remember the love which my parents lavished on me - it was a love that cannot possibly be forgotten. Despite a few blips from time to time, theirs was a love which never wavered and never judged. It was heartfelt love, a mother's love, a father's love.

Why do I mention my parents' love? Well, it's because of a parallel: the love which I believe the Lord has shown me throughout my lifetime cannot possibly be forgotten - it was the sort of love one would expect from a Heavenly Father. Why did Mr Sparrow visit me day by day during my outdoor illness? Why did Jesus stand at my bedside a little while later and gently touch me? How come I was back at school a month later? How did I learn maths so quickly? How come someone approached me in *Woolworth's* and gave me money?

And how come I've managed to get up again after I'd been knocked down by accusations and other problems? Was it mere determination? No, I believe that God came 'downstairs' in love, and enabled me.

Despite my numerous queries, concerns and muddles, and despite the fact that I understand so little and that I only have a childlike faith, I believe that His love towards me has never wavered. It's also been far from analytical, and what a good thing too, considering all my faults and failings.

With my childlike faith, there's no wonder that I love children's hymns - I feel that they are just about within my spiritual grasp. This one by Susan Warner is a great help to me:

Jesus bids us shine with a pure clear light,
Like a little candle burning in the night.
In this world of darkness, so let us shine,
You in your small corner, and I in mine.

In theory, evangelicals agree that a simple faith is all that is needed, but in practice I think there is often an expectation of much more. 'But do you believe so-and-so, and what about this, and what about that?' It begins to feel more like a checklist. Mind you, not all evangelicals are so analytical. I think there are many who bypass all things analytical and controversial, and just have a simple faith in the Lord.

As for myself, I think I must have been 'up there' for many years carefully sorting out various doctrines. Maybe I looked down on those who seemed content with not knowing much about doctrine. Surely I needed to come down from that position.

More recently I have definitely been 'up there' as an elder, working hard in that capacity; but I now felt unable to remain in the heights. No, I wasn't pushed down, far from it. However, it was becoming clear that I didn't quite fit in at the top, with my many concerns and questions, and so I simply made a decision to descend.

Unfortunately, my resignation wasn't accepted, and I was given a year's 'sabbatical' instead, and told not to accept any preaching engagements. This preaching ban felt a bit like a rule without a reason.

At the end of my sabbatical, I offered my resignation once again, and this time it was accepted, though it was something which was unheard of in the history of the church.

"What?" said the senior elder, "someone resigning in full working order?"

So am I back in my little bedroom in Torquay, as a child, where my searching began, when I first believed in infinite space and infinite time? Maybe the end of all my exploring was to arrive where I started, but this time round my journey could begin with a simple faith in an infinite and loving God.

On New Year's Day 2005 Mary and I resigned from formal membership of the church, with every intention of attending the services Sunday by Sunday, and continuing to help, but soon we came face to face with a 'no entry' sign!

This sign was erected a few days later when three elders came to see us - but they seemed rather like detectives to me! After some investigating, they told us that our help was no longer required. It was now 'inappropriate' for me to cook for the Luncheon Club, for Mary to play the piano, and for me to play the organ.

Yes, in plain terms, we'd been sacked! No reasons were given, but I think it all boiled down to our vagueness in answering their many questions about what we believed. I think we didn't answer all their questions with the firmness and dogmatism that was required of us.

Let me emphasise once again that the elders genuinely believed that they were obeying the Lord, and their ban was based on what they believed the Bible taught. I feel sure that they were acting with sadness in their hearts.

We weren't pushed out of the church itself. Nonetheless, it was a big bump when I was pushed out of the kitchen and knocked off the organ seat. And it was a big bump for Mary too, when she was knocked off the piano stool.

Mind you, we still came in useful at times, as we've been asked to play for several funerals and weddings subsequently, and we've always been pleased to accept.

A few days after Mary and I resigned, Ruth resigned, and she too had a visit from the elders, and was told that it was now 'inappropriate' for her to work in the kitchen.

Not surprisingly, our dismissal from the Luncheon caused quite a problem. Ruth and I certainly didn't want to stop doing the work we loved so much, and we both felt extremely sad to be leaving. We missed everybody - even little Jimmy in his jersey! We never said our 'good-byes' to our diners, and they must have wondered why we'd departed so suddenly, without any explanation. But what could we do?

Well, that's it! I'm no longer working in the kitchen, no longer playing the organ, and only a matter of months after this, no longer attending the church. It all seemed so abrupt and unreal. And now, many years later, I'm attending a small Methodist Church nearby. Who would have expected me to travel 'full circle' back to my old Methodist days?

I've lived near the city boundary for some time now, and some folk might think I've actually stepped over the boundary, but they are wrong! Whatever I've stepped over, it's certainly not the boundary of belief and trust, but it's more like the boundary of debate and dogmatism. I'm thankful not to be bogged down any more with doctrinal minutiae, and I've thrown away all the labels except this one:

In any case I'm unable to choose one interpretation over another, because even within the Evangelical City there are districts of dogmatisms within dogmatisms, each with 'clear' Biblical backing. I've discarded all the posh words describing different viewpoints, because I no longer need to know whether I'm Calvinistic or Arminian, amillennial or premillennial. On and on it goes - different views on baptism, on the future of the Jewish nation, on this, that and the other.

As I write, Mary and I have just played the piano and organ for another funeral at the church. By now it's quite a few years since we resigned our membership, but what a welcome we received, with lots of hugs for us both!

"We miss you so much, and we wish you still played for the services."

I had a lovely chat with *Rita* after the funeral - we talked with ease about our simple faith. She told me she understood nothing about all these different interpretations, and she believed that 'not knowing' didn't matter at all. I felt very much at one with her. Maybe there are many other church members who feel like *Rita*. I was reminded of the two Elim wives who had visited us at Ackhill, and who were ignorant about doctrinal niceties. All those years ago, I'd begun to wonder whether in their 'ignorance', these two ladies were the ones who knew best. If that's what I wondered then, how much more so now. Do you remember Mary's Mum's angry retort when we quoted the Bible to her?

"Just leave me alone with my simple faith!" I've learnt a lot since then. Perhaps Mum was right after all.

When someone says that "this IS what the Bible teaches in verse so-and-so," followed by a big full stop, I feel I can hardly cope these days - all the more so when I know that others have a different interpretation, having used the same Bible and the same prayerful approach. I definitely prefer commas to full stops, especially when it comes to answering big doctrinal questions or the 'why' of all the suffering in the world.

But maybe God isn't the slightest bit interested in all our full stops, anyway, and is less analytical with our beliefs than we are with each other's. Maybe He looks at our hearts rather than our 'heresies'. Does God smile upon our love and our trust, rather than examine our divided doctrines? Or is that the kind of question I'm not supposed to ask?

So here I am in a wide-open space, believing that God accepts my simple faith, and has forgiven my sins, believing too that the Lord has helped me over and over again, even though I'm just a muddled green bottle.

I don't wish to be irreverent, but in a sense the Lord reminds me of Humble Grandpa, who was always happy to have a muddled green bottle as his grandson - a wonderful Grandpa, who used to chat with me as we munched our Crunchie Bars together, sitting on a bench overlooking the beach.

In the first chapter of this book I asked whether my questions about the meaning of life were too hard for me to answer. Well, if my questions require deep answers, doctrinal answers, dogmatic answers, then I have to say, yes, they are too hard for me. But then, do I need to answer them?

The American physicist Richard Feynman admitted that he could live with uncertainty and not knowing. He claimed that it is better to live not knowing than to have answers that might be wrong. What an admission from a scientist!

For some, knowing the big answers might well be their ultimate prize, but for me at any rate, not knowing these answers has become my ultimate humbling. 'Life is a long lesson in humility,' writes James Barrie, and that's certainly been my own experience.

I have at long last learnt to be content with not knowing, and to be happy with simply trusting, and no more.

Simply trusting every day,
Trusting through a stormy way;
Even when my faith is small,
Trusting Jesus, that is all.
(Edgar Stites)

7950331R00131

Printed in Great Britain
by Amazon.co.uk, Ltd.,
Marston Gate.